Linguistic theory and adult
second language acquisition

European University Studies
Europäische Hochschulschriften
Publications Universitaires Européennes

Series XXI
Linguistics

Reihe XXI Série XXI
Linguistik
Linguistique

Vol./Bd. 226

PETER LANG
Frankfurt am Main · Berlin · Bern · Bruxelles · New York · Oxford · Wien

Carolina Plaza Pust

Linguistic theory and adult second language acquisition

On the relation between the lexicon and the syntax

PETER LANG
Europäischer Verlag der Wissenschaften

Die Deutsche Bibliothek - CIP-Einheitsaufnahme

Plaza Pust, Carolina:

Linguistic theory and adult second language acquisition : on the relation between the lexicon and the syntax / Carolina Plaza Pust. - Frankfurt am Main ; Berlin ; Bern ; Bruxelles ; New York ; Oxford ; Wien : Lang, 2000
  (European university studies : Ser. 21, Linguistics ; Vol. 226)
  Zugl.: Frankfurt (Main), Univ., Diss., 1998
  ISBN 3-631-36101-7

D 30
ISSN 0721-3352
ISBN 3-631-36101-7
US-ISBN 0-8204-4732-3
© Peter Lang GmbH
Europäischer Verlag der Wissenschaften
Frankfurt am Main 2000
All rights reserved.

All parts of this publication are protected by copyright. Any utilisation outside the strict limits of the copyright law, without the permission of the publisher, is forbidden and liable to prosecution. This applies in particular to reproductions, translations, microfilming, and storage and processing in electronic retrieval systems.

Printed in Germany 1 2 3 4 5   7

For my parents

Acknowledgements

How do we acquire knowledge of language, how do we use it - what is knowledge of language? These questions are central to the *generative paradigm*. But in a more or less conscious way many of us come across these questions in our day-to-day life, for example, when we observe early child utterances, when we produce speech errors, when we are confronted with foreign languages we do not understand or when we speak different languages. My personal curiosity regarding these issues is rooted in the multilingual surrounding in which I grew up and which is still important to me.
I dedicate the present study to my parents who gave me, among many other things, the opportunity or, better, the precious gift of two languages. It goes without saying that I would never have gone all the way along without their continuous encouragement and support. Thanks also to Roberto for his help in every domain. This dissertation is as much theirs as it is mine.

The precisation of the issues which would be subject to the present dissertation matured as I became more and more acquainted with linguistic theory. Many ideas which I had had vaguely in my mind took their shape in the framework of a research paradigm which goes, in my view, to the heart. In this respect Helen Leuninger deserves my deepest gratitude. Her expertise and support have been decisive for the fulfillment of this dissertation. She has been my teacher in many ways. I admire her personal engagement and her commitment as well as the way in which she makes us understand the relevance of linguistic research. I have gained from every course, from every conversation I had. Without her teaching, many aspects of linguistic theory would have remained obscure. Thanks also for giving me the possibility of leading a working group at Frankfurt University on the topic of the present study. This has been an enriching experience, which provided me with additional motivation for persevering with this work. Thank you also to the students, for their active participation and fruitful discussions.
I also want to extend my gratitude to Jürgen Meisel for providing me the empirical data which have been of great value for this dissertation.
Many of the ideas related to a dynamic approach to language acquisition emerged out of stimulating conversations with Annette Hohenberger. I am very grateful for her encouragement and the useful advice she gave me.

I am indebted to Mark Towner for going through the woods of a linguistic dissertation, sorting out errors of any kind and contributing to the fluidity of the text. Naturally I accept the responsibility for any remaining errors.

Finally I want to emphasise my gratitude to the many friends around me who have been at my side during this time with comprehension and patience. Their support has been an invaluable contribution to the progression of the present study.

Contents

1	**Introduction**	13
1.1	General objectives and scope of the present study	13
1.2	The cognitivist approach to ASLA	17
1.2.1	Functionalist hypotheses	17
1.2.2	General processing strategies	20
1.2.3	The developmental sequence of L2 German	20
1.2.4	Critical appraisal of the cognitivist approach to (AS)LA	24
2	**The UG Hypothesis**	26
2.1	The autonomy assumption	26
2.2	The Logical Problem of language acquisition	27
2.3	The modular organisation of grammar	30
2.4	Functional categories and the Functional Parametrisation Hypothesis	32
2.5	The interface between lexicon and syntax	36
2.5.1	Argument structure	36
2.5.2	Theta theory	38
2.5.3	Projection Principle	39
2.5.4	Case theory	39
2.6	German sentence structure	42
2.6.1	The Symmetry Hypothesis	44
2.6.2	The Asymmetry Hypothesis	47
2.7	Language acquisition and the modularity of grammar: Narrowing the focus	48
3	**Modularity and ASLA**	50
3.1	The Lexical Learning Hypothesis and German word order in child language acquisition	50
3.2	Lexical learning and German word order in ASLA	54
3.3	The Fundamental Difference Hypothesis	57
3.4	The Competition Model	59
3.5	Modularity of mind: Critical remarks about the centralist approach to ASLA	63
4	**The Principles and Parameters model and ASLA: Core issues of the UG Hypothesis of ASLA**	69
4.1	Linguistic theory and ASLA	69
4.2	Logical Problem and ASLA	70
4.3	Learnability considerations	73
4.3.1	L2 input	74

4.3.2	Mother tongue knowledge	75
4.3.3	Parameter setting	76
5	**The Developmental Problem of child language acquisition**	**80**
5.1	The Maturation Hypothesis	81
5.1.1	Maturation of UG	81
5.1.2	Maturation of the Functional Module	84
5.2	The Continuity Hypothesis	91
5.2.1	The lexical learning approach	91
5.2.2	The syntactic learning approach	93
5.2.3	Strong vs. Weak Continuity Hypothesis	97
5.3	Conclusion	101
6	**The Developmental Problem of ASLA**	**105**
6.1	Adult language acquisition devoid of maturation	107
6.2	The No-Functional-Module Hypothesis	108
6.3	Structure-building or restructuring in ASLA: The Initial State Debate	113
6.3.1	The Full Transfer View	144
6.3.2	The Gradual Development View	122
6.3.3	The assumption of ASLA-specific triggers	128
6.3.4	Modularity revisited	133
7	**Language development and the mirror-world of chaos and order**	**139**
7.1	Variation in child language acquisition	139
7.1.1	Variation in the development of the early grammar	139
7.1.2	Variation and the emergence of complex structures	141
7.1.3	Learner types	145
7.1.4	Bilingual bootstrapping	148
7.1.5	Implications for the Principles and Parameters theory	150
7.2	Linguistic variation and the theory of self-organisation: Preliminary considerations	151
7.2.1	The temporal dimensions of organisation	151
7.2.2	The anticipatory and reconstructive potential of a structure	153
7.2.3	Differentiation and integration	154
7.2.4	Some preliminary conclusions on non-linearity and language development in its multiple forms	157
7.3	Chaos theory and language development	160
7.3.1	The dynamics of chaos and order	160
7.3.1.1	Feedback, attractors and fractals	160
7.3.1.2	Bifurcations and the irreversibility of time	163

7.3.2	Dynamic conceptions of language development	168
7.3.2.1	Gradualness, catastrophes and language change	169
7.3.2.2	The tripartite algorithm of language acquisition	171
7.3.3	Conclusion and preliminary outlook at a dynamic approach to ASLA	173
8	**Intra-individual variation in ASLA: A case study**	**177**
8.1	Preliminary considerations	177
8.2	Developmental milestones	178
8.2.1	VP headedness	178
8.2.1.1	VP initial	178
8.2.1.2	Restructuring of the VP headedness	182
8.2.1.3	Conclusion	191
8.2.2	Verb raising	193
8.2.2.1	Subject-verb agreement and verb raising	193
8.2.2.2	The finiteness distinction and the implementation of the inflectional paradigm	203
8.2.2.3	Conclusion	214
8.2.3	Nominative case checking	216
8.2.3.1	Restricted verb raising and nominative case-checking	217
8.2.3.2	Implementation of the government option	223
8.2.3.3	Conclusion	226
8.2.4	Non-subject topicalisation	229
8.2.4.1	Non-subject V2	229
8.2.4.2	Topic drop and pro-drop	235
8.2.4.3	Conclusion	240
8.2.5	IP-headedness	244
8.2.5.1	Symmetric V2	244
8.2.5.2	Restructuring of IP	257
8.2.5.3	Conclusion	264
9	**Final remarks or "opening the windows"**	**268**
9.1	Linguistic theory and ASLA: The dynamics of their relationship	268
9.2	Lexical and syntactic development: What triggers what?	271
9.3	The "shifting web": Hysteresis effects and bifurcations in ASLA	274
9.4	ASLA: A window onto the whole	277
10	**Bibliography**	**278**

1 Introduction

1.1 General objectives and scope of the present study

It is typical for adult second language acquisition (henceforth ASLA) that from the beginning learners try to convey quite complex thoughts with the few lexical items they have acquired so far.
The following passage of an interview between a German and a Spaniard is quite illustrative:

Interviewer:

Vor	50	Jahren,	ist	da	in	der	Stadt
before	*50*	*years*	*is*	*there*	*in*	*the*	*town*

Gallego	oder	Castellano	gesprochen	worden?
Galician	*or*	*Castilian*	*spoken*	*been*

'What did they speak in the town fifty years ago, Castilian or Galician?'

Baltasar F.:

in	estadt?	in	estadt	in	estadt	in	unsere	estadt
in	*town*	*in*	*town*	*in*	*town*	*in*	*our*	*town*

normal	in	estadt	normal	castellano	sprechen,	aba
normally	*in*	*town*	*normally*	*Castilian*	*speak*	*but*

viel	aba	viel	leute	gallego	sprechen	in	estadt.
many	*but*	*many*	*people*	*Galician*	*speak*	*in*	*town*

'In town? In our town they normally speak Castilian. But there are still people speaking Galician.'

äh	alte	alte	leute	alle	gallego	sprechen	aber
eh	*old*	*old*	*people*	*all*	*Galician*	*speak*	*but*

junge	leute	so	will.
young	*people*	*so*	*want*

'All the elder people speak Galician. But the young want it so.'

ja,	ja,	en	schule	castellano	sprechen,	no,
yes	*yes*	*in*	*school*	*Castilian*	*speak*	*no*

kein	gallego	kein	gallego.
no	*Galician*	*no*	*Galician*

'Yes, in school they speak Castilian not Galician.'

13

in e	schule	kein	gallego	sprechen,	verboten
in	*school*	*no*	*Galician*	*speak*	*prohibited*

gallego.
Galician

'In school they do not speak Galician because it is banned.'

(Rieck 1989: 209, my transl.)[1]

Utterances like these suggest that learners initially lack many of the complex linguistic means which are necessary for an utterance to be considered a wellformed sentence in German. Nevertheless, early learner utterances will be properly understood given the right context and a cooperative attitude on the side of the interlocutor(s).

Quite commonly, the observation that formal linguistic devices are missing at the beginning of language acquisition has been taken as evidence that the early language is somehow *deficient*. As a consequence, the question arises as to (a) how grammatically encoded concepts and relations are being expressed during the initial stages of ASLA, if at all and (b) how formal linguistic devices of the L2 are eventually learned.
What do learners know of the L2 at the beginning of ASLA? The passage quoted above suggests that for a certain period of time learners only know a few lexical items of the L2. Note that the use of these lexical items is not completely target-like yet.
It has repeatedly been pointed out (cf. Klein 1986) that learners initially use invariant forms which cannot unequivocally be assigned to a syntactic category. The form "abai", for example, could refer to 'Arbeit' (*work*) or 'Arbeiter' (*worker*) or to 'ich arbeite' (*I work*).
These considerations suggest that the first lexical items learners use are underspecified for the different functions they fulfill in the target language system.

The complexity of the learnability task the language learner faces becomes evident once we acknowledge that linguistic forms are embedded in different structural contexts such as the semantic, the phonological, the morphological, the syntactic or the pragmatic context. How does the learner acquire this information?
Adult learners do fully master (at least) one language, namely their mother tongue. On the basis of their mother tongue knowledge adult

---

[1] The original version provided in Rieck contains a number of typographic cues as to the intonation contour of the utterances which I omitted here. Note, additionally, that I subdivided the passage into sequences for ease of comprehension.

learners may thus seek to embed the lexical items they learn into the relevant structural contexts because they already know that linguistic forms fulfill different functions at different linguistic levels, the communicative function being only one among these. Apart from this knowledge, however, they are faced, as children are, with the task of determining the language-specific properties of the lexical items in question.

So far, the question has been left open as to whether there is any relationship between the different structural levels lexical items are embedded in. One may also ask whether the properties of these levels stand in a relationship to extra-linguistic phenomena. If such inter-relations exist, what role do they play in language acquisition?
One possible inter-relation will be at the heart of the present analysis, namely, the relationship between the lexicon and syntax. How do adult learners acquire the regularities of the L2 word order? In which ways is the development of the L2 syntax related to the acquisition of the L2 lexicon?
In the following sections I will discuss some of the proposals made in this respect in the realm of linguistic theory and their implications for a theory of ASLA. When analysing ASLA general considerations as regards the human language faculty come into play. By the same token research in the field of ASLA contributes to our understanding of what constitutes our language faculty. These are the basic tenets underlying the present study.

We will see in chapters 1 and 2 that there are basically two different views on the nature of our human language faculty. According to the *Cognitivist Hypothesis* presented in chapter 1, language is based on the regularities of general cognitive capacities. Consequently, language acquisition is assumed to be determined by general processing constraints. I will discuss the weaknesses of the cognitivist approach on the basis of one of the most frequently cited longitudinal studies on ASLA, i.e. the ZISA project (cf. Clahsen, Meisel and Pienemann 1983). Later on we will see that this criticism is still of relevance for a critical evaluation of many contemporary hypotheses put forward in the field of ASLA.
In chapter 2 I will argue in favour of the assumption that our knowledge of language is represented in the form of a universal grammar (*UG Hypothesis*). There are two basic issues I will focus on. On the one hand, I will be concerned with the theoretical considerations underlying the so-called *autonomy assumption*, which claims that grammatical knowledge cannot be reduced to other linguistic or extra-linguistic regularities. Here I will also present the UG-based model of grammar. In this model special attention will be payed to the relation between the lexicon and syntax. On the other hand, I will discuss the learnability considerations which follow

from the UG Hypothesis for a theory of language acquisition, especially as regards the *Principles and Parameters* model. Here I will focus on the potential relation between the acquisition of a specific sort of lexical elements (i.e. *functional categories*) and the development of a language-specific grammar. If cross-linguistic variation is tied to functional categories, as is assumed in the *Functional Parametrisation Hypothesis*, the appropriate determination of functional categories will be of crucial relevance in language acquisition. Before dealing with the empirical hypotheses put forward in this respect I will discuss recent proposals regarding the analysis of German sentence structure. These will be relevant for our understanding of the different studies of the acquisition of German in childhood and in adulthood which will be subject to discussion.

In the course of the subsequent chapters we will see how current hypotheses on ASLA are linked to research in the field of child language acquisition. Many times this relation takes the form of a contrast between the general "achievements" of children as opposed to the adults' alleged general "failures". More specific accounts have sought to determine the underlying reasons for the differences between child and adult language acquisition.
According to the *Lexical Learning Hypothesis* presented in chapter 3 syntactic development in childhood is *triggered* by specific lexical items in the input. However, lexical learning of this sort is claimed not to hold in ASLA. Therefore, language learning is assumed to be different in adulthood. This claim is based on the assumption that there is a *critical period* for language acquisition. Presently, there are two different hypotheses which claim that child and adult language acquisition cannot be alike due to a difference in their cognitive capacities, namely the *Fundamental Difference Hypothesis* and the *Competition Model*. Basically, they claim that adults have no or only partial access to the language-specific module.
I will discuss the weaknesses of both hypotheses by reconsidering current assumptions regarding the modular nature of the human mind (*Modularity Hypothesis*). I will show that the alleged dichotomy of language-specific learning mechanisms available in child language acquisition *versus* general learning mechanisms in adult language acquisition cannot be maintained. We will see that the criticism of the cognitivist hypothesis put forward in chapter 1 is of relevance here as well.

If adults face learnability problems which are specific to ASLA, the question is whether they can be explained in terms of the Principles and Parameters model. I will focus on this issue in chapter 4 where I also provide an overview of the critical aspects of the so-called *UG-access debate.* In this context logical and empirical arguments in favour of a UG-based approach to ASLA shall be recapitulated. Many of the opponents of a UG-based approach to ASLA point to a crucial contrast between child and adult language acquisition: whilst the first is "deterministic" in the sense that every child attains the knowledge of her mother tongue, adults vary considerably as to their degree of success. But what determines the apparent developmental "schedule" in child language acquisition? We will see in chapter 5 that there are different proposals under discussion with regard to the so-called *Developmental Problem.* Chapter 6 highlights the related discussion in the field of ASLA and points to some persistent inconsistencies in both fields.

Subsequently, we will see that many of the inadequacies of current hypotheses result from too static a learning concept underlying the Principles and Parameters model.
Many of the alleged differences between adult and child language acquisition which have been part of the UG-access debate gain a new significance in the light of recent studies on variation in child language acquisition. As it turns out, variation is not an exclusive property of ASLA. So, *variation* is the head-word of chapter 7. Here, many of the longstanding learning-theoretic assumptions implicit in the Principles and Parameters model will be given up in favour of a more dynamic approach to language. We will see to which extent *self-organisation* plays a role in language acquisition. Furthermore, I will outline some of the properties of dynamic systems to which language apparently belongs.

These considerations will be contrasted with the empirical findings discussed in chapter 8. This chapter is dedicated to a close analysis of intra-individual variation in the acquisition of L2 German by an adult Italian learner. The revision of traditional learning concepts will be at stake here. For example, I will contrast the lexical learning hypothesis with a dynamic learning concept.
Parallels to other forms of language development shall provide additional evidence against the long-standing prejudice that in ASLA everything is "fundamentally different".

1.2 The cognitivist approach to ASLA

1.2.1 Functionalist hypotheses

According to the *functional approach* formal linguistic devices are directly related to the communicative needs and intentions of learners (cf. Bates and MacWhinney 1982).

Slobin (1973), for example, claims that

> "[t]he emergence of new communicative intentions must bring with it the means to decode those intentions in the speech the child hears, and this makes it possible for him to discover new means of expressing those intentions."
> (ibid.: 186)

As pointed out by Givón (1985), this causal relationship extends to all other temporal dimensions of language development:

> "Syntactic structure (...) arises ontogenetically, diachronically, and probably also phylogenetically by syntactization of another communicative mode, the pragmatic/paratactic mode."
> (ibid.: 1017/8)

The correlations between syntactic and semantic or pragmatic functions are considered to be so strong that they should be easily discovered during the learning process (cf. Bates and MacWhinney 1982, Clahsen 1984). Following Givón (1979) proponents of the functionalist approach (cf. Dittmar 1982, Rieck 1989, among others) claim that the developmental process underlying language acquisition is a continuum from a *functional pragmatic mode* to a *syntactic mode*. The development towards the syntactic mode is characterised by the progressive acquisition of formal linguistic devices such as the morphological paradigm, pronominalisation or the target language word order rules (cf. Clahsen 1984, Rieck 1989).

It is assumed that *functional pragmatic principles* such as (1) - (3) underly the organisation of the early learner grammar (cf. Klein 1986: 82).

(1) Principle of theme-rheme segmentation:
Put what is spoken about before what is to be said about it.

(2) Principle of semantic connectivity:
Keep elements linked in terms of meaning close together.

(3) Principle of orientation:
Place orientational elements (place, time, modality) at the beginning of an utterance.

Further, the lack of formal-linguistic devices is said to be compensated by *lexicalisation*, a process whereby free lexical items take over the function of some grammatical encodings (cf. Dittmar 1982).

According to Klein (1986) and Rieck (1989) the lexical component undergoes a first differentiation process already in the initial stage of ASLA. The authors observed that certain lexical items (*morphs*) are "*predomi-*

nantly used as content words and other predominantly as function words" (Klein 1986: 81). The assumption is that in the latter case concepts like temporality, quantity, quality and negation, which would have to be encoded in grammar, are lexicalised. Modality, for example, is expressed by means of lexical items like 'vielleicht' (*perhaps*) or 'normal' (*normally*), cf.

(4) **vielleicht** kollege Deutsch keine Arbeit - macht
 perhaps colleague German no work does
 Spanien
 Spain
 'when the German colleague does not work he may go to Spain'

(5) **normal** Zementwerk vierzig Stunden Arbeit -
 normally concrete-factory forty hours work
 vielleicht Reparatur, **vielleicht** mehr Stunden
 perhaps repair perhaps more hours
 'normally we work forty hours per week, but if we have to do some repair we may work more hours'
 (Dittmar 1982: 23, my transl.[2])

Similarly, the lack of temporal markings on the verb is compensated through temporal specifications like 'samstag' (*Saturday*), cf.

(6) **samstag** ... bisele spazier
 Saturday a-bit walk
 'Saturdays I walk a bit'
 (Rieck 1989: 55, my transl.)

Functionalist linguists further acknowledge that strategies of this sort may only partly compensate for the lack of a formal linguistic system. According to them, successful communication at this stage strongly relies upon a cooperative attitude on the side of the interlocutors, i.e. much of what is not being explicitly said will have to be understood on the basis of the context in which the fragmentary utterances are expressed (cf. Dittmar 1982).
As pointed out above, it is assumed that reliance on discourse context declines in the course of *grammaticalisation*, i.e. the process through which morpho-syntactic devices are introduced in the learner language.

---

[2] Note that the free translations provided represent one of the various possible interpretations of the utterances.

1.2.2 General processing strategies

Functionalists assume that the pragmatic mode not only represents "*a more TRANSPARENT communicative system*" but also that it "*is a slow means of processing*" (Givón 1985: 1018). Two predictions follow for language acquisition: whereas the emergence of grammatical devices is held to be functionally driven, the overall linguistic development is said to be constrained by general processing constraints, i.e. extra-linguistic mechanisms. So this is the *cognitivist* dimension of the model of ASLA outlined so far.

Following Slobin (1973) learner systems are the product of general principles and constraints of the information processing system. In other words, the general information processing system determines which linguistic structures may be acquired when and by means of which strategies. The format of the general perceptual or information processing strategies is determined by the alleged limited capacity of the information processing system. As the constraints on this system are believed to be "*universal limitations on sentence processing*" (ibid.: 196) it is assumed that they will guide both child and adult language processing.

The crucial assumption underlying the cognitivist approach is that language processing principles such as the *operating principles* proposed by Slobin underlie not only the development of perceptual or production strategies. They also play a crucial role in the acquisition of linguistic rule systems. Guided by the *Processing Economy Principle* (cf. Clahsen 1982), which results from the limited capacity of the processing system, the learner will first acquire the less complex formal linguistic devices of the target language, since these are held to require less processing capacity. Cognitive complexity is defined by taking into account the following: the shorter the mapping of underlying structures onto surface structures, the lighter the burden on the language processing system. This correlation is reflected in learning strategies like Slobin's (1973: 199) *Operating Principle D*, cf.

(7) Operating Principle D
Avoid interruption or rearrangement of linguistic units.

1.2.3 The developmental sequence of L2 German

Clahsen, Meisel and Pienemann (1983) (henceforth CMP) (cf. also Clahsen 1984) suggest the following developmental sequence for the acquisition of L2 German word order by adults:

- Stage I: One constituent stage
  Mainly elliptical utterances.

- Stage II: SVO
  Word order at this stage strictly follows the subject-verb-object pattern, cf.

  (8) die   leute   arbeiten hier
      the people   work   here
                                              (Antonio S.)
      'the people work here'
      (CMP 1983: 101, my transl.)

- Stage III: ADV-PREP
  A facultative rule moving adverbials into a position left of the subject (ADV-PREP) is responsible for the sentence-initial position of the adverb at this time, cf.

  (9) acht uhr   ich   kommen zuhause
      eight ó clock I   come   home
                                              (Zita P.)
      (Clahsen 1984: 59, his transl.)

- Stage IV: PARTICLE
  Participles, infinitives and uninflected separable verb parts are moved to the end of the sentence at this stage by means of the rule PARTICLE, cf.

  (10) die   will   immer   kommandieren
       this-one wants   always command
                                              (Raffaela I.)
       'she always wants to command'
       (CMP 1983: 139, my transl.)

  (11) die   schmeißt mi   schon   jetzt raus
       this-one throws   me   already now   out
                                              (Benito I.)
       'she throws me out already now'
       (ibid.: 137, my transl.)

- Stage V: subject-verb INVERSION
  At this stage CMP observe the productivity of the obligatory

INVERSION rule, which requires the verb to precede the subject in the following cases
- object NP at the beginning of the sentence
- preposed adverbial
- preposed embedded sentence
- questions
cf.

(12) jetzt   kann   sie   mir   eine   frage   machen
     now   *can* *she* *me* *a*   *question* *make*
                                                  (Pietro I.)
     'now she can ask me a question'

     (ibid.: 141, my transl.)

- Stage VI: ADV-VP
  At this stage learners acquire a further permutation rule, which moves the adverb or a further prepositional phrase into a position inside the VP (i.e. between the verb and the object), cf.

(13) das   is'   immer   schwierigkeit
     this *is* *always* *difficulty*
                                              (Giovanni I.)
     'this is always difficult'

     (ibid.: 152, my transl.)

- Stage VII: V-ENDE
  Verbs in embedded clauses (subordinate clauses, indirect questions or relative clauses) are placed in final position, following the V-ENDE rule, cf.

(14) wenn   jetzt die   papiere   kommen
     when *now* *the* *papers* *come*
                                              (José S.)
     (Clahsen 1984: 60, his transl.)

One of the main methodological observations advanced in CMP (1983) concerns the assumption that in analysing word order in the learner's language both the type and the pattern of learner errors provide evidence for the processes going on in ASLA. Their claim runs as follows:

"Certainly, word order errors cannot be taken generally as indications of language use strategies. However, we are of the opinion that the type of

error may provide a clue about the strategies of language use (...) On the one hand, the "place" at which the deviances occur indicates which of structural features are problematic for the learner (in acquisition and/or in use). On the other hand, the type of deviancy provides a clue for the solution to the problem, which the learner probably prefers to a possibly more difficult problem."
(ibid.: 179, my transl.)[3]

The basic assumption underlying CMP's account of the above mentioned developmental sequence is that it is determined by general processing strategies in the sense of Slobin's operating principles. According to CMP the acquisition of word order or, in their terms, *permutation rules* starts out at Stage II. At this stage the syntactic constituents are placed in a strict order, namely SVO. The initial word order SVO results from a strategy whereby learners first determine the *canonical order*[4] of the L2, i.e. the sequence which is a direct mapping of the underlying structure. This learning strategy, which corresponds with Slobin's *Operating Principle D* (see above), is termed Canonical Order Strategy, cf.

(15)   Canonical Order Strategy (COS)
In underlying sequences $[X1 + X2 + ... + Xn]C_X [ ]C_{X+1} ... [ ]C_{X+m}$ in which each subconstituent $X_1, X_2, ... X_n$ contributes information to the internal structure of the constituent C_X, no subconstituent is moved out of C_X, and no material from the subsequent constituents $C_{X+1}, C_{X+2}, ..., C_{X+m}$ is moved into C_X.
(Clahsen 1984: 221)

CMP claim that SVO is the basic structure which will be subject to all other structural changes in the learner's system.
The remaining development is explained by means of two further strategies, i.e. the *Initialization/Finalization Strategy* (IFS) and the *Subordinate Clause Strategy* (SCS).
The postposing or preposing of syntactic constituents is put down to the IFS, which prevents the movement of constituents into positions which

---

[3]   The original passage quoted reads as follows:
"Sicherlich können Wortstellungsfehler nicht generell Indizien für Sprachverwendungsstrategien sein. Wir meinen aber, daß die Art der Fehler Aufschluß über die Strategien des Sprachgebrauchs geben kann (...) Während der 'Ort', an dem die Abweichungen auftreten, zeigt, mit welchen strukturellen Merkmalen die Lerner Schwierigkeiten haben (im Erwerb und/oder im Gebrauch), liefert die Art der Abweichung ein Indiz für die Lösung des Problems, die der Lerner für ein möglicherweise schwieriges Problem bevorzugt."

[4]   The canonical word order is given in neutral sentences, i.e. in simple, active, affirmative sentences (cf. Slobin and Bever 1982). According to this definition the canonical word order in German is SVO.

would interrupt the underlying word order, movement into initial or final positions being allowed,[5] cf.

(16) Initialization/Finalization Strategy (IFS)
In underlying sequences [XYZ]$_S$ permutations are blocked which move X between Y and Z and/or Z between X and Y.
(Clahsen 1984: 222)

The acquisition of word order rules concerning the initialisation or finalisation of syntactic constituents, such as ADV-PREP, TOPI, and PARTICLE thus fit into this strategy. The late acquisition of INVERSION is regarded as a result of this rule violating both the COS and the IFS. Similarly, the *Subordinate Clause Strategy* is responsible for the fact that the correct word order rule for embedded sentences (V-ENDE) is only acquired later on.

1.2.4 Critical appraisal of the cognitivist approach to (AS)LA

... *the point is to detect what determines what.*

(Henning Wode 1981: 30)

There is no doubt that language is a medium of communication. But it is certainly questionable whether this (obvious) statement provides a sufficient basis for a theory of (second) language acquisition as claimed within the functional approach (cf. Meisel 1990). It seems fairly trivial to claim that anybody who wants to learn a foreign language tries to be as communicatively efficient as possible (cf. Adjemian 1976). Considering the complexity of language it is debatable to view communicative efficacy as the only motor of language development. Nor is there a causal relationship between the high complexity of grammatical regularities of language and the fact that we use it for communication (cf. Fanselow and Felix 1990a). So what needs to be distinguished is the communicative function linguistic devices may fulfill and the nature of the linguistic system acquired, in which linguistic elements have different functions on different structural levels. As a consequence, the analysis of the grammatical properties of learner systems, the way they are acquired and the form they have, is only secondarily concerned with the question of what pragmatic functions the incipient L2 knowledge may fulfill. This is not to say that extra-linguistic factors do not play a role in language acquisition.

---

[5] Additional empirical support for the validity of this strategy is taken from studies on perception (Clahsen 1984: 222 refers to Neisser 1967). According to these studies, initial or final positions are perceptually more salient.

We all know that adult learners differ as to how successfully they learn a second language. But it is certainly questionable to assume that learners only acquire the linguistic devices they need for the realisation of their respective communicative needs. Whatever the reasons for why not all adult learners achieve full competence, their L2 is a linguistic system following language-specific principles.

As for the mechanisms underlying language development, do general processing mechanisms in the form of Slobin's operating principles really predict how learners will proceed on their way to the target? Do they not rather describe what remains to be explained, that is, the actual structural development?

Contrary to the central claim of the allegedly "general" processing account cognitive complexity is defined with respect to *linguistic* complexity. Recall that the operation principles presented above operate on linguistic structures and as such they presuppose the identification of features and elements of these structures (cf. Tracy 1991). Consequently, we have to look at the nature of linguistic knowledge, how it comes into being and how it is used (cf. Chomsky 1981). In fact, these are the crucial questions discussed in the framework of the *UG Hypothesis* presented in the next section.

2 The UG Hypothesis

2.1 The autonomy assumption

In German the finite verb may appear in initial position, as in interrogative or conditional clauses, cf.

(1) wird David heute ein neues Auto kaufen?
    will David today a new car buy
    'will David buy a new car today?'

(2) kauft David heute ein neues Auto, so wird
    buys David today a new car so will
    er mit seiner Freundin nach München fahren
    he with his girlfriend to Munich go
    'if he buys a new car today, David will go to Munich with his girlfriend'

Apparently the initialisation of the verb is related to the functional type of a sentence. But, as sentences (3) and (4) below show, German word order does not only follow semantico-functional criteria. In embedded clauses introduced by a conjunction, the finite verb has to appear in final position:

(3) ich glaube, daß David gerne liest
    I think that David with-pleasure reads
    'I think David reads with pleasure'

(4) ich glaube, David liest gerne
    I think David reads with-pleasure
    'I think David reads with pleasure'

In main clauses finite verbs are placed in second position and may be preceded by any syntactic constituent:

(5) David liest heute ein Buch über den
    David reads today a book about the
    Zweitspracherwerb
    second-language-acquisition
    'today David reads a book about second language acquisition'

26

(6) heute liest David ein Buch über den
    today reads David a book about the
    Zweitspracherwerb
    second-language-acquisition
    'today David reads a book about second language acquisition'

For further illustration, interrogative clauses containing a verb with a separable prefix may be considered. In such sentences only the finite verb appears in the initial position leaving the prefix behind (cf. (7)). Note that there is no functional-pragmatic reason whatsoever which could explain why the prefixes cannot be initialised together with the verb (cf. (8)) (cf. also Fanselow and Felix 1990a).

(7) zieht heute Thomas die grüne Hose an?
    put today Thomas the green trousers on
    'will Thomas put on the green trousers today?'

(8) *anzieht heute Thomas die grüne Hose?
    on-put today Thomas the green trousers
    'will Thomas put on the green trousers today?'

Therefore we have to conclude that whilst certain sentence configurations have semantic effects, the rules generating these sentences are clearly independent of such semantic considerations.

These are but a few of many grammatical regularities which may only be described on the basis of grammatical categories and explained through grammatical principles.

If regularities underlying the syntactic and phonological domains of language cannot be reduced to regularities of some other non-language-specific systems, they must belong to an independent, that is, *autonomous* system of mental representations. Over the last decades researchers working within the paradigm of *generative grammar* have sought to determine the rules and principles which adequately describe possible human grammars and which fulfill a further, crucial condition, namely the *learnability criterion*.

2.2 The Logical Problem of language acquisition

The assumption that language learning cannot be based solely upon *inductive* generalisations from the input is supported by evidence that the linguistic input with which children are confronted is

- finite as opposed to the infinite set of possible linguistic sentences,
- partly degenerate without however having any effect on the emerging capacity,
- not explicit with respect to the information necessary for the induction of the principles and the generalisations characteristic of the mature language competence.

For example, if children relied on inductive generalisations from the input they could mistakenly conclude, in hearing sentences (9) to (11) that English interrogative clauses are formed by replacing an expression with a wh-word and subsequently positioning it at the beginning of the sentence (cf. Grewendorf et al. 1987: 18).

(9)   Peter kissed Mary.

(10)   Who did Peter kiss?

(11)   Who did you say that Peter kissed?

However, such a generalisation would fail to account for the ungrammatical status of (12).

(12)   *Who did you say that kissed Mary?

(12) shows that subjects of embedded clauses may not be questioned in this way. It also illustrates that generalisations based upon surface phenomena do not cover the *structure dependency* of grammatical rules (cf. Chomsky 1988).
So we are faced with the problem of explaining how all children acquire their mother tongue in a relatively short time despite the underdetermination by input data (*Poverty of Stimulus Problem* or *Logical Problem of language acquisition*, cf. Chomsky 1986, Lightfoot 1991, White 1982 among others).[6] As pointed out by Chomsky (1986) this problem represents a (test) case of *Plato's Problem*, cf.

> "The problem is to account for the specificity and the richness of the cognitive systems that arise in the individual on the basis of the limited information available."
> (ibid.: xxv)

---

[6]   Consider the relevance of these considerations (Chomsky 1986: 7):
"This difference of perception concerning where the problem lies - overlearning or poverty of evidence - reflects very clearly the effect of the shift of focus that inaugurated the study of generative grammar."

Research over the last decades has shown that children do not get systematic information as to the grammatical or ungrammatical status of the generalisations they make (*no negative data assumption*, cf. Atkinson 1992, Lightfoot 1991). And wherever children are corrected, corrections prove to have no relevant impact, unless the respective construction is, as pointed out by Hohenberger (1996: 39), "*within reach*".[7] Further, many hypotheses which would lead to ungrammatical output, are never considered by children.

In view of this evidence it is plausible to assume that human beings are equipped *a priori* with a set of principles and rules constraining the form of natural languages, i.e. with a *universal grammar* (henceforth UG). In other words, the human language faculty is believed to be part of the genetic endowment, which guarantees - together with minimal data in the input - the acquisition of the language-specific grammar in question, i.e. the *steady state* of the adult speaker. In this way, language acquisition resembles the process of growth of other organs:

> "... universal grammar is an element of the genotype that maps a course of experience into a particular grammar that constitutes the system of mature knowledge of a language, a relatively steady state achieved at a certain point in normal life."
> (Chomsky 1980: 65)

As for ASLA, the crucial question to ask is whether this process is unique to language acquisition in childhood (henceforth L1A) or not. Linguistic theory has focused on mother tongue knowledge when analysing human language faculty. But we can assume that our language faculty is also involved in the acquisition, knowledge and use of other languages. As trivial as this assumption may seem - it lies at the core of the ongoing debate in the field of ASLA research. This is an issue to be dealt with shortly. Firstly, however, I turn to the understanding of grammar in the realm of UG theory.

---

[7] These considerations go against the claims advanced by proponents of the *Motherese Hypothesis*. According to this hypothesis parents adapt their utterances to children's needs. There are two critical aspects of this hypothesis. Firstly, it is unclear how reduced input could ever result in the development of complex language knowledge. Further, the learnability load would be increased as the set of possible grammars which could account for the simplified data would be far larger (cf. Gleitman and Wanner (1982) for a discussion of the central arguments).

2.3 The modular organisation of grammar

As pointed out above, research within the framework of UG theory has concentrated on the determination of the rules and principles underlying the *universal* knowledge of grammar, which is assumed to consist of the components in (13) (cf. Chomsky 1981).

(13)
- lexicon
- syntax:
  - X-bar theory
  - move-α
- PF component
- LF component

According to this model syntactic structures are represented on the levels listed in (14).

(14)
- D-structure
- S-structure
- PF (Phonetic form)
- LF (Logical Form)

S-structures are derived from underlying (D-)structures. The latter result from the information of the lexicon and the X-bar theory constraints. S-structures become phonetic forms through the interpretation at PF. They are further assigned logical forms by the LF component.

As opposed to traditional versions in which grammar was a system generating an infinite number of rules, current accounts following Chomsky's (1981) *Government-Binding theory* (henceforth GB theory) or *Principles and Parameters theory* (henceforth PP theory) state that UG is a system that determines the universal conditions on the wellformedness of linguistic structures, thus constraining the number of possible human languages (cf. Fanselow and Felix 1990b, Grewendorf 1991, among others).

A fundamental idea underlying GB theory is that UG is *modular* in character, each of the sub-systems listed in (15) consisting of a number of principles, which interact so as to derive wellformed structures (cf. Chomsky 1981).

(15)
- bounding theory
- government theory
- theta theory
- binding theory

- case theory
- control theory

Universal principles have to fulfill a dual requirement. On the one hand, they have to be as far reaching as to include all the possible human languages, on the other hand they have to be as constrained as required by the learnability criterion (cf. Chomsky 1986).
That is, when determining universal principles both logical and empirical grounds have to be taken into account. If a certain linguistic regularity cannot be deduced from the input, this has to be drawn back to a universal principle on the background of the no negative data assumption. The question as to whether this principle holds in any language is to be decided on empirical grounds. As a consequence,

> "... there is a tension between the demands of descriptive and explanatory adequacy. To achieve the latter, it is necessary to restrict available descriptive mechanisms so that few languages are accessible... To achieve descriptive adecuacy, however, the available devices must be rich and diverse enough to deal with the phenomena exhibited in the possible human languages. We therefore face conflicting requirements." (op. cit.: 55)

The idea that some universal principles are *parameterised* in order to cover cross-linguistic variation meets this dual requirement (cf. Chomsky 1981, Rizzi 1982). The *pro-drop parameter* (cf. Hyams 1986) is a case in point. Cross-linguistic research has evidenced that languages differ as to whether a subject position may be left lexically empty or not. Whilst the former option, i.e. *[+ pro-drop]*, is realised in both Spanish and Italian, it is excluded in languages such as German and English, i.e. in *[- pro-drop]* languages.
As pointed out by Hyams there are some further grammatical properties which seem to go along with the possibility of leaving the subject position lexically empty: free subject-verb inversion, expletives are not required and subjects of embedded finite sentences may be extracted. Interestingly, all these phenomena lead to ungrammaticality in the second group of languages, i.e. in [- pro-drop] languages. Considerations like these have lent credence that several grammatical properties or deductive consequences follow from the respective parametric options.

Note that UG determined properties of a language have to be distinguished from idiosyncratic ones. Consider, for example, the categorial selection of lexical items, which succeeds language-specific *subcategorisation* requirements specified in the lexical component, thus not pertaining to the domain of grammar.
A language-specific instantiation of universal principles and parameters, i.e. a particular *core grammar* is distinguished from idiosyncratic proper-

ties of the language in question, i.e. the *periphery*. On learnability grounds it is assumed that the core grammar has an *unmarked* status and is thus easier to learn than the *marked* periphery (cf. Chomsky 1981, White 1982).

As for parameter-setting, the idea is that language-specific parametric options are *triggered* by minimal data in the input.
Note that the differentiation between *triggered* as opposed to *learned* target language properties is crucial to the model at hand: the development of structural knowledge is guided by universally determined language-specific mechanisms as opposed to the idiosyncratic properties of the target language which have to be learned.

Presently, the traditional assumption that parameters are associated with universal principles has been replaced by the hypothesis that certain lexical items are subject to parametrisation (cf. Chomsky 1989, Ouhalla 1991, Pollock 1989). We will turn our attention to the details of this proposal in the next section.

2.4 Functional categories and the Functional Parametrisation Hypothesis

As anticipated in the previous section, the central idea underlying current versions of the PP model is that cross-linguistic variation is tied to a restricted set of categories, namely to *functional categories* (henceforth FCs), rather than to grammatical principles (cf. Chomsky 1989, Pollock 1989, Ouhalla 1991). Note that the central argument underlying the *Functional Parametrisation Hypothesis* is in tune with the traditional idea whereby elements of the open class (i.e. N, A, V, P) primarily determine the semantic aspect of an utterance as opposed to elements of the closed class which are mainly involved in the determination of the formal aspect of the utterance (cf. Guilfoyle and Noonan 1988, Hohenberger 1992, Radford 1990).

Following Pollock (1989), Chomsky (1989) and Ouhalla (1991) features such as agreement and tense, which had been previously subsumed under the category INFL (*inflection*), project their own maximal projections AGRP and TNSP, as illustrated in (16). [8]

---

[8] For a detailed discussion of the empirical motivation of this analysis the reader is referred to Pollock (1989) and Chomsky (1989).

(16)
```
                    CP
                   /  \
                Spec   C'
                      /  \
                     C    AGRs"
                         /  \
                       Spec  AGRs'
                            /  \
                         AGRs   TP
                               /  \
                              T    AGRo"
                                  /  \
                                Spec  AGRo'
                                     /  \
                                  AGRo   VP
```

(Chomsky 1992: 10)

Which are the properties of FCs which make them have a different status than substantive categories?

Firstly, functional elements are limited in number as opposed to the elements of the open class. Note that functional elements cannot be affected by conscious coining of new lexical entries (cf. Ouhalla 1992). Secondly, the properties of FCs are subject to cross-linguistic variation as opposed to the properties of substantive categories. Thirdly, substantive and functional categories differ as to their selectional properties in the following way:

- S-selectional properties
  Substantive categories, as opposed to FCs, assign thematic roles.[9] Thus, only substantive categories have s-selectional (s = semantic) properties.[10] The lack of theta-role assignment has been taken as the crucial criterion for determining whether a category belongs to the class of FCs. In this respect there is agreement that auxiliary and modal verbs, pronouns and some prepositions belong to the class of functional categories.

---

[9] See section 2.5.2 for a further insight into theta theory.

[10] As it is only substantive categories assigning or receiving theta-roles, functional categories are excluded from the predicate phrase, the VP being the domain of such processes. As a consequence modal and auxiliary verbs have to be generated outside the VP. The same applies to expletives and futher non-theta receivers.

- M-selectional properties
  There are a number of languages in which functional categories like determiners or complementisers are realised as free morphemes. Yet it is quite common for FCs to be instantiated as affixes.[11] Thus, FCs must be specified as to the category they attach to.[12] This property will also allow for FCs to appear as free, i.e. non-affixal, morphemes.
  Note that m-selection is not a distinctive property of FCs since substantive elements also have m-selectional properties.
  Whenever functional categories are realised as affix categories they will have to move or host another category, depending on the hierarchical position they have in the clause.[13]
  Note that this movement is subject to the *Head Movement Constraint* whereby a head category can only move to the head position immediately preceding it.[14, 15]

- Grammatical features
  Functional categories have the grammatical features listed in (17).

  (17) • AGR:
  - agreement features (person, number and gender)
  - case features:
  [+ nominative]   in subject AGR-S
  [+ accusative]   in object AGR-O

  • TNS:
  - tense features   [+/- past/future]

  • C and Det:
  - wh-features   [+/- wh]

---

[11] Cf. Baker (1988), Marantz (1984).

[12] Note that derivational affixes belong to the functional categories also. Consequently, with respect to verbs only verbal roots are substantive categories (cf. Ouhalla 1991: 203, footnote 8).

[13] This follows from the *Extended Projection Principle* (see section 2.5.3 below), which stipulates that the m-selectional properties of affix categories must be satisfied.

[14] Cf. Ouhalla (1991: 43).

[15] There is an important conclusion following from these considerations. The assumption that inflectional affixes are represented syntactically and that the processes by which they are derived take place in syntax, implies that much of the morphological component enters syntax. For further discussion of the relation between morphology and syntax see Ouhalla (1991, section 4.5), Baker (1988) and Marantz (1984).

- C-selectional properties
  FCs are specified for categorial selection (c-selection) as opposed to substantive categories.[16]
  The fact that languages vary as to the relative order of TNS and AGR - in VSO languages AGR is inside TNS, while in SVO languages AGR is outside TNS - shows that cross-linguistic word order variation is related to the c-selectional properties of FCs (cf. Ouhalla 1991, Grewendorf 1991). The *AGR/TNS parameter* is a case in point:

(18) AGR/TNS parameter:
  - TNS c-selects AGR
  - AGR c-selects TNS

In summarising the preceding considerations we can conclude with Ouhalla (1991:8) that functional categories

> "... represent the flesh and blood of grammar, in the sense that they are the locus of grammatical information which determines the structural representation of given constructions, as well as the various grammatical processes they may undergo."

Note that functional categories play a crucial role in *movement processes*. As a consequence of their m-selectional properties and in order to satisfy the morphological wellformedness principle, verb-movement out of the VP obtains if FCs are bound morphemes. Pollock (1989), for example, considers the possibility that verb raising depends on whether AGR is opaque or transparent to theta-role transmission in a language.[17]

Further, specifier positions of FCs provide the appropriate landing sites for arguments which have to move in order to satisfy the *Case Requirement*: subjects in active sentences or objects in passive sentences move into SpecAGR-S, objects in active sentences into SpecAGR-O (cf. Ouhalla 1992).[18]

Cross-linguistic variation with respect to these and other grammatical processes is a progression from the language-specific specification of the FC in question.

---

[16] C-selectional specification in the case of substantive categories would be redundant as the categorial realisation is predictable (cf. *Canonical Structural Realisation*, section 2.5.3 below).

[17] For a discussion of some possible implications following from this analysis in terms of learnability for ASLA see section 6.3.1.

[18] A more detailed analysis of the role of AGR categories with respect to agreement relations and case checking will be given in section 2.5.4.

As for language acquisition, we can advance the relevance of the determination of the language-specific properties of FCs by virtue of being *"the patients and agents of syntactic change at the same time"* (Hohenberger 1996: 45).

We also have to consider a more modular view of the lexical component. In fact, Ouhalla (1992) proposes a sub-division as follows: (a) the *UG lexicon*, made up by the finite set of functional categories, (b) the *mental lexicon* belonging to the conceptual system, which is independent of UG, and (c) the *grammatical lexicon*, containing the lexical representations of the categories of both the UG- and the mental lexicon, whereby "... *the grammatical lexicon can be conceived as a level of representation on a par with D-structure, S-structure, ... etc*" (ibid.: 9).

2.5 The interface between lexicon and syntax

2.5.1 Argument structure

The introduction of X-bar theory (cf. Chomsky 1970) marked a crucial step in the history of generative grammar insofar as the universal format of the structures generated by possible human grammars was conceived. Given the universally constrained architecture of phrase structure, language-specific information concerning the contextual features of a lexical item need not be specified in UG. Note that this information is encoded in the lexicon, i.e. in the respective *subcategorisation frames*.

The lexical representation of the grammatical information about a predicate is represented in the form of the *argument structure* (henceforth a-structure) of a lexical item (cf. Grimshaw 1990). It is thus expected that this information is "*critical to the syntactic behavior of a lexical item*" (ibid.: 1, cf. also Zubizarreta 1987, di Sciullo and Williams 1987).[19] If we consider, additionally, that a-structure is projected from lexical semantic structure we may advance that a-structure represents the *interface* between lexical semantic structure and syntax (i.e. D-structure), as Jackendoff (1990: 48) puts it:

> "In short, "argument structure" can be thought of as an abbreviation for the part of conceptual structure that is "visible" to the syntax."

---

[19] I will not go into the details of further differentiations proposed in the literature regarding the levels of lexical representation (cf. Zubizarreta 1987 and Demonte 1991 for an extended discussion of the relevant arguments).

In this context the central concept is that of a *thematic role*. Thematic roles such as *agent, patient, goal, source* or *location* provide information about the thematic relations in a sentence. It is generally agreed, however, that a-structure is "blind" against the thematic role *labels*, although they are often used for ease of comprehension, cf.

> "Substantive notions like theme, patient, experiencer have no grammatical import: rules and principles of grammar are never formulated in terms of these notions."
> (Zubizarretta 1987: 12, cf. also Grimshaw 1990)

There is one way, however, in which these thematic role labels play a role, namely in the organisation of a-structure which is assumed to depend on the *thematic hierarchy* (cf. (19)). More precisely, this relationship holds at the interface between lexical-conceptual structure and a-structure (cf. Grimshaw 1990).[20]

(19) (Agent (Experiencer (Goal / Source / Location (Theme))))
      (Grimshaw 1990: 6)[21]

Following Grimshaw this organisation relates to *prominence relations* which are based on the hierarchy in (19). It is assumed that this relation plays a crucial role in processes like passivisation or in the differentiation among psychological verbs.[22]

Implicit in these considerations is the assumption that semantic representations obey universal regularities as much as syntactic representations do (cf. Jackendoff 1972, 1983, 1990, Chomsky 1988). The relevance of this assumption may be summarised as follows:

> "Universality is necessary so that representations are language-independent; we must be able to compare meanings of sentences across languages. Put more strongly, to suppose a universal semantic representation is to make an important claim about the innateness of semantic structure."
> (Jackendoff 1972: 1)

In view of these considerations we can further delimit the learnability task along the lines exemplified in Chomsky (1988: 31/32):

---

[20] Cf. also Jackendoff (1990).
[21] I will ignore here the discussion surrounding the problem of determining the relative order of *Theme* and *Goal/Source/Location* which is mentioned by Grimshaw (1990: 175).
[22] According to Grimshaw (1990) we have to assume two different dimensions of prominence relations, i.e. the thematic and the aspectual dimension, in order to embrace the relevant differences among the verbs in question.

"The child must have enough information to determine that the form *persuadir* ['to persuade', CPP] is the one that corresponds to the preexisting concept but need not discover the precise bounds and intricacies of this concept, which is already available, before experience with language."

We will now turn our attention to the relevance of thematic information in syntax.

2.5.2   Theta theory

Within the framework of GB theory subcategorised positions are in a thematic relationship with the lexical head of the syntactic construction. Thematic relations encoded in the form of *thematic roles* or *theta-roles* are assigned by the verb. The totality of theta-roles selected by a verb is called its *theta-grid*.
This allows for a crucial differentiation regarding the status of expressions. Expressions which are assigned a theta-role are *arguments*. Impersonal 'it' or other non-referential expressions do not have the status of arguments because they are not assigned a theta-role. They are in no thematic relationship to the verb. Expletive elements, for example, only fulfill the function of lexically filling the syntactic subject position. These expressions are *non-arguments*.
Each syntactic position which is assigned a theta-role by the lexical head of a construction is a *theta-position*. Note that theta-role assignment of a head to its complements occurs obligatorily. The subject position, on the other hand, is not always a theta-position as illustrated in (20) where 'there' is a non-argument subject lacking any thematic role (cf. Chomsky 1986: 90):

(20)   there is a man in the room

Consequently, syntactic positions differ as to whether they are assigned a theta-role. Positions which may be assigned a theta-role are *A-positions*. The pleonastic element 'there' in (20), for example, is in an A-position. Positions like SpecC and adjunct-positions, on the other hand, are *Non-A-positions*.

Theta-role assignment and argument-status are constrained by the *Theta-Criterion* which has to be fulfilled on all representation levels:

(21)   Theta-Criterion
       Each argument bears one and only one theta-role, and each theta-role is assigned to one and only one argument.
       (Chomsky 1981: 36)

Sentence (22) below illustrates the case in point. We can see that ungrammaticality results from the destruction of the thematic structure of a verb at S-structure: by virtue of being moved from a theta-marked position into another theta-marked position, one of the verbal arguments (i.e. 'John') receives two theta-roles (the theta-roles of the direct and the indirect argument respectively) (cf. Felix and Fanselow 1990b: 132).

(22) *a book was given John$_i$ to t$_i$

2.5.3 Projection Principle

The above mentioned requirement on the maintainance of thematic information at all representational levels is guaranteed by the *Projection Principle*.

(23) Projection Principle
Representations at each syntactic level (...) are projected from the lexicon, in that they observe the subcategorisation properties of lexical items.
(Chomsky 1981: 9)

Following the Projection Principle, the Theta-Criterion, which originally is conceived as a wellformedness condition at the level of LF, has to be fulfilled at every syntactic level. It was shown above that this requirement is, in fact, needed in order to explain the ungrammaticality of sentences like (22).

Since subjects are not subcategorised, a further principle ensuring that every sentence has a subject has to be stipulated. *The Extended Projection Principle* (cf. Chomsky 1982) results from the integration of this principle into the Projection Principle.

It is important to note that the language-specific categorial realisation of the thematic roles selected by the verb results from their respective *CSR(C)*, i.e. their *canonical structural realisation* (cf. Chomsky 1981, Grimshaw 1981).

2.5.4 Case theory

The relationship between theta theory and case theory is quite demonstrative of the modular organisation of grammar. In GB theory case features fulfill an identificational function related to the Theta-Criterion. In fact, the latter is only fulfilled if arguments are assigned case. This constraint on theta-marking is captured by the *Visibility Condition*:

(24) Visibility Condition
An element is visible to theta-marking only if it is assigned case. (...) A lexical argument must have Case, or it will not receive a theta-role and will not be licensed.
(Chomsky 1986: 94)[23]

It should be noted that case theory has only recently received attention. For a long time, case was assumed to be a morphological phenomenon, and as such it belonged to a grammar-independent component (cf. Stechow and Sternefeld 1988).

Within GB theory case features have a function both in morphology and in syntax. In this respect it is important to acknowledge the distinction drawn between a case feature and a case morpheme. The two are differentiated terminologically as follows:

- *abstract case* or *a-case* refers to a certain case feature

- *morphological case* or *m-case* refers to the actual case morpheme.[24]

Note that there is cross-linguistic variation as to the categories which may assign case. [- N] categories, i.e. verbs and prepositions, universally assign case. Case assignment by nouns and adjectives, i.e. [+ N] categories, only applies in some languages. For example, Spanish differs from German in that in German but not in Spanish [+ N] categories may also assign case, as illustrated in (25) and (26). The Spanish construction in in (26) is ungrammatical as the appropriate case assigner is missing.

(25) die   Ablehnung   meines   Antrages...
     the   rejection   my-gen.   application
     'the rejection of my application'

---

[23] This constraint is a more detailed version of the earlier *Case Filter* (cf. Chomsky 1981: 49):
(i)   Case filter
      *NP, if NP has phonetic content and has no Case
[24] For a detailed analysis of case morphemes, agreement features and hereditary principles see Sternefeld and Stechow (1988: 160).

(26) *la denegación solicitud
     the rejection application

Since nouns and adjectives do not assign case in neither English nor Spanish, these languages make use of so-called *dummy case markers*. The English preposition 'of', for example, functions as an assigner of objective case to an object NP in the PP. This preposition is inserted in the mapping of D- to S-structure following the *of-insertion rule*. Similarly, the insertion of *de* is needed in Spanish.[25]

In some languages certain verbs govern a specific case. As illustrated in (27) and (28) the German verb 'helfen' (*to help*) governs the dative case unlike the verb 'unterstützen' (*to support*).

(27) Paul hilft   ihm   ('ihm' = dative)
      Paul helps him

(28) Maria unterstützt sie   ('sie' = accusative)
      Maria supports   her

Dative and objective genitive (as well as the case assigned by adjectives and prepositions) represent *idiosyncratic or inherent cases* closely tied to theta-role assignment. They have to be specified in the lexical entries and are realised at D-structure. They are termed *lexical* or *oblique* cases. As opposed to these oblique cases, nominative and accusative are assigned under certain structural or syntactic conditions (thus they are denominated *structural cases*). Note that AGR categories play a decisive role here: AGR categories agree with and assign case to the noun-phrases occupying their specifier position (cf. Chomsky 1986, Ouhalla 1992). The spec-head agreement relation is illustrated in (29).

We will additionally follow Koopman and Sportiche (1991) and Roberts (1993) in the assumption that there is a further possibility, namely, nominative case-checking under government. Consequently, we expect cross-linguistic variation regarding the choice among these alternatives. The government relation is illustrated in (30). Note that the respective language-specific choice among these options bears on the surface word order realised in a particular language. In Romance languages, for example, nominative case is checked under spec-head agreement.

---

[25] This phenomenon applies as well in French and in Italian. It is interesting to note with respect to German that this language not only allows for structural case assignment by N and A. Under particular idiosyncratical conditions prepositions are also needed as case-assigners (cf. Stechow and Sternefeld 1988).

(29)　spec-head agreement　　(30)　government

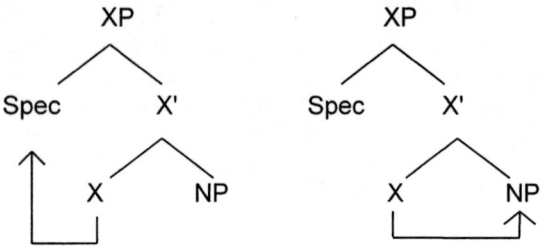

```
        XP                        XP
       /  \                      /  \
     Spec  X'                  Spec  X'
      ↑   /  \                      /  \
      |  X    NP                   X    NP
      |__|                         |____↑
```

In these languages the subject must leave the VP and move into the SpecAGR position in order to be case-checked. This will derive the surface word order SVO. In a language like German, subjects and verbs need not obligatorily be in a spec-head relation as nominative is checked under government. Therefore, the specifier position may also serve as a landing site for other topicalised elements.[26]

2.6　German sentence structure

One of the crucial characteristics of Germanic languages (with the exception of Modern English) is that the finite verb obligatorily appears in the second position in main declarative clauses (cf. (31) - (33)). This phenomenon is commonly denominated *Verb-Second* (V2).

(31)　Danish:　　Hulken　bog　　har　Peter　læst?
　　　German:　 Welches　Buch　 hat　Peter　gelesen?
　　　English:　 Which　　book　has　Peter　read?

(32)　Danish:　　Denne　　bog　　har　Peter　læst.
　　　German:　 Dieses　　Buch　 hat　Peter　gelesen.
　　　English:　 *This　　 book　has　Peter　read.

(33)　Danish:　　Måske　　har　　Peter　læst　denne bog.
　　　German:　 Vielleicht　hat　　Peter　　　 dieses Buch gelesen.
　　　English:　 *Maybe　　has　　Peter　read　this book.

(examples from Vikner 1995: 39)

This is not to say, however, that all German clauses are V2 clauses as the topological model in (34) illustrates.

---

[26]　In section 8.2.3 I will discuss the implications following from this contrast for the acquisition of L2 German by an adult Italian learner.

(34) Topological model of German word order generalisations (cf. Fritzenschaft et al. 1991: 57)

'Vorfeld' (pre-field)	'linke Satzklammer' (left sentence bracket)	'Mittelfeld' (middle field)	'rechte Satz-klammer' (right sentence bracket)	'Nachfeld' (post-field)
topicalised constituents	verb in initial or second position	constituents that have not been extracted	clause-final verbs	extraposed constituents
Ungern (reluctantly)	gab (gave)	Jill ein Stück von dem Apfel (Jill a piece of the apple)	ab (away)	den er für sie gepflückt hatte. (which he for her picked had)
	Gab (gave)	Jill ein Stück... (Jill a piece...)	ab (away)	................?
	Obwohl (although)	Jill ein Stück... (Jill a piece...)	abgab (away-gave)	................,

The following generalisations are valid:

- Topicalised constituents appear in the *pre-field*.

- Extraposed contituents appear in the *post-field*.

- No constituent appears in the *pre-field* in the following cases:
  (a)   yes/no questions
  (b)   imperatives with and without subjects
  (c)   conditional V1 structures
  (d)   structures in which the verb-initial position is licensed by a further verbal context.

- Verbs appear in the position of the *right bracket* in clauses which are introduced by a complementiser, relative pronouns or wh-phrases.

43

There is no one-to-one correspondence between the verb-placement asymmetry and the main/embedded clause dichotomy as German allows for verb-final structures with main clause character and unintroduced embedded V2-clauses. Note that the sentence-final position of the verb is obligatory in embedded clauses introduced by a complementiser[27] and, conversely, is ruled out in the case of unintroduced embedded clauses as shown in (35) and (36).

(35) ich   hoffe,   daß   er   heute   kommen kann
      I   *hope*   *that* *he* *today* *come* *can*
      'I hope he can come today'

(36) *ich   glaube, er   keine Zeit   hat
      I   *think* *he*   *no*   *time* *has*
      'I think his has no time'

Interestingly, colloquial German allows for V3 in embedded clauses introduced by 'weil' (*because*) and 'obwohl' (*although*), e.g.

(37) weil   er   hatte keine Zeit
      because   *he* *had* *no*   *time*

(38) obwohl   er   hatte keine Zeit
      although *he* *had* *no*   *time*

Now, the crucial question is how these generalisations may be captured by a sentence structure conforming to the X-bar schema.
Two main analyses have been subject to discussion throughout the last years, namely the *Symmetry Hypothesis* and the *Asymmetry Hypothesis*.

2.6.1   The Symmetry Hypothesis

According to the Symmetry Hypothesis (cf. Grewendorf 1988, Vikner 1995 among others) (39) is the underlying structure of both main and embedded clauses. Following this analysis, the verbal head will move to I, where affixes are allocated, and remain there in verb-final structures. V2 and V1 structures, on the other hand, result from the subsequent movement of the verbal complex into C and of a topicalised constituent into SpecC.

---

[27]   There is one exception to this generalisation, namely the conjunction 'denn' (*because, for*) which rules out V-End.

(39)
```
           CP
          /  \
       SpecC  C'
             /  \
            C    IP
                /  \
             SpecI  I'
                   /  \
                  VP   I
                 /  \
               Spec  V'
                    /  \
                   ...  V
```

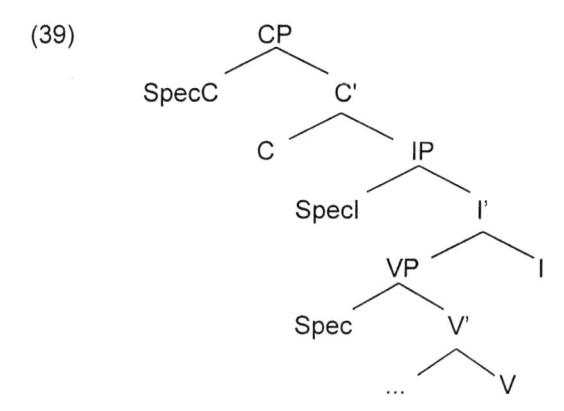

According to Platzack and Holmberg (1989) it is the different placement of the finiteness operator [+ F] which accounts for cross-linguistic variation with respect to V2 phenomena. In languages not exhibiting V2 like, for example, French, the finiteness operator appears in I. In languages like German [+ F] appears in C.[28] Müller (1993) points out that SpecC has a dual status in V2 languages insofar as subjects and non-subjects may appear there, i.e. SpecC may function as an A- or a Non-A-position. According to her this follows from [+ F] appearing in C.

Note that the Symmetry Hypothesis of German sentence structure suggests that lexical complementisers and finite verbs at the left periphery of the sentence are "mutually exclusive".[29] There are a number of ways in which finite verbs in V1 and V2 and complementisers in VE structures behave similarly. What remains unexplained, however, is why wh-phrases behave differently in main and in embedded clauses (cf. Gawlitzek-Maiwald et al. 1992). Wh-phrases, representing maximal projections, choose specifier positions as their landing sites (cf. (40)).
But, in embedded clauses introduced by a wh-phrase (cf. (41)) the verb does not move into C although this position would be available in principle.
If wh-phrases are generated in the specifier position of the CP it is unclear why they prevent the verb from appearing in C in embedded clauses.

---

[28] This is but one of different analyses proposed. For a detailed discussion see Vikner (1995, chapter 2).

[29] Certainly, this mutual exclusiveness is only a superficial account of a phenomenon still to be explained. Insofar as finite verbs and complementisers do not belong to the same category they cannot be mutually exclusive in the strict sense of the term (see Gawlitzek-Maiwald et al. 1992, Stechow and Sternefeld 1988).

(40)   [CP Werk [C'   hat_ij [IP[I'[VP t_k   einen   Brief   gelesen t_j] t_ij]]]] [30]
       who   has   a   letter read

'Who has read a letter?'

(41)   Ich   weiß,   wer   den   Brief   gelesen   hat.
       I   know   who   the   letter   read   has

'I know who has read the letter'

(op. cit.: 151)

It has been suggested that wh-phrases may appear in C in subordinate clauses, which would further explain why in some German dialects wh-words and complementisers may absorb inflectional features (cf. Grewendorf 1988, Müller 1993). Note, though, that this analysis goes against the tenets of the Structure Preserving Principle as a maximal phrase would be moved into a head position.

As a way out of the dilemma it has been proposed (cf. Grewendorf 1988 and references therein) that finite verbs and complementisers occupy the same position in the sentence. This claim is based on the assumption that in languages like German C and I (I being head-initial) merge to one position termed CONFL. However, this assumption faces the problem of explaining how verbs in embedded clauses may remain in a position not specified for finiteness and agreement features, viz. in V. In this respect it is claimed that in embedded clauses the INFL features lower down to V. This analysis implies that INFL features are realised as affixes in COMP. But, the crucial weakness of this hypothesis remains, however, i.e. how INFL and COMP can be base-generated in one position at once (cf. Rothweiler 1993).

The verb placement asymmetry in German raises a more general question, namely, why finite verbs have to move into C in main declarative and interrogative clauses. As pointed out by Rothweiler, if movement into C was optional, the grammar would overgenerate unintroduced sentences with a finite verb in sentence-final position, as illustrated in (42).

(42)   *Ich   das   jetzt   überlegen   muß.
       I   that   now   think-over   have-to

(op. cit.: 14, my transl.)

---

[30] (40) represents the S-structure including the traces of moved categories. The authors assume that moved affixes also leave traces following Strict Structure Preservation.

It seems (42) is excluded because C is not lexically filled. So the crucial point about the C position in German main declarative and interrogative clauses would be that it must be lexically filled with a finite verb. Consequently, Rothweiler assumes, if C remains empty no sentence is generated, working on the assumption that sentences represent CPs.

This analysis does not give a satisfactory account of why finite verbs do not move into C in subordinate wh-clauses. As an empty complementiser position would be ruled out a 0-complementiser has been postulated, which realises the relevant subcategorisation features of subordinate clauses (cf. Grewendorf 1988).

Additionally there is the issue of why there is no initial field in the case of embedded clauses introduced by a complementiser. Rothweiler (1993) suggests that the initial field is created in case SpecCP inherits the wh-feature of C.[31]

2.6.2 The Asymmetry Hypothesis

According to the Asymmetry Hypothesis (cf. von Stechow and Sternefeld 1988) main clauses project to IP only (cf. (43)). Note that IP has to be head-initial in this case. Embedded sentences, on the other hand, project to CP.

(43)

```
            IP
           /  \
       SpecI   I'
              / \
             I   VP
                / \
            SpecV  V'
                  / \
                 XP  V
```

Following this analysis the verb moves to I, topicalised constituents to SpecI. Consequently, this analysis presupposes that subjects need not show up in SpecI as they remain in their base-generated position in case some other constituent is topicalised into SpecI. By the same token, SpecI also functions as an A-bar-position, since it may serve as a landing site for topicalised constituents.

In this way, the Asymmetry approach to German sentence structure does

---

[31] SpecCP is believed to inherit these features in case C is filled by a lexical complementiser. Note that this does not apply for the case of the 0-complementiser.

not need to explain why verbs move into C in V2 and V1 structures and, conversely, why V2 structures are incompatible with complementisers. Unfortunately, this analysis does not provide a solution to the problem concerning wh-phrases either (cf. Gawlitzek-Maiwald et al. 1992).

Furthermore, there is some disagreement as to whether the IP is also head-initial in the structure provided for embedded clauses. Recall that the verb appears in final position in complementiser-introduced embedded clauses. The following options have been considered (cf. op. cit.):

- IP is head-initial and INFL-features lower to the verb in sentence-final position.
- IP is head-initial and INFL features are generated in the VP and checked for compatibility.
- IP is head-final in embedded clauses introduced by a complementiser and head-initial in embedded V1 and V2 structures.

None of these options, however, is completely satisfactory. While the first two pose descriptive problems (cf. Müller 1993), the latter one is questionable on learnability grounds as it is generally assumed that the headedness parameter is set either to the initial or to the final value.

The preceding considerations show that any of the descriptive analyses of German sentence structure proposed so far faces a number of problems. It was shown that much controversy centres around the problem of adequately capturing the grammatical processes concerning the left periphery. With respect to language acquisition it may be assumed that the task of discovering the target-like regularities pertaining to the left periphery will not be an easy one (cf. Fritzenschaft et al. 1991, Müller 1993, Gawlitzek-Maiwald et al. 1992). In chapter 7 (section 7.1) we will see that this prediction is borne out by the data.

2.7 Language acquisition and the modularity of grammar: Narrowing the focus

The considerations outlined in this chapter show how the relation between the lexicon and syntax is closely tied to the modular nature of our language faculty. More specifically we could see that in UG the relation between lexicon and syntax is subject to universal constraints or wellformedness conditions on representations, cf.

> "The representations that appear at the various levels are those that can be projected from semantic properties of lexical items in such a way as to

accord with the various principles of UG with their parameters set. Every element that appears in a well-formed structure must be *licensed* in one of a small number of available ways."
(Chomsky 1986: 93)

We have also learned how a modular concept of grammar embraces universal and language-specific aspects of natural languages.
While the former are the result of the inter-relation among the different subcomponents of grammar, the latter are derived by language-specific information in the lexicon. This in turn is further differentiated into thematic as opposed to grammatical information which is associated with substantive and functional categories respectively. As regards substantive elements, we learned that they have uniform properties across languages and that there are universal principles which ensure that the thematic structure associated to them is retained in syntax.

Furthermore, we need to consider the relevance of functional categories as outlined in the Functional Parametrisation Hypothesis. We could see that they play a crucial role in our understanding of grammar. Following this assumption cross-linguistic variation is tied to the language-specific properties of FCs. Consequently, the acquisition of a particular grammar will depend on the appropriate specification of these properties.

Note that this approach calls for a precise differentiation between the learning of lexical idiosyncracies as opposed to the triggering of parametric properties associated with FCs. This issue is of special relevance in the present analysis as outlined in chapter 1. Recall that there we highlighted the learnability problem associated with the plurifunctionality of lexical items. So a critical review of the different concepts of lexical learning will be one of the main points subject to discussion in the following sections.

What we have learned in this section is that the structural levels lexical items are embedded in cannot be reduced to each other. But we may assume that the determination of their inter-relation is crucial for any explanation which considers the possibility that the acquisition of elements of one level may trigger off properties of some other level, as is the case in the framework of the lexical or functional parametrisation hypothesis.

3 Modularity and ASLA

3.1 The Lexical Learning Hypothesis and German word order in child language acquisition

The central assumption underlying Clahsen's *Lexical Learning Hypothesis* is that there is a correlation between the acquisition of certain lexical items and the development of syntactic structure (cf. Clahsen 1988a, 1988b, 1990a, 1992, Clahsen et al. 1990), cf.

> "A parameterized theory of grammar requires that such restructurings are triggered by relatively simple kinds of positive data which are readily available to the child. Ideally, we would therefore like to restrict the kinds of triggering data to particular lexical items and their associated properties." (Clahsen 1988b: 49)

Clahsen draws on Pinker's (1984) hypotheses regarding the inter-relation of the acquisition of the lexicon and the development of syntax (i.e. what he denominates as the *"lexicalist version of learnability theory"*, Clahsen 1992: 59), which may be summarised as follows:

- The child's *intake* (i.e. the perception of the input data) varies in the course of language acquisition.
- Some UG principles, although present from the beginning, operate vacuously until the identification of the relevant triggering elements.
- As soon as the child has categorised these lexical items the respective universal principles and the deductive consequences associated with them become immediately operative.

Consequently, his analysis of child data is dedicated to the identification of the lexical items, whose acquisition induces major changes in the child grammar.

Clahsen's studies of child German word order development are based upon the *Double Movement analysis* of German sentence structure. According to this analysis, verbs provided with the INFL feature [+ agreement] in main declarative sentences have to move to COMP. This is achieved by means of the *Finite-Fronting rule*. In affirmative sentences a further constituent may be moved into a position preceding the verb via the *Topicalisation rule*. Verbs cannot be moved in embedded clauses, in which the COMP position is filled with a lexical complementiser. Clahsen (1988b: 51, my transl.) provides the examples in (1) (his (2)) for further illustration:

(1) a. D-structure:
S' [COMP [(daß)] Adrian gerade das Radio
(that) Adrian just the radio
angestellt hat]
turned-on has
'(that) Adrian just turned on the radio'

b. Finfronting:
S' [COMP [Hat$_i$] Adrian gerade das Radio angestellt e$_i$]
has Adrian just the radio turned-on
'Did Adrian just turn the radio on?'

c. Topicalisation:
S" [TOP [Adrian$_j$] S'[COMP [hat$_i$] e$_j$ gerade das Radio
Adrian has just the radio
angestellt e$_i$]]
turned-on
'Adrian just turned the radio on'

Clahsen further assumes that the Double Movement analysis is motivated by two parameters in the following way:

- COMP/INFL parameter
Following Platzack (1983) Clahsen states that there is cross-linguistic variation as to whether COMP and INFL are realised as one or two syntactic nodes. The former option is applicable to German, i.e. COMP and INFL are merged in one syntactic node, namely CONFL. This position may host either inflected verbs or complementisers.

- INFL/V parameter
In line with Kratzer (1984) Clahsen assumes that INFL/V parameter determines whether INFL is weak or strong in a language in relation to its morphological properties. Depending on the status of INFL, inflected verbs will be categorised either as INFLs, i.e. [$_{Infl}$ V INFL], or as Vs, i.e. [$_V$ INFL]. In German INFL is strong (verbs being strongly inflected). So inflected verbs appear in the CONFL position unless this position is filled by a lexical complementiser.

Clahsen's account of the developmental stages of the child acquisition of German word order is as follows (cf. especially Clahsen 1988a). (For ease of comprehension I provide an overview of the German person/number verb endings in (2)).[32]

(2)

Person	number	suffix	example	
1st	singular	-e/-0	ich spiel-e	(*I play*)
2nd	singular	-st	du spiel-*st*	(*you play*)
3rd	singular	-t	sie spiel-*t*	(*she plays*)
1st	plural	-n	wir spiel-*e-n*	(*we play*)
2nd	plural	-t	ihr spiel-*t*	(*you play*)
3rd	plural	-n	sie spiel-*e-n*	(*they play*)

Clahsen observes that constituents do not appear in a fixed linear order at *stage II*[33]. Although verbs appear alternatively in initial or in final position he acknowledges a preference for verb-final structures. Furthermore, children already distinguish between inflected and uninflected verbal forms at this stage. According to Clahsen, the verbal inflections used, which reduce to root *-0* and infinitive *-n* (some children already use *-t*), do not correlate with grammatical persons. He assumes that children use inflections following semantic criteria instead, especially in order to mark the semantic transitivity of a sentence. In this respect Clahsen claims that *-t* functions as a marker of intransitivity. Note that his assumption is that such inflected verbs and modals are categorised in the lexicon as INFLs and correctly placed in INFL.[34] Uninflected forms as Vs, on the other hand, would remain in V since main verbs cannot be fronted into the INFL position as long as the agreement system has not been acquired. Following these considerations Clahsen claims that children have specified INFL as head-initial following evidence in the input, like, for example, the order *Mod...Inf*.

As for the VP Clahsen remarks that although children find evidence for both ...XV and ...VX... in the input, they recognise that in VX... structures V is in the INFL position. They correctly conclude that the VP is head-final upon exclusion of the VP-initial option. The latter option is excluded as it would require further movement rules. Such rules, in the case of XVS right dislocation of the subject, would violate the configurational matrix.

---

[32] The following distribution disregards morphological irregularities as well as the suppletive forms of the copular verb 'sein' (*to be*) and the forms of modal verbs.

[33] Clahsen's analysis starts out with stage II where children produce two to three constituent utterances after a period of one-word utterances, which would represent stage I.

[34] Clahsen (1992) assumes that the early categorisation of modals as INFLs is a consequence of their meaning. Their later recategorisation to V at stage III is assumed to follow the acquisition of the subject-verb agreement paradigm.

Clahsen acknowledges that children can produce the correct word order for main clauses at *stage IV*[35], i.e. finite verbal elements appear in the second position. This correlates with the fact that children now master the target agreement paradigm.

Clahsen remarks that a number of inflectional forms have been learned at *stage III*. According to Clahsen the children's need to mark the finiteness of verbs at this stage is reflected in the overgeneralisation of the verbal inflection form *-e* (cf. (3) - (4)) and the use of anaphoric pronomina as verbal suffixes (cf. (5) - (6)).[36]

(3) ich   kann**e**   drinsitzen
     I   *can*   *inside-sit*

(4) du   ma   auch   zeig**e**
     you *ADV* *also* *show*

(5) fels   noch   nicht   is**er**   putt
     rock *yet*   *not*   *is-he*   ['kapputt' = *broken*]

(6) das   is**er**   großer fisch
     that *is-he*   *big   fish*

(Clahsen 1988a: 77, my transl.)

Note that Clahsen assumes that children are not yet aware of the formal status of inflectional endings. Nevertheless, he takes pronominal copies as an indicator of a possible correlation between the acquisition of verbal inflection and the pronominal system.

At *stage IV* children have acquired the inflectional ending *-st*, which they use without error.[37] As all other inflections have been acquired by this time the acquisition of the agreement system is fulfilled at this point in the process. Clahsen assumes that the child has discovered the *strong* nature of German verb inflection, which allows her to correctly analyse finite verbs as INFLs.

In view of these findings Clahsen concludes that the acquisition of target-

---

[35] Clahsen (1988a) points out that no significant, i.e. qualitative, changes take place in the learner grammar of stage III. Rather, the learner grammar of stage III is understood as a transition of stage II to stage IV.

[36] Clahsen further refers to the fact that in some languages pronominal marking represents a means of agreement marking, for example, in Swahili.

[37] Furthermore, grammatical function words, like auxiliaries, prepositions and articles are no longer omitted. The acquisition of these items is said to proceed concurrently.

like word order in being related to the target-like fixation of the INFL/V parameter is dependent on the development in the morphological component of the lexicon (op. cit.: 81).

Finally, as soon as embedded clauses are produced at *stage V* they occur with correct word order. According to Clahsen the presence of lexical complementisers in the input trigger the correct setting of the COMP/INFL parameter.

3.2 Lexical learning and German word order in ASLA

According to Clahsen (1988b, 1988c, 1990b) and Clahsen and Muysken (henceforth CM) (1986, 1989), if adult learners of German had access to UG, they would have to find out, as children do, that German word order depends upon the correct fixation of (a) the Head parameter, (b) the COMP/INFL parameter and (c) the INFL/V parameter. And they should do so by means of *lexical learning* in the sense outlined previously, e.g. the learning of the target language agreement system should trigger the correct verb movement rules.

CM claim that the UG-based prediction is not borne out by the empirical data. They argue that the acquisition of L2 German follows other regularities.[38] The hypothesis that ASLA is not guided by UG but rather by general learning mechanisms is based on two empirical arguments:

- The learners posit SVO as the underlying word order throughout the whole development.
- Lexical learning in the sense outline above does not induce any restructurings in the learner's grammar.

These considerations are based on the developmental sequence in (7).[39]

---

[38] Clahsen and Muysken refer to the empirical data gathered in the ZISA project mentioned in section 1.2.3.

[39] It should be noted that Clahsen (1988b) assumes that there are 4 rather than 6 stages. This he already stated in Clahsen (1984). The original developmental sequence (see section 1.2.3 above) is repeated here for further illustration (the initial one-constituent stage is omitted here):
(i) Stage I: SVO
     Stage II: ADV-PREP
     Stage III: PARTICLE
     Stage IV: INVERSION
     Stage V: ADV-VP
     Stage VI: V-END

(7) Phase I: SVO, adverb preposing
Phase II: PARTICLE, extraposition of subject
Phase III: subject-verb inversion, ADV VP
Phase IV: V END

As already mentioned, CM state that adult learners assume that SVO is the underlying word order of German throughout the whole development as opposed to children who discover correct SOV quite early. In line with the earlier assumptions put forward in CMP (1983) (see section 1.2.3), adult learners are said to choose SVO in accordance with general processing principles. CM's main claim is that the L2 German development, i.e. the *permutation rules* subsequently learned, cannot be explained in terms of UG.

The rule PARTICLE acquired at stage II is given as an illustrative example. Clahsen (1988b) points out that the movement of separable prefixes, participles and infinitives to the sentence-final position cannot be the result of a single *universal* rule as it pertains to different syntactic constructions: separable prefixes are generated before the verb, participles and infinitives after the verb. No local rule, such as the English *particle shift* rule could apply as movement takes place over several constituents. Similar considerations apply to the rules V END and INVERSION.

As for the mechanisms guiding the course of adult L2 development, *lexical learning* is ruled out, since no relation between the acquisition of the agreement system and verb placement is acknowledged.
This claim is based on the following empirical findings (cf. Clahsen 1988b *pace* Köpcke 1987):

- Stage I:
  Verb endings produced: *-0, -n, -e* (*-t* and *-st* also acknowledged).
  Strong individual variation as to the preferred verb ending.

- Subsequent stages:
  Decrease of previously predominant *-st*.
  Root and infinitive forms replaced by inflected forms.

Clahsen remarks that the use the endings *-t* and *-st* is correct from the beginning although he observes differences with respect to "*the extent to which these forms are produced by the learners*" (op. cit.: 63).
Conversely, learners are said to have difficulties in the acquisition of the correct use of the ending *-n*, this form being overgeneralised "*irrespective of the person and number of the subject up to Phases III/IV*" (ibid.). Clahsen suggests that *-n* is analysed as [- AGR], i.e. "*it functions as in-*

finitive" (ibid.). Conversely, the endings *-0* and *-e* are overgeneralised only with the 2nd and 3rd pers. sing. Clahsen takes this as evidence that leaners only distinguish the person feature, rather than person *and* number.
In general, he claims that individual variation as to the use of inflected and non-inflected forms reflects differences in language use.

Clahsen concludes that rather than the notion of agreement, it is the realisation of the morphological paradigm of agreement markings, especially regarding the differentiation of person and number, which poses learnability problems in ASLA. Since the verb placement rules of stages II and III are acquired without having established the target-like agreement paradigm yet, lexical learning in the sense of UG is ruled out.
Clahsen claims that this hypothesis is further supported by the empirical data concerning embedded clauses, which evidence a high grade of individual variation as to when learners begin to use complementisers and embedded clauses. He considers the possibility that this variation is related to the different exposure to German. As regards the word order in embedded clauses he acknowledges generalised SVO until the acquisition of V END. In view of these findings he concludes that complementisers do not trigger the correct fixation of the COMP/INFL parameter. This he takes as further evidence against a possible restructuring of underlying SVO to SOV in L2 German development (cf. also CM 86).[40]

Nevertheless, Clahsen concedes that there might be a relationship between the full implementation of the agreement paradigm and the acquisition of V END: the data suggest that no learner acquires V END without having established the agreement paradigm. In view of this finding he concludes that

> "[t]he rule V END obviously presupposes the notion 'finiteness' in its structural description. Therefore, we may conclude that the emergence of this rule requires the (previous) acquisition of the agreement system." (ibid.: 64)

But he remarks (ibid.) that such a relationship does not hold at the former stages as

> "[t]he verb-position patterns of Phase II (similar to those of III) can be acquired without having established the German agreement paradigm."

---

[40] The possibility that learners may have taken over their L1 word order is explicitly rejected in CM (1989) as they claim that Turkish-speaking learners of German (Turkish is an SOV language) also treat German as an SVO language. I will discuss recent findings suggesting that L2 learners with a Turkish L1 initially posit SOV as the underlying word order in section 6.3.

Unfortunately, no further reasons as to why these generalisations should hold are provided. Instead, the fact that the acquisition of verb placement rules and the development of the agreement paradigm proceed separately up to stage IV is taken as empirical evidence against a UG based approach to ASLA.

As CM claim that L2 grammatical rules do not conform to universal constraints they conclude that L2 *knowledge* is not grammatical knowledge in the sense of UG. Consequently, they argue that language acquisition in adulthood follows different mechanisms. These are the main arguments put forth within the framework of the *Fundamental Difference Hypothesis*, which I will discuss in the following sections. We shall see how the interpretation of the empirical data hinges on these considerations and how these are challenged by alternative analyses in the realm of the UG Hypothesis. Furthermore, I will also discuss some critical issues pertaining to the domain of the theory of child language acquisition and point to the implications following thereof for ASLA. So it is in this context where some of the weaknesses of Clahsen's *Lexical Learning Hypothesis* will be dealt with. By means of this rather intricate procedure, I aim at providing some insight into the intricacy of our language faculty in the belief that we cannot do away with ASLA in simply claiming that adults rely on mechanisms other than UG.

3.3 The Fundamental Difference Hypothesis

Following Lenneberg (1967)[41], proponents of the *Fundamental Difference Hypothesis* (cf. Bley-Vroman 1989, Clahsen and Muysken 1986, 1989, Schachter 1989) assume that there is a *critical period* for language acquisition and that language-specific learning mechanisms are lost after this period. Adults, then, are said to only rely upon *general problem-solving mechanisms* while dealing with the acquisition of a foreign language. Such general problem-solving mechanisms are assumed to be involved in the solution of problems for which no specific module is available.

The general character of these learning mechanisms, in other words their *non-task-specifity qua* mechanisms of the *central systems*, is assumed to be the reason for why these mechanisms generally fail to

---

[41] For a discussion of Lenneberg's *critical period hypothesis* in his study about the recovery of aphasia see Felix (1987). There it is pointed out that according to Lenneberg this *critical period* coincides with the end of the lateralisation process, that is, more or less at the onset of puberty.

completely master the problem at hand.[42] Consider, for example, Bley-Vroman's claim that

> "[l]ack of inevitable perfect mastery is, of course, a characteristic of general adult learning in fields for which no domain-specific cognitive faculty is thought to exist, especially in areas of substantial complexity."
> (Bley-Vroman 1989: 44)

The problem with claims of this sort is that they are highly speculative, not only in view of the fact that we know so little about the mechanisms underlying cognition but also because concepts like *lack of success* are not further specified. Therefore, it is questionable if this "all-or-nothing" attitude, exemplified in the passage quoted subsequently really is constructive if a theory of ASLA is to be developed at all, cf.

> "Any model which entails uniform success - as child first language acquisition models must - is a failure of adult language learning."
> (ibid.: 44)

Unfortunately, a more precise account of the predictions following from the assumption that language learning in adulthood is guided by general learning mechanisms is not given.[43] Bley-Vroman's claim is representative in this respect:

> "Some of its characteristics, however, are apparent. It must, for example, be goal-oriented. It must have ways of utilizing feedback and instruction. There must be some way of understanding explanations. A variety of mechanisms must clearly be available, including distributional analysis, analogy, and hypothesis formation and testing. The indeterminate intuitions of adult learners suggest something vaguely probabilistic and non-monotonic. There ought to be some way to move from controlled to automatic processing."
> (ibid.: 54)

Whenever a more concrete analysis of the general problem-solving strategies applying in ASLA has been sought, reference to *learning strategies* in the sense of Slobin's *Operating Principles* is made. In other words, the analysis favoured by Clahsen (1988b) and Clahsen and

---

[42] Note that the differentiation between *central* as opposed to *modular* systems is based on the *Modularity Hypothesis* put forth in Fodor (1983) which I will discuss below in section 3.5.

[43] Bley-Vroman's comment is illustrative of the *attitude* within the framework of this hypothesis:
"A consideration of the precise nature of an adequate model of general adult cognitive problem solving as it functions in foreign language learning would take us too far afield." (ibid.: 54)
Comments like these suggest that there is no serious interest in analysing ASLA.

Muysken (1986, 1989) is the same as the one given in CMP (1983). Note that in some ways these considerations are not really in the spirit of the claims underlying the cognitivist approach presented above. Whilst the cognitivist hypothesis states that general processing constraints in the form of learning strategies guide both L1A and ASLA, the crucial hypothesis put forth within the *Fundamental Difference Hypothesis* is that only ASLA is *exclusively* determined by general cognitive mechanisms. But, why should adults but not children rely only on these mechanisms? Further, as I pointed out above in section 1.2.4 no extra-linguistic correlates to the general-problem solving mechanisms have been determined so far. Anyway, if they have the form of Slobin's Operating Principles, as suggested, general problem-solving mechanisms are not as *general* as proponents of the FDH would like them to be. As noted above, if processing strategies operate on properties of linguistic structures, they presuppose, at least to a certain extent, a "*rudimentary knowledge about a structural criterion*" (Tracy 1991: 29, my transl.).

The FDH implies that these mechanisms undergo the task of language acquisition because language-specific learning mechanisms are no longer available in adulthood. The FDH further predicts that adult learners can only aim at learning target *surface* structures by means of general problem-solving mechanisms. Yet, it is unclear what this really means.

If we abstract away from CMP's descriptive generalisations in the form of *permutation rules*, we can see that at a certain point in time learners correctly place finite verbs in the second and infinitive verb forms in sentence-final position in matrix clauses. Later on, the target word order for embedded clauses is also mastered. Thus, there are two critical questions to answer. Firstly, is there any empirical evidence proving that late learner grammars differ in a relevant way from the target language norm? As for the constraints underlying these grammars, how may a "*surrogate of UG*" (Bley-Vroman 1989: 52) be distinguished from real UG? Secondly, is it justified to exclude a UG-based account on the basis of differences between children and adults regarding the developmental path? None of these questions are appropriately answered by the FDH.

3.4 The Competition Model

There is a further hypothesis which relates differences between child and adult language acquisition to differences underlying the cognitive capacities of children and adults. As opposed to the FDH, however, Felix' *Competing Systems Hypothesis* or *Competition Model* (1985, 1987, 1991) states that language-specific mechanisms are also involved in

ASLA. According to Felix, the *Language-specific System* (*LS-system*) becomes active as soon as learners are exposed to L2 input (Felix 1987: 160). Even when confronted with data from such languages as Latin or Ancient Greek, an activity of this system, though minimal, is expected. Felix argues that the availability of the LS-system in ASLA is supported by numerous empirical studies, the developmental sequences, which are quite similar between L1A and ASLA, being a case in point.

On the other hand, he argues that individual variation with respect to the *ultimate attainment* in ASLA shows that the LS-system does not work as in child language acquisition. Felix assumes that this is due to the fact that adults, as opposed to children, have access to a further processing system, namely the *Problem-Solving System* (*PS-system*).

Roughly speaking, the PS-system is hypothesised to underly the ability to tackle formal abstract operations. Felix believes that this new ability which develops at the onset of puberty[44] may also be involved in the processing of linguistic data, as, for example, in metalinguistic operations:

> "... any type of metalinguistic ability in which thinking about language rather than using it is the primary focus draws upon the PS-system, just as thinking about any other subject matter does."
> (op. cit.:156)

In ASLA, learners are expected to recur to the PS-system especially during the initial stages, when faced with communicative pressure.
In comparing utterances of child *L2* acquisition and ASLA Felix arrives at the following conclusion:

> "... one crucial difference between the child and the adult learning has to do with the fact that during the early stages of acquisition adults tend to form utterances on the basis of general conceptual and semantic considerations while children conform more strictly to syntactic organizations of sentence structure."
> (Felix 1985: 61)

He assumes that the adult's resort to problem-solving strategies results from the communicative pressure they are subject to, cf.

> "Social conventions and norms require that the adult find some other communicative means to convey his message, if his proper grammatical

---

44 Felix draws upon findings within the field of developmental psychology, in particular, upon Piaget's work on the four major stages of cognitive development given in (i) (cf. McShane 1991).
   (i)   - sensorimotor stage (up to 2 years)
         - preoperational stage (from 2 to 6 or 7 years)
         - concrete operational stage (from 6 or 7 to 12 or 13 years)
         - formal operational (onset at age 12 or 13)

competence proves to be insufficient (...) It seems plausible to assume that the adult will approach this problem by using strategies and solutions that his general intellectual capacities permit him to exploit, i.e. he transfers his problem-solving capacities to the domain of language learning. In other words, he tries to solve a problem which happens to be of linguistic nature."
(ibid.: 63)

But, as opposed to the mechanisms underlying the LS-system, problem-solving strategies may never lead to successful language acquisition. This line of thinking leads on to the crucial idea underlying Felix' Competition Model, namely, that these two processing systems do not cooperate but rather *compete* (thus the term *Competing Systems Hypothesis*) in the acquisition of the L2:

"The adult, then, has available two types of cognitive systems which, in a sense, compete in processing language data for the purpose of acquisition (...) The competition beween the LS- and the PS-system in the acquisition of formal language properties thus seems to be the reason why adults are inferior to children with respect to how successfully they can achieve a native-like command of a second language."
(Felix 1987: 161/2)

Following these considerations, differences as to the rate of success in ASLA are expected depending on which of the two systems takes over the learning task:

"... the more the PS-system controls the learning process at the expense of the LS-system the smaller the chances will be for the learner to achieve a native-like command of the second language. Conversely, the more the LS-system determines the course of development the more likely it is that the learner will reach his goal."
(ibid.: 162)

Felix claims that socio-psychological factors such as motivation and integration into the target language community represent filter mechanisms which may enhance the activity of the LS-system insofar as they determine how much language input is processed. Conversely, traditional foreign language teaching is assumed to mainly address the PS-system. Felix believes that on general grounds learning in the classroom setting is condemned to fail. A natural linguistic environment, on the contrary, will have a most positive influence on the activity of the LS-system.

The problem with these considerations is that much confusion stems from the PS-system which is seen to *interfere* with the proper work of the LS-system. On the one hand, general problem-solving mechanisms are described as formal abstract operations involved in metalinguistic processes, while on the other, with respect to early utterances, they are

referred to as semantico-conceptual processing strategies. As seems likely despite their general character, general problem-solving mechanisms do provide different and thus possibly specific solutions to the different learnability problems adults face in the course of language acquisition. There is, additionally, an apparent contradiction in Felix' reasoning regarding the differences between child and adult language acquisition: when comparing child and adult L2 learners he observes that only the former produce syntactically structured utterances and concludes that the production of semantically organised utterances of adults are the result of problem-solving mechanisms. We will see, however, that Felix' model of child first language acquisition states that child early language is also semantically organised prior to the maturation of the relevant universal principles (see section 5.1.1).
The question as to how general processing mechanisms may deal with linguistic data at all is only vaguely answered.
Indeed, Felix himself does acknowledge this shortcoming:

>"The question of whether the PS-system is as effective and adequate as LS-processing is a much more serious issue. In absence of clear experimental evidence we have to rely on more general observations which are admittedly quite speculative".
>(op. cit.: 158)

Certainly, Felix' model is a first attempt to develop a theory of ASLA on the basis of current assumptions concerning the human mind and the language faculty in particular. Yet his ideas concerning the interaction of the mechanisms involved in ASLA are rather imprecise. The predictions do not go beyond general considerations. The expected developmental differences depending on whether ASLA takes place in a formal or in a natural setting are not determined. The idea that successful language acquisition depends on the nature of the input is not fully fleshed out. In the light of the PP model this is a crucial issue worth further scrutiny. As restricted input in the classroom may mean that adult learners are not furnished with the relevant primary linguistic data, the failure of the linguistic system to become operative is predestined. But this is no competition at all!
It is, in fact, unclear how competition between cognitive processes which are different in nature should happen at all. In view of the fact that the mechanisms in question address different linguistic areas the question arises as to how they should *compete*, if they are, in principle, not designed to assume each other's function. Note that no real competition in the acquisition of UG based knowledge can take place because general learning mechanisms are designed in such a way that they do not have access to this kind of knowledge.
Too much uncertainty surrounds what has become a kind of *key* to ASLA

specific learnability problems, namely the differentiation between central and modular systems. It seems differences between adult and child language acquisition have been too readily interpreted as a consequence of the wrong cognitive system being involved in ASLA.

3.5 Modularity of mind: Critical remarks about the centralist approach to ASLA

Clearly, the hypothesis that the human language faculty is an autonomous cognitive component goes along with the assumption that the human mind is modular in character. Interestingly, this basic tenet underlying UG theory has been the point of departure for the claim that ASLA is guided by different mechanisms than child LA.
Simplifying somewhat, the following arguments are the crux of the two hypotheses outlined in the preceding sections:

- Task-specific mechanisms may be operative for a certain (critical) period of time only.

- Beyond this critical period non-task-specific mechanisms may aim at taking over the function of task-specific mechanisms either because the latter have been lost (= FDH) or because it is in their nature to compete with task-specific mechanisms (= Competition Model).

- Non-task-specific mechanisms will never achieve what is their objective, namely, successfully taking over the job of task-specific mechanisms. Thus their product will be different in nature from the product of task-specific mechanisms.

As attractive as the correlation between two forms of language acquisition and two forms of cognitive processes may seem at first sight, it is questionable whether it really conforms to the "architecture" of the human mind. Consider, for example, the well-known fact that when listening to a sentence in one's own mother tongue, it is understood without any (active) effort. We can conclude that perceptual processing of (mother tongue) linguistic data is triggered in the same manner as reflexes, i.e. *automatically*. This automaticity, in other words, this *obligatoriness* of processes like the perceptual computing of linguistic data has led to the assumption that processes like these are guided by task-specific cognitive mechanisms. Both input systems, as, for example, the components of the perceptual and the language understanding system, and output systems, such as the systems playing a role in motor control and language production, are held to be modular.

While there is common agreement as to the task-specificity of modular systems such as the auditory or visual perceptual system, the determination of the implications following from this property has led to some controversy.[45] Fodor (1983) claims that as a consequence of their *vertical* character modular systems have well-defined properties which distinguish them from horizontally organised, i.e. *central* processes:

> "Roughly, modular cognitive systems are domain specific, innately specified, hardwired, autonomous, and not assembled. Since modular systems are domain-specific computational mechanisms, it follows that they are species of vertical faculties."
> (Fodor 1983: 37)

Modular systems are domain-specific due to their task-specificity. Consider, for example, Fodor's statements regarding sentence perception:

> "All the available evidence suggests that the computations which sentence recognizers perform must be closely tuned to a complex of stimulus properties that is quite specific to sentences. Roughly, the idea is that the structure of the sentence recognition system is responsive to universal properties of language and hence that the system works only in domains which exhibit these properties."
> (ibid.: 50)

While there is much agreement about the assumption that there are specific mechanisms involved in the processing of linguistic input, research throughout the last years shows that the question of whether and if so to what extent general knowledge is involved in natural language understanding or processing still remains.[46] According to Fodor both obligatoriness and speed are consequences of the fact that modules are *informationally encapsulated*. In other words, modules are held to only have access to locally represented information. As a consequence of the modules' *shallowness*, central processes do not have any access to the intermediate representations computed by the modules. It is important to keep these two properties apart, as pointed out by Garfield (1987a: 5):

> "Domain specifity has to do with the circumstances in which a module comes into use; encapsulation has to do with the information that can be mobilized in the course of that use."

Much of the controversy surrounding the *Modularity Hypothesis* outlined in Fodor (1983) results from the question of whether modular systems are informationally encapsulated at all and if so to what extent.

---

[45] The reader is referred to to the articles in Garfield (1987b) for an extensive overview of the different positions in this discussion.

[46] For a through examination of the different hypotheses put forward in this respect see Leuninger (1989).

Marslen-Wilson and Tyler (1987: 38), for example, disagree with Fodor along the following lines:

> "But what is compelling about our real-time comprehension of language is not so much the immediacy with which linguistic form becomes available as the immediacy with which interpreted meaning becomes available. It is this that is the target of the core processes of language comprehension, of the processes that map from sound onto meaning."

Do top-down processes interfere with bottom-up processes and, if so, is this evidence against the impenetrability ascribed to modular systems? According to Fodor (1983), top-down processes within a module are compatible with the hypothesis that input systems are informationally encapsulated. He considers the phoneme restoration effects observed in experiments with distorted stimuli, where predictive, expectation-driven mechanisms play a role:

> "If (...) the 'background information' deployed in phoneme restorations is simply the hearer's knowledge of the words in his language, then that counts as top-down flow within the language module; on any remotely plausible account the knowledge of a language includes knowledge of its lexicon."
> (ibid.: 77)

This is to say that the language module as a whole is autonomous in the sense that non-linguistic information may not interfere with the operations in the module (cf. Marslen-Wilson and Typler 1987). Much controversy has arisen from the empirical testing of these claims. During the last decades several models of language processing have been conceived. Roughly, the issue is whether language processing is the product of serial and independent or rather interactive processing of word-level, syntactic and message-level processes (cf. Marslen-Wilson and Tyler 1987). Irrespective of this discussion, research in the field of ASLA has concentrated on the question of whether the language module plays a role at all when acquiring a second language in adulthood. As pointed out by Zobl (1990: 40) the *centralist approach* to ASLA claims that

> "... the structure of the adult language faculty is significantly less modular inasmuch as central processes assume the computational work performed by the domain-specific module in L1 acquisition."

Keeping with this reasoning, ASLA should exhibit the properties assumed to be characteristic of central processes, to which long-term memory and further processes making up general knowledge are assumed to belong. Consider the following characterisation of the processes in question:

> "Central systems, in contrast, are slower and more subject to voluntary control in their operation, are unencapsulated, are typically neurally

scattered, and operate with a semantically richer set of representations. Modular processes are blind; **central processes are deliberate**."
(Garfield 1987a: 7, my emphasis)

Consequently, if ASLA were based on central processes alone we should observe an asymmetry with respect to the nature of the knowledge attained, i.e.

> "[a]dults might be expected to have a fair degree of success in aspects of language that are semantically more interpretable. On the other hand, abstract syntax, being semantically shallow, should represent a domain where reliance on central processes results in markedly lower levels of attainment."
> (Zobl 1990: 41)

This asymmetry is not the one attested in studies of near-native competence where failure to achieve target language norm was more pronounced in areas of referential and lexical semantics and discourse-functional aspects (cf. Coppietiers 1987, loup et al. 1994).

In her study about *processes of self-organisation in linguistic ontogeny* Karpf (1990) criticises the strong version of the modularity hypothesis and argues in favour of a concept of modularity which also embraces the interaction which occurs among systems and sub-systems (cf. also Tracy 1991). On the basis of evidence regarding neuronal information processing Karpf acknowledges that in complex systems such as language a hierarchical organisation is needed, which begins at the primary sensory data and ends in the cognitive domain (Karpf 1990: 31). She stresses that the concept of cognitive module should apply only to the latter level.

Her warning against a too global concept of a cognitive module is especially relevant in the light of ALSA hypotheses like the FDH or the Competition Model. Her understanding of a module departs from a concept in which a module is a *"functionally and above all topologically delimited unity"* (ibid.: 31, my transl.). Instead, she conceives modules as

> "... autonomous subsystems with a specific function in the overall system, which manifest themselves neurophysiologically as more or less complex, co-operating neuronal groups with the same preference of orientation."
> (ibid.: 242, my transl.)[47]

---

[47] The original reads as follows:
"Module sind autonome Teilsysteme mit spezifischer Funktion innerhalb eines Gesamtsystems, die sich neurophysiologisch als unterschiedlich komplexe, kooperierende Neuronengruppen mit gleicher Orientierungspräferenz manifestieren."

In the light of this differentiated view of modularity we can see that both the FDH and the Competition Model suffer from an understanding of modularity which disregards the complexity underlying modularly organised information processing. According to Karpf the relevant differences between adult and child language acquisition lie

> "... rather in the age-specific. i.e. in the more or less highly dissociated neuronal organisation and in the processes resulting thereof than in the activity of separate cognitive organisation systems."
> (ibid.: 240)[48]

Consequently, we may emphasise here the relevance of *internal* processes concerning the interaction among systems and sub-systems of one or more languages in language development. In other words, it seems we have to allow for processes of *differentiation* and *integration* to take place on different levels in the course of language acquisition, i.e. for modularisation on different levels to be *the result* of such processes (cf. Karpf 1990, Tracy 1991). And we expect learning processes to be related to such processes of modularisation (see chapter 7)!

As pointed out by Karpf (1990: 55) there is empirical evidence supporting the assumption that there is a *critical period* in the sense

> "... that there are temporarily determined, genetically triggered development phases, in which the maturation of the function systems is critically bound to the adequate stimulus."[49]

Note that, so defined, the assumption of a critical period does not imply the *loss* of the relevant learning mechanisms.
It seems that the first two years in ontogeny are *critical* with regard to the plasticity, the sensitivity and the growth of the central nervous system (cf. ibid.). We also know about the dramatic consequences following from the lack of the relevant environmental stimuli during this phase. But, on neurophysiological grounds the learning processes are identical in early and late learning.
In terms of language development this would be manifest in the form of a *similar* developmental sequence. As pointed out by Karpf (ibid.: 69f.) the emphasis is put on *similarity* because the different forms of language

---

[48] The original reads as follows:
"... eher in der altersspezifischen, d.h. der unterschiedlich stark dissoziierten neuronalen Organisation und den daraus resultierenden Prozessen als in der Aktivität getrennter kognitiver Organisationssysteme."

[49] The original reads as follows:
"... daß es zeitlich determinierte, genetisch getriggerte Entwicklungsphasen gibt, in denen die Ausreifung der Funktionssysteme hochsensitiv an eine adäquate Reizstimulation gebunden ist."

acquisition occur on a different cognitive and linguistic basis on which the different sets of principles operate (ibid.: 67).

In fact, recent research in the fields of child language acquisition, ASLA and language change shows that *self-similarity*, a notion from chaos theory, is of relevance in our understanding of language development in its different forms. I will go deeper into this issue in chapters 7 and 8 where I will explore the necessity of a reevaluation of the traditional learning concepts which also lie at the heart of the UG access debate discussed in the following section.

4 The Principles and Parameters model and ASLA: Core issues of the UG Hypothesis of ASLA

4.1 Linguistic theory and ASLA

"UG or not UG?" - put bluntly, this has been "the" question in recent ASLA research.[50] It is important to note in this respect, as obvious as it may seem, that the nativist approach has - so far - concentrated mainly on native language knowledge and its acquisition (see chapter 2). That is to say, on the side of linguistic theory, competence or acquisition of more than one language, has been largely neglected although the knowledge or the acquisition of a second language is common to the majority of human beings (cf. also Cook 1991, Tracy 1994/5).
Only recently, the far-reaching implications of UG theory have encouraged further research initiatives that aim to include various forms of language acquisition (as well as its knowledge, use and possible loss), as envisaged in Felix and Wode (1983: 6):

> "The ultimate aim must be to characterize and specify man's ability to learn languages and to determine how this ability responds to different learning conditions and behaves at different age levels. These goals require an essentially new aporach to the study of language acquisition. It should no longer be limited to one or the other individual type of language learning. Research on language acquisition should be carried out under an integrated perspective. The idiosyncracies of one acquisitional type need to be related to those of other types, while, at the same time, commonalities of different types must be determined in order to specify the universal basis of language acquisition."

Yet, while research in the area of child bilingual acquisition centres on how bilingual competence, its acquisition and use is to be explained in terms of UG theory (cf. Meisel 1992, Hyltenstamm and Obler 1989, Tracy 1994/5), the ongoing debate in the field of ASLA underlines the more fundamental question of whether a UG based account of language acquisition in adulthood is possible at all. In section 3.3 we learned that the Fundamental Difference Hypothesis rejects the possiblity of a UG-based account of ASLA without providing a clear explanatory alternative, thus obscuring rather than furthering the integrative approach to the human language faculty.
Conversely, proponents of a UG-based account of ASLA (henceforth UG Hypothesis) assume that

---

[50] Cf. DuPlessis et al. (1987), who chose this as the title for their article: "UG or not UG: that is the question."

"[t]hose linguistic models that aim to provide psychologically relevant explanations of human language behaviour must ipso facto be relevant to our understanding of L2 linguistic behaviour."
(Sharwood-Smith 1988: 173)

We will see in the following sections in which way empirical and conceptual considerations of UG theory are relevant for our understanding of ASLA.

4.2 Logical Problem and ASLA

The matter of whether ASLA is guided by the same learning mechanisms as L1A is related to the question of whether adult second language competence also has the form of an internalised grammar. In this respect, proponents of the UG Hypothesis claim that

"... unless we can show that the psychological mechanisms that underlie the individual's L2 (viz. the mental representations of L2 knowledge) are substantially different from those in L1, then we are also committed to claim that L2 acquisition and processing have the same psychological mechanisms/mental representations as in L1. The above implication follows from the fact that the most rational null hypothesis about L2 knowledge is that it has the same status as L1 knowledge."
(Schwartz 1986: 140)

Schwartz's claim that the UG Hypothesis should be the *null hypothesis* is based on the assumption that if a domain-specific language faculty is claimed to exist for the L1, the same must be assumed to hold for the L2:

"The formulation of a null hypothesis depends on the assumptions and theoretical apparatus implicated in the research question. If one can make a further hypothesis without adding to and complicating the already existing assumptions and theoretical constructs (which have independent motivation), this is, then, technically, the null hypothesis. It is the simplest, most logical hypothesis, the one that requires the fewest additional assumptions (Ockham's razor) for its formulation (...) The next step in the research programme should be to try to prove this hypothesis (...) wrong."
(ibid.: 140, footnote 20) [51]

Following this line of reasoning, the burden of proof lies in showing that L1 and L2 do not involve the same form of knowledge. Conversely, if the

---

[51] Note that, so defined, Schwartz's notion of a null hypothesis differs from the common understanding of a null hypothesis in the statistical analysis of research. There the null hypothesis represents the alternative hypothesis to a statistical hypothesis regarding the distribution of test scores, *viz.* their correlation. Commonly, the analysis is designed to disprove the null hypothesis that there is no relationship between two features.

assumption that L1 and L2 are different in nature is taken as null hypothesis, evidence favouring the sameness of L1 and L2 knowledge has to be found. Unfortunately, proponents of this consideration do not have a clear idea as to the kind of evidence needed to disprove the latter null hypothesis (see section 3.3).

Certainly, the well-known individual variation concerning the final state in adult second language acquisition calls into question whether the logical arguments underlying the nativist assumption apply in ASLA at all.
According to the FDH, failure to achieve the *ultimate attainment* has to be considered as the most compelling evidence against UG access in ASLA. Conversely, proponents of the UG Hypothesis have indicated that before tackling the issue of whether the inborn language faculty is lost in adulthood, different external factors leading to a possible interruption of the learning process have to be excluded.
Further, the nature of the properties of learner languages, which are subject to *fossilisation*[52] has to be determined in the light of the differentiation between idiosyncratic language properties, which have to be learned (in the literal sense of the word) and those linguistic properties which follow from universal rules or principles. Clearly, with respect to the Logical Problem of language acquisition (see section 2.2), only fossilisation of the latter is of interest.
But, one of the most lamentable shortcomings of ASLA research lies in the ignoring of native-like speakers of an L2. The few exceptions (cf. Birdsong 1991 and 1992, Coppietiers 1987, Ioup et al. 1994, Johnson and Newport 1991, Sorace 1993, White and Genesee 1996) seem to provide a contradictory picture regarding the question of whether ultimate attainment is possible in ASLA. A review of these studies reveals, however, that this contradictory evidence is partly related to the criteria determining the choice of the subjects which were analysed (cf. White and Genesee 1996). My general impression is much in line with White and Genesee's (ibid.: 235) conclusion that

> "[i]t is interesting to note in this regard that some studies which argue that there is an upper limit to the competence that can be attained by late learners have ignored or even made excuses for cases of native-like competence in their samples."

In sum, as long as we do not have extensive and adequate studies on native-like adult L2 speakers any consideration regarding the impossibility of attaining full competence of the L2 remains speculative.

---

[52] The notion of *fossilisation* refers to those (target-deviant) linguistic forms from earlier stages which are still used at later points in the acquisition process. So these forms seem to be *fossilised* as they are not subject to further development (cf. Selinker 1972).

Now, if the *Poverty-of-Stimulus Argument* is to apply in ASLA, the question is whether adult learners attain abstract and deep properties of the L2 which they could not have learned by inductive generalisations of the input alone. In other words,

> "[i]f the L2 learner goes beyond the input, even though not as far as the native speaker, then there is potentially an L2 equivalent of the projection problem. That is, knowledge is attained on the basis of impoverished input, and this requires explanation."

(White 1989: 39)

Vivian Cook (1991) has explicitly pointed to a logical differentiation concerning the *Poverty-of-Stimulus Argument* (see section 2.2). He proposes two versions of this logical argument.
The first variant pertains to the knowledge of some speaker Y' of a language X, the second variant pertains to the whole community Y of speakers of a language X. These variants are summed up in (1) and (2).

(1)   *Narrow* poverty-of-stimulus argument:
     Step A. A native speaker knows X.
     Step B. X could not have been learned from the
               forms of evidence plausibly available.
     Step C. X is not learned.
     Step D. X is built-in to the mind.

(2)   *Broad* poverty-of-stimulus argument:
     Step A'. Native speakers know X.
     Step B'. X could not have been acquired from forms of evidence
               plausibly available to all children.

According to Cook the differences between these two variants correlate with the differences between child and adult language acquisition. Cook points out that the "broadening of the argument" (ibid.: 107) applies to child language acquisition only, as both step A' and step B' can be deduced from step A and B respectively. Clearly, the knowledge of a native speaker of X is representative for the knowledge of the whole community of native speakers of a language X. And with respect to B' he states that

> "... since all children acquire competence, whatever evidence is necessary to do so must be available to all of them, essentially cutting the possibilities down to positive evidence."

(op. cit.: 106)

Cook argues that a differentiation along these lines shows why the poverty-of-stimulus argument also applies to adult second language acquisition, if only in the restricted sense of the *narrow* variant. This variant applies for every speaker's knowledge of those linguistic properties which he could not have induced from the L2 input. As for the deduction of the *broad* variant of the *narrow*, this is clearly not possible for ASLA, as variation concerning the ultimate attainment is empirically well founded.

Most authors seem to agree on a differentiation along these lines, the general idea being that if there is a discrepancy between input and knowledge in ASLA this calls for an explanation (see White above). This is not to say that the question of why ultimate attainment is often not achieved in adult second language acquisition could be ignored. But to conclude that there is no access to UG in ASLA because there is learner variation regarding the ultimate attainment would be the wrong path to take. As Flynn and Manuel (1991: 134) put it:

> "The argumentation to support such a conclusion must precisely demonstrate that UG does not constrain an adult learner's hypotheses about the new target grammar and not simply that the end-states attained differ between adults and children (...)."

In general, researchers within the framework of the UG Hypothesis agree on the assumption that failure to achieve the final state, i.e. *fossilisation* of structural properties of the learner system which defer from the target (under exclusion of any deficit in the input), may result from adult learners facing different learnability problems than children. It is important to note that this latter consideration marks the difference between the UG based and the non-UG-based analysis: only the former seeks a *linguistic* solution to the question of why ultimate attainment is not achieved across the board.

4.3 Learnability considerations

One of the fundamental learnability considerations following from the assumption that the PP model applies also in ASLA concerns the triggering of the L2 target grammatical properties by primary linguistic data in the L2 input, as illustrated in (3).

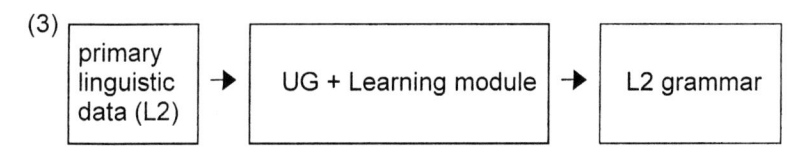

(3) primary linguistic data (L2) → UG + Learning module → L2 grammar

In order to ascertain that the PP model applies also in ASLA, we have to prove both the availability of the components of this model and their alleged interaction.

4.3.1 L2 input

Adult second language acquisition may take place under quite different conditions. In this respect two main modes of ASLA have to be distinguished: *natural* or *untutored* as opposed to *tutored* second or *foreign* language acquisition. Whilst the former refers to L2 acquisition in the L2 community with none or only minor teaching influence, the latter refers to second language acquisition mainly taking place in a formal (teaching) setting, possibly in a language community, in which the L2 is not spoken. Since different adult learners are exposed to different L2 input[53] (positive evidence alone, or both positive and negative evidence) the question arises as to whether the poverty-of-stimulus argument applies to all forms of ASLA. This issue pertains especially to ASLA in a formal environment. Does the linguistic evidence provided in the classroom have any implications on the learning model presented above?

Within the framework of the UG Hypothesis there is a general consensus that although information concerning the grammatical properties of the L2 is provided in tutored SLA, it is quite plausible to assume that this form of *negative evidence* is irrelevant for the Projection Problem as the information does not concern the deep and abstract properties of the L2.[54] It appears this assumption is further supported by research evidencing that both tutored and untutored ASLA follow (roughly) the same developmental path.[55]

But there is still much uncertainty regarding the question of delimiting which kind of input we may consider as *insufficient* in the sense of the learning model at hand. That is, we still have to determine what we understand as structurally impoverished input in the classroom (Sharwood-Smith 1988) or to what extent contact to the L2 community may be severely restricted and the implications following thereof.[56] But, while there may be several *external* reasons for why parameter setting may not be triggered at all, we also have to look at the *internal* factors for a grammar to be *resistant* to change (see chapters 7 and 8).

---

[53] That is to say, adult learners of a certain L2 may only have in common the very fact of being learners of this L2 and differ as to all other variables like mother tongue, age, learning conditions, etc. In other words, the concept of a "community" of learners of a second language clearly differs from the common notion of a language community.

[54] This is not to say that negative evidence may not have any implication for the learning process. The issue of whether negative evidence plays a role in parameter setting will be resumed below.

[55] Cf. Felix/Weigl (1991), Pienemann (1989).

[56] This clearly seems to be the case for the subjects analysed within the HPD studies (cf. HPD 1977). It is the more surprising that these learners largely proved to follow the same developmental path as the one given in CMP (1983).

4.3.2 Mother tongue knowledge

In the analysis of the grammatical knowledge developed in ASLA it is of fundamental importance to ascertain whether mother tongue knowledge has a pervading influence, and if so, to what extent in the acquisition of the deep and abstract properties of the L2. On the basis of the PP model the issue boils down to the question of whether the target-like fixation of the relevant parameters is achieved irrespective of the parametric options realised in the mother tongue.
There are two fundamental issues to be addressed at this stage:

- In which ways is the L2 learner grammar related to the L1 grammar?
- What are the consequences for the learnability of the L2?

It goes without saying that the long-standing generalised assumption that "... *it is because the L2 and the L1 are related in the mind that the L2 cannot be learned as a second L1*" (Cook 1992: 578) needs further elaboration.
What is noteworthy in this respect is that most of the studies dealing with the parameter-setting issue in ASLA assume that the determination of the L2-specific parametric properties occurs on the basis of the L1 grammar. This is evident in the generalised notion of the *re*-setting of parameters wherever the L1 and the L2 value differ. For proponents of the UG Hypothesis this necessity lies at the heart of their empirical studies which seek to prove that this necessity is, in fact, realised.
What remains unclear, however, is the question of whether parameter resetting implies the development of an L2 grammar which would be *independent* of the L1. Suzanne Flynn's (1988: 78) statements, for example, seem to suggest that the L2 learner grammar is not completely independent of the L1, cf.

> "In short, my claim is that L2 learners will not duplicate structural properties already available to them from their L1s. In support of this claim I argue that two distinct patterns of acquisition should emerge in L2 acquisition."

It seems, researchers working in the framework of the UG Hypothesis have not paid too much attention to the distinction of the assumption that the L1 serves as a part of the *initial state* in ASLA (see section 6.3) from the question of how L1 and L2 properties are related in the mind. This is possibly due to the fact that they have concentrated on the analysis of the learnability task specific to adult learners.
Those researchers pursuing the validity of the Fundamental Difference Hypothesis, on the other hand, have repeatedly pointed out that the idea

of a re-setting of parameter values goes against the original PP model. This claim can be traced to learnability considerations put forward in the field of child language acquisition, as, for example, Clahsen's (1990a: 365f.) *parameter-setting constraint* which states that

> "... once a parametric setting (consistent with the available input) has been chosen by the child, the remaining unexercised options are no longer accessible. Therefore, parameter resetting is not possible during development."

On the basis of this assumption Clahsen (1990b: 151) concludes that *"[i]f the child cannot reset, it is hard to imagine how the adult could."*
Clahsen's reasoning teaches us in which ways the notion of parameter re-setting is misleading. First, his learnability consideration put forward in the field of child language acquisition does *not* naturally extend to ASLA. Put bluntly, adult learners are *not* restructuring their L1 grammar for the sake of embracing new or unnoticed properties of L1 input, which would amount to the original learnability problem which the *parameter-setting constraint* intends to circumvent. Rather, the idea of parameter re-setting implies that adults start out with a set of default hypotheses (which happen to be determined by their L1 grammar), as much as Clahsen allows such default settings to occur in child LA. And, in both cases it is expected that this initial grammar is restructured where need be. I will come shortly to the "deterministic" aspect implicit in the parameter-setting constraint.

In sum, the misguided notion of parameter re-setting exemplifies the intricacy of determining the status of L2 grammars. The common notion of interlanguage or interim L2 grammars apparently circumvents this problem. Similar shortcomings are characteristic of the understanding of *cross-linguistic influence*. Interestingly, while there is common agreement that

> "... the ability to transfer must be regarded as part of the people's competence when they know a language just like their ability to paraphrase or make grammaticality judgments"
> (Wode 1988: 181)

there is less of a consensus as to the nature and the consequences of this "ability". Note that this is an issue which is of equal importance in the field of bilingual acquisition (cf. Tracy 1994/5, see section 7.1.4).

4.3.3 Parameter setting

As mentioned previously, most of the empirical studies carried out in the course of the last decade focus on the question of whether adult learners manage to correctly set the target-language parametric values.[57] At first sight, the empirical evidence gained seems not to support a clear-cut answer:

- Some data suggest that L2 learners have not (yet?) recognised the respective parameter values of the L2.
- Other studies show that L2 learners take over parameter values of their mother tongue.
- It has also been reported that some learners resort to neither the L1 nor the L2 value but to another possible UG option.
- There is also evidence for the learners target-like parameter-setting.

Does this "contradictory" evidence suggest that UG is not accessible in ASLA?
Firstly, however, we have to take into account possible methodological shortcomings. Note that most studies consist of just one cross-sectional data gathering. As such they provide information about the learner's *current competence* at a specific point in time. So any conclusion about further development remains somewhat speculative. ASLA, like child language acquisition, is not *instantaneous* as the idealisation implicit in learning model underlying the PP theory seems to suggest, but a *process*. We have to reconsider learner hypotheses under a developmental perspective. Learner hypotheses may be of *provisional* character. If we allow for this possibility, we could accommodate - to a degree yet to be defined - wrong parameter settings, or, put differently, *possible errors*.

Lydia White, for example, assumes that transitory hypotheses offer no reasonable evidence against a UG driven ASLA as long as these hypotheses conform to the options of UG:

"The fact that parameters can be set differently suggests that a possible error would be for language learners to select an inappropriate parameter setting for the language being learned."
(White 1988: 146)

Taking this reasoning further, learner violations of UG principles represent *impossible errors* as opposed to a non-target-like but UG-constrained parametric choice. Such possible errors may result from L1 parametric options serving as initial or *default* hypotheses in ASLA.

---

[57] Cf., for example, Zobl's (1990: 42) statement that "the litmus test for claims on behalf of the domain-specific acquisition is bound up with the concept of parameter-setting."

Suzanne Flynn, for example, makes the following predictions in this respect:

> "Where principles involve parameters, L2 learners from early stages of acquisition recognize a match or a mismatch in the values of parameters between the L1 and the L2. In the cases in which the L1 and the L2 differ, L2 acquisition is disrupted as learners must and do assign new values to cohere with the L2 grammar. In the case in which they match, L2 acquisition is facilitated as learners do not need to assign a new value to this parameter. They can, instead, rely upon the L1 value in guiding their construction of English."
> (Flynn 1988: 78)

Going one step further, Schwartz and Sprouse (1994) concede that in ASLA the relation of L1 and UG may be such that

> "... the lack of success may arise exactly because the sole hypotheses that an L2er can employ in the construction of an L2 grammar are those that UG makes available, but as they apply in conjunction with the L1 grammar, these hypotheses will in certain circumstances miss the mark and without (the necessary) negative data, the L2er will be unable to retract."
> (ibid.: 356)

While the distinction between possible and impossible errors, on the one hand, and the assumption that the L1 is part of the initial state, on the other hand, are quite appealing, it is questionable whether the implications of these considerations really conform to the PP model. We learned above that the idea of learners choosing incorrect parameter values seems to run counter to the PP model in which the nature of parameter setting is claimed to be *deterministic* (cf. Clahsen 1990a, Randall 1992). Such determinism has been claimed to hold irrespective of whether there is a necessity for parameter resetting in child LA.

In the field of child language acquisition research, attention has been drawn to the question of whether children are equipped with initial or default options, and if so, which criteria determine the status of parametric options. Learning principles based on *markedness* considerations, like, for example, the *Subset Principle* (cf. Wexler and Manzini 1987) were taken to ensure that children would not choose grammars they could not *unlearn* with positive evidence alone.

Studies investigating whether learning principles like the Subset Principle apply in ASLA have shown that they do not work as in L1A. Adult learners do not always start out with the most restrictive parameter setting. Instead there is evidence for the adoption of parameter settings which could not be unlearned under the presupposed learnability conditions.[58] There is some disagreement as to whether these data suggest that the *learning module* is not available at all in ASLA or rather that the learning module may not work in the same way because of the interference of L1 knowledge (cf. White 1989).

The preceding observations suggest that if L1 options serve as default options in ASLA, not only the role of learning principles may have to be reconsidered but also the nature of the *triggers* needed in order to retract from wrong initial hypotheses. The implications of what may be considered as the ASLA specific *Delearning Problem* (cf. Schwartz and Sprouse 1994) have to be further analysed as this problem may prove to be one of the main reasons for why ASLA is not deterministic[59] to the extent that child language acquisition is (according to Schwartz and Sprouse this is the ASLA specific *Determinacy Problem*).
Clearly, longitudinal studies of ASLA should prove revealing in this aspect.
On a theoretical level, we must conclude that the study of ASLA needs to be based on a more precise account of the universal constraints guiding language *development*.

---

[58] Cf. White (1989) for an extended discussion of the relevant studies.
[59] We will see in section 7 that we need to reconsider our understanding of the apparent determinism in child LA.

5   The Developmental Problem of child language acquisition

Child language acquisition research over the last decades has focused on the determination of learner grammars and the changes they undergo. The empirical observation that the developmental process consists of a fixed order of changes, seems to run counter to the fundamental idea underlying the PP model, namely, that minimal data in the input trigger the relevant properties of the target language grammar *instantaneously*.

If UG represents the initial state and if, in addition, children have access to enough linguistic input from the very beginning of language acquisition, the question has to be asked as to why the child has to pass through developmental stages at all (cf. Felix 1987) or, put differently,

> "[w]hy does language acquisition take time at all when it consists of setting parameters on the basis of simple evidence?"
> (Verrips 1990: 12)

The following thought experiment may serve as an illustration of the fact that the developmental problem has to be solved in the domain of linguistic theory:

> "Just imagine a situation in which linguistic theory has worked out a full theory of Universal Grammar, and a complete list of the triggers that enable the child to set the parameters. In this situation, we take a two-year old in separation for a few days or maybe a week and systematically present these relevant data to him, or - even better maybe - we instruct parents to do this. Would the child acquire full knowledge of the grammar of the language? Very few researchers would predict that this would actually be the case, even those who adhere to parameter theory. This shows that the developmental problem is real. Apparently, **there is something time-consuming** in the process of language acquisition."
> (op. cit.: 13, my emphasis)

Now, the idealisation of language acquisition as an "instantaneous" event has to be understood in the light of the Logical Problem of language acquisition (see section 2.2). That is, this idealisation is necessary in order for linguistic theory to provide a principled account of how language acquisition is possible at all.[60]

Yet in order for a theory of language acquisition based on the PP theory to provide a satisfactory account of real time language acquisition the following questions have to be addressed:

---

[60]   It was already mentioned above that Chomsky's theory is not an acquisition theory. The relation between the two results from the requirement that a grammar has to be learnable given the primary data of the input.

- Why do child grammars change?
- Why are not all parameters fixed concurrently?
- How is each stage structured?
- How do transitions take place?
- Why does the developmental sequence take the form it actually does?

In current language acquisition research two main hypotheses for the solving of the developmental problem have sway in the current debate:

- Maturation Hypothesis
  Universal principles and parameters become available only successively, according to an innately specified maturational schedule.

- Continuity Hypothesis
  Universal principles and parameters are available from the onset of language acquisition. It is only target language properties which have to be triggered.

5.1 The Maturation Hypothesis

5.1.1 Maturation of UG

The *Maturation Hypothesis* claims that analogous to the development of biological systems the acquisition of language is subject to maturation. Borer and Wexler's (1987: 124) considerations are representative in this respect:

"The claim that certain linguistic properties mature is consistent with what is known about many innate biological systems - that they mature... It is well-known that many aspects of the brain mature after birth. On the assumption that linguistic properties are situated in the brain, it is quite plausible that linguistic properties mature."

In its traditional version (cf. Felix 1984) the Maturation Hypothesis claims that the emergence of universal principles is determined by a maturational schedule. Restructurings in the learner's grammar take place as principles of UG mature.

Felix (1984, 1987) gives the following account of the developmental sequence for the acquisition of German word order as given in (1).

(1)   stage I   variable constituent order

stage II   random use of SOV and SVO with finite verb forms and SOV with non-finite verb forms
stage III   SOV discovered as the underlying word order, finite verb forms stabilise to SVO, non-finite verbs forms only in SOV[61]

According to Felix, variable constituent order at *stage I* is a result of the missing X-bar theory. The child's grammar at this stage is not a possible grammar in terms of UG as it is not syntactically structured yet. Felix claims that the early child grammar is semantic in nature since

> "[t]he child's grammar during the two-word and three-word stage is based on a small set of semantic categories which enter into combinations that express semantic relations."
> (Felix 1987:17)

Among these combinations, he finds the semantic relations *agent-action*, *entity-locative*, *possessor-possession* (cf. Felix 1984).

Felix argues that the emergence of X-bar theory at the onset of *stage II* introduces two new restrictions into the child language affecting (a) the choice of lexical categories entering categorial projections (N, V, A and P) and (b) possible word orders. Felix states that the emergence of X-bar theory imposes the restriction where a complement has to either precede or follow its head. Following this reasoning OVS orders should be expected to occur as well. As Felix (1987) points out it is unclear why children do not produce this order at all.

Following the requirements of Case theory, which according to Felix has also matured at this stage, children will realise that free word order without morphological case-marking is excluded by UG.

As a consequence, children will restrict possible word orders to those combinations in which the object is adjacent to the verb as long as morphological case is lacking.[62] This is empirically supported by Felix's finding that only SOV and SVO qualify as base-generated word orders at this stage.

Finally, Felix assumes that once the notion of government emerges in the transition of stage II to *stage III*, the child will know that a grammar cannot base-generate two different word orders, as government may only work in one direction.

---

[61] The sequence is based up on the empirical data in Clahsen (1982) and T. Park (1974) *The acquisition of German syntax*. Ms. Bern. Unfortunately, Felix does not quote any data for further illustration of the development in question.

[62] According to Felix only languages with overt case marking allow for relatively free word order combinations, German being such a language.

Felix hypothesises that upon the maturation of the Structure Preserving Constraint the child will correctly decide that SOV is the underlying word order of German.[63]

Unfortunately, Felix's analysis does not cover a number of verb placement asymmetries acknowledged during the initial stages of the development. For example, it has been attested that inflected verbal elements and modal verbs appear in sentence second position. Conversely, non-finite verb forms occur sentence-finally only (cf. Clahsen 1992, see sections 3.1 and 5.2.2). Further, as noted by Felix, some word orders which would be predicted to occur do not show up.

On general grounds, the most controversial consequence following from Felix's analysis is that learner grammars may not conform to UG as principles which have not matured yet may be violated. The assumption that UG only plays a relevant role at later stages of development reduces the relevance of UG in linguistic theory (cf. Guilfoyle and Noonan 1988). It also implies that learner grammars might not belong to the set of possible human languages, i.e. they would represent *wild grammars* (cf. Goodluck 1986). In other words, the child would be ascribed a state of language knowledge which should be impossible (cf. Grewendorf 1991).
Why do early grammars have a different status than later grammars? The assumption that the transition from a semantic to a syntactic grammar is biologically driven is problematic in terms of falsifiability. Insofar as any change in the learner grammar may be explained by maturation this theory loses much of its explanatory power (cf. Guilfoyle and Noonan 1988). Note that no adequate explanation as to why some principles mature before others is offered (cf. Ouhalla 1992).

If cross-linguistic variation of the grammatical properties of languages is tied to functional categories, it is their target-like specification which is expected to play a central role in structural development. In line with this hypothesis, more recent versions of the Maturation Hypothesis claim that it is the items belonging to the *Functional Module*, which mature in the course of language acquisition, the principles of UG being present from the onset of LA. The assumption that FCs are missing in early child grammar is the main tenet of the so-called *Small Clause* or *VP Hypothesis* presented in the following section.

---

[63] Felix claims that the V2 rule which has to move the verb into the second position in main clauses does not violate the *Structure Preserving Constraint* insofar as root transformations (those applying to the highest S) need not be structure preserving. On the other hand, if SVO were chosen this constraint would be violated as there is no base-generated final V-position to which the verb could move.

5.1.2 Maturation of the Functional Module

In his analysis of child language acquisition Radford (1990) distinguishes three main phases as listed in (2).

(2) 1. precategorial stage: around the 12th month
     2. lexical stage: around the 20th month
     3. functional stage: some 4 months later

According to Radford during the *precategorial stage* children only produce single words, which they have not yet analysed as to their grammatical or categorial properties.[64] As shown in (3) - (4) children produce categorially inappropriate answers at this stage:

(3)   What's that? *There.* (19)

(4)   Who rides the car? *Gone.* (16)

   (op. cit.: 32)

Radford claims that children start out with word combinations consisting of lexical categories (i.e. N, V, A and P) and their projections only around the 20th month.[65] He holds that the following empirical evidence supports the assumption that lexical categories are already present in child language at this stage, contrary to Felix's claim (cf. op. cit.: 43):

- Morphological endings like plural *-s* or gerundive *-ing* are not bound to particular semantic roles but to certain grammatical categories.

- Child word combinations follow *cross-categorial structural symmetry*, for example, nouns are combined with other constituents in order to construct a noun phrase, verbs to a verb phrase, etc.

---

[64] Interestingly, Radford (op. cit.: 23) draws a comparison to adult second language initial utterances:
"It seems reasonable to suppose, that (in some ways) the young child is just like our linguistically naive tourist: that is he communicate with words, but although these words have constant phonological, pragmatic and (perhaps) semantic properties, they lack grammatical properties and hence are purely acategorial in nature."
The question as to whether Radford is right in his claim with respect to the acategorial nature of such utterances shall be resumed at a later point as *child language acquisition* is the subject of this section.

[65] According to Radford a vocabulary spurt takes place during this phase.

According to Radford, early utterances are *categorial-thematic*[66] inasmuch as all constituents belong to the inventory of lexical categories and all sister constituents are in a thematic relationship to the head. He thus assumes that early categorial-thematic structures directly reflect thematic relations among lexical items. [67] Radford hypothesises that utterances at this early stage do have a hierarchical, endocentric, i.e. a *syntactic* structure in the sense of X-bar theory.

(5)　"pussies chasing birdies"

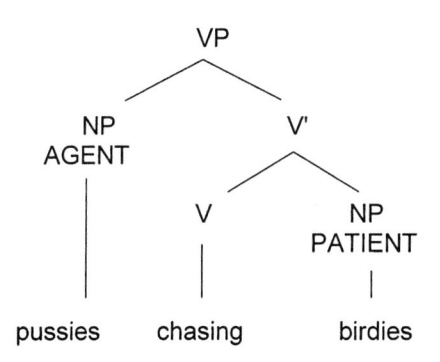

```
              VP
             /  \
           NP    V'
          AGENT / \
           |   V   NP
           |   |  PATIENT
           |   |   |
        pussies chasing birdies
```

As illustrated in (5) (op. cit.: 45) the assumption that early structures are syntactically organised does not exclude the relevance of semantic, i.e. thematic relations in these structures. Thus, as opposed to Felix's model in which UG is (partly) missing during early stages of language acquisition, Radford's model is based on a more modular view of the human language faculty in language acquisition.

So far (*stage II*), two modules, i.e. the lexicon and the categorial component (and possibly a third, i.e. an *interface* component[68]), operate in the child's grammar. Universal principles are not violated but rather operate vacuously. As we will see shortly, proponents of the VP- or Small-Clause

---

[66]　Radford (ibid.: 47) proposes the following definition of a *thematic constituent*:
"... a given word-level category X is thematic just in case X theta-marks any syster subject specifier it has; conversely, X is nonthematic if X has a nonthematic complement, or a nonthematic specifier, or both."

[67]　As a consequence non-thematic constituents like, for example, expletives are absent at this stage.

[68]　Cf. op. cit.: 244: "Since the categorial component defines a class of syntactic structures which (inter alia) serve to 'express' the predicate-argument structures specified in the lexicon, it is clear that the child's grammar at this point must also contain an interface between the lexicon and the categorial component - that is, a set of mechanisms which map (thematic) argument structures into syntactic structures (...)."

Hypothesis assume that this is due to the relevant structures (or FCs) not having matured yet.

The syntactic status of early structures of the form [NP XP][69] is claimed to be further supported by their resemblance to adult *small clauses*.[70] But, as opposed to adult small clauses, children's structures do not consist of a DP but an indeterminate NP. The second, and more fundamental difference is that child small clauses as opposed to the adults' may function as independent, i.e. as matrix clauses.
According to Radford, child small clauses may function as matrix clauses because case requirements, which would rule out small clauses as independent clauses in adult grammar, are not operative in the child grammar as long as the D-system is absent.[71]
Radford's main prediction, i.e. the absence of functional categories in early child grammar, has been agreed upon by a number of authors. Yet there is some disagreement over the appropriate description of early child utterances (cf. Müller 1993).
Ouhalla (1992), Grewendorf (1991), and Tsimpli (1992), among others, have favoured the alternative *VP analysis* (cf. Guilfoyle and Noonan 1988). According to this analysis, children's early structures only consist of a VP due to the lack of FC's. This is in line with the crucial claim underlying the FPH (see section 2.4), cf.

> "This theory implies that all aspects of linguistic variation are manifested outside the predicate phrase in terms of, for example, the directionality of complementation and the order of functional categories... etc. As far the organisation of the constituents inside the predicate phrase is concerned languages are expected to exhibit uniform properties."
> (Ouhalla 1992:10)

---

[69] The predicate XP may be represented by one of the four lexical projections AP, NP, VP, PP, NP being the subject.

[70] Following Stowell (1981) it is assumed that small clauses, like, for example,
(i)   we mustn't let [*the campaign* come to nothing]
consist of a DP subject and a predicate phrase, i.e. they are assumed to have the structure given in (ii)
(ii) [xp [DP subject] [x' [x head] complement/s]]
where the head of the overall structure would be a non-finite predicative lexical category.

[71] The ungrammaticality of independent small clauses in the adult grammar may be illustrated by the following contrast:
(i)   I consider [him unsuitable for the post]
(ii) *him unsuitable for the post
The pronominal DP 'him' is licensed in (i) as a subject of the SC because it is within the case domain of the preceding transitive verb 'consider'. Conversely, the objective pronoun 'him' in (ii) has no objective case assigner.

Because of the absence of any of the relevant VP-selecting FCs (AGR, TNS or NEG) child VPs are unselected (cf. Ouhalla 1991, Hohenberger 1992) and may thus function as matrix clauses in child language at this stage. A further consequence of the lack of FCs, specifically AGR (i.e. AGR-O) is that the linear order of the head and its complements is free at this time (cf. Ouhalla 1991, Grewendorf 1991). Note that neither the subject nor the object are case-marked yet due to the absence of AGR-categories. In other words, there is a grammatical reason for why word order in the VP in early child language is variable: the lack of FCs allows children to exhaust all possible combinations within the VP. Note that this analysis does not exclude the possibility that pragmatic factors may determine a preference for a certain word order (cf. Grewendorf 1992).

Now, the crucial empirical claim underlying the assumption that FCs are absent up to *stage III* is that the grammatical processes which depend on the presence of FCs are not operative yet.
Proponents of the VP- or Small-Clause Hypothesis claim that this prediction is borne out by the data (cf. Radford (1990) for English, Parodi (1990) for German and French, Hohenberger (1992) for German, Guilfoyle and Noonan (1988) for English and German data).
(6) gives an overview of the missing grammatical processes pertaining to the respective lacking functional category systems and some of the implications following for child language at this stage (cf. Radford 1990):

(6)   Missing functional categories and absent grammatical processes

   D-system:

   Lack of
   - morphosyntax of referential determinants
   - morphosyntax of case-marked pronominal determinants
   - binding properties of pronouns and nouns

   Consequences:
   - The Case Filter applies vacuously in early child language as children have no D-system.
   - Move-α is vacuous at this stage: as the relevant case requirements are absent there is no motivation for movement (there would be no landing sites as these are allocated in functional projections - and these are missing!).

   I-system

   Lack of
   - tense and agreement inflection
   - do-support, copula, modal verbs

- empty categories
- case assignment to subject position

Consequences:
- No V-to-I movement
- No landing sites for movement

C-system

Lack of
- syntax of complementisers, auxiliary verbs and preposed wh-constituents

Consequences:
- wh-words are analysed as phrasal adjuncts
- no inversion in questions
- no V2 effects

It is certainly striking, how far-reaching the absence of one of the grammatical modules, namely the UG lexicon, is. But this is only a natural consequence, if we acknowledge the crucial role of FCs in grammatical processes. Certainly, the VP-analysis is a more restrictive hypothesis than Felix's Maturation Hypothesis. Early child grammars differ from adult grammars in predictable ways, cf.

"This view implies that children's grammars must be optimal with respect to the tools they have access to and not necessarily with respect to the final and complete adult grammar."
(Guilfoyle and Noonan 1988:5)

In line with the modular view of the human language faculty, the absence of one of the grammatical modules is responsible for why early child grammars look the way they do. Consider, for example, the fact that move-α is predicted to be vacuous at this stage:

"The argumentations are highly redundant and interdependent. No functional categories, no landing sites, no case system, no motivation. No matter how one argues, the sub-aspects imply each other. The origin of this network is given in the lack of functional categories. Thereof consistently results the diversity of implications."
(Hohenberger 1992: 80)[72]

---

[72] The original reads as follows:
"Die verschiedenen Argumentationen sind hochredundant und bedingen sich gegenseitig. Keine funktionalen Kategorien, keine Landeplätze, kein Kasussystem, keine nicht-thematischen Positionen, keine Motivation. Egal wie man argumentiert, die Teilaspekte implizieren einander. Die diesem Netzwerk zugrundeliegende Ursache ist das Fehlen Funktionaler Kategorien. Daraus ergeben sich folgerichtig die vielfältigen Konsequenzen."

But the crucial question to ask is why functional categories develop only after lexical categories. In terms of learnability one could ask for *"the linguistic properties of functional items which make them more difficult to learn"* (Radford 1990: 263). As mentioned throughout the preceding sections, proponents of the Small Clause Hypothesis, the VP-Hypothesis or the Structure Building Hypothesis rule out a learning-based approach. Thus, alternative explanations have to be sought.

We could assume that the delayed acquisition of FCs depended on their formal or semantic complexity. However, the irregularity and the complexity of lexical categories should also be reflected in a delayed acquisition, which is not the case.
Alternatively, the consideration that FCs are acquired late because of their cognitive complexity must be ruled out because of the present unavailability of a language-independent way of determining (a) the cognitive complexity of the items in question and (b) the child's cognitive capacity at any given stage in the development (cf. Radford 1990).
Therefore, proponents of the VP- or Small-Clause Hypothesis assume that the implementation of functional category systems must be subject to maturation. Although this is a more restrictive hypothesis than the Maturation Hypothesis in its traditional version (cf. Felix 1984) it still suffers from shifting the triggering problem into a non-linguistic, i.e. into the biological domain.
There is no *a priori* reason why this should not be valid, but theory-internal considerations as to why functional categories are not available in the initial stages would be more valuable in terms of both falsifiability and predictive power. Before resorting to a maturation-based explanation, grammar-internal accounts of why some sub-parts of the modular language faculty come into play later than others should be considered.

Could there be a reason related to the structure of grammar for why lexical category systems are in place before functional category systems? Note that both autonomy *and* interaction play a role in grammar as conceived in GB theory: it is the interaction of independent sub-systems or modules which constrains grammatical competence. This interaction, in other words, this interdependence of the sub-parts of grammar could be the reason for why some modules must be in place before others may become operative. An analysis along these lines has been suggested, for example, by Roeper and de Villiers (1992).

Radford (1990) himself has pointed out that the architecture of grammar allows for a *teleological* view of language development.
The interrelation of lexical and functional categories - functional projections serving the function of f-projecting lexical categories into functional

categories - allows for the assumption that the acquisition of lexical categories must precede functional categories on logical grounds.

Radford also considers a *parametric explanation* which would be in line with the assumption that the properties of lexical categories are acquired first because they are universal as opposed to functional categories which are subject to parametrisation. According to this argument the acquisition of the latter would be delayed because it would require far more linguistic evidence.

Radford rejects both these hypotheses because of their incompatibility with his empirical claims, namely, (a) that all four lexical categories are acquired before the FCs and (b) that FCs emerge concurrently. Yet he also points out that these empirical facts are not predicted by either the maturationally based or the grammar-internal hypotheses.

Further empirical studies suggest that, contrary to Radford, a gradual emergence of FCs may have to be considered. Guilfoyle and Noonan (1988), for example, suggest that COMP may be implemented after INFL, and DP before IP. A potential problem for any of the maturationally based accounts is cross-linguistic variation with respect to the order of emergence of the grammatical phenomena which would be subject to a maturational schedule.

Interestingly, much of the controversy around the question of whether the Functional Module becomes available in its entirety at a certain point in time is based on the empirical findings of researchers analysing the acquisition of languages other than English.[73]

Not only has Radford's "concurrent-implementation-assumption" been questioned, the absence of the Functional Module has been challenged by proponents of the *Continuity Hypothesis* who claim that there is empirical evidence that some or all functional categories are present in early child grammar. We will have a critical look at their arguments in the following section.

---

[73] Hyams (1994) is quite radical in her assumption that the concentration on English data has narrowed the scientific view of many researchers. Here is her claim (ibid.: 22):
"... there is a broad range of acquisition data from other languages which cannot be readily accounted for under the assumption that early grammars lack all functional heads. In fact, it is fair to say that the characterization of early language as 'telegraphic', the 'asyntactic', and finally 'small-clause-like' is in large measure a historical accident. Had the grammatical study of early language begun with German and Dutch, for example, rather than English a very different picture would have emerged."
There are many ways in which this is too radical a claim. Some of them will be dealt with in the following section.

5.2 The Continuity Hypothesis

One of the main tenets of the *Continuity Hypothesis*[74] is that UG imposes a fundamental constraint upon learner grammars from the beginning, namely *UG conformity*:

> "Implicit to the approach is the hypothesis that while the early grammar may differ from the adult grammar, the variation between the two systems falls within well-defined limits, as determined by the principles and parameters of UG, i.e. grammatical development is a "continuous" process."
> (White 1982: 148-9)

Implicit to this approach is the assumption that the full range of universal principles and parameters is available from the onset of language acquisition. What learners have to acquire is the target-like specification of the parameterised properties in question. There have been different proposals as to how this may be achieved.

Traditionally (cf. White 1982, Hyams 1986, Clahsen 1988a), the correct fixing of parameterised principles is understood to be determined by *lexical learning* (*Lexical Learning Hypothesis,* see section 3.1).
Alternatively (cf. Weissenborn 1990), target grammatical properties have been considered to be triggered by *syntactic learning* (*Syntactic Learning or Bootstrapping Hypothesis*).
Furthermore, there is some disagreement as to the specification of the phrase structure in the initial state. With respect to this issue two different versions of the Continuity Hypothesis have to be distinguished:

- The Strong Continuity Hypothesis
- The Weak Continuity Hypothesis

I will discuss each of these variants in the following sections.

5.2.1 The lexical learning approach

Some of the main tenets of this approach have already been mentioned in the context of Clahsen's account of the acquisition of German word order (see section 3.1).
Roughly speaking, this hypothesis follows from the traditional triggering concept claiming that the acquisition of language-specific properties is

---

[74] Cf. White (1982), Pinker (1984), Hyams (1986), Clahsen (1988a, 1990a) and Weissenborn (1990) among others.

input driven. The idea that there is a correlation between the acquisition of certain lexical items and the development of certain grammatical structures is appealing as cross-linguistic variation is assumed to be related to the properties of a specific sub-part of the lexicon, i.e. the UG lexicon. Yet, this approach faces the problem of explaining why development takes the form it actually does. If the relevant information, i.e. the lexical items in question, belong to the child's input from the beginning of the acquisition process, the question arises as to why the correct fixing of parameters is not immediately triggered (*Triggering Problem*, cf. Borer and Wexler 1987, Lightfoot 1991).

The traditional response to this question (cf. White 1982) is based on the assumption that the triggering function of lexical items may only become operative once they are actually perceived, i.e. once they belong to the child's *intake*. The delayed perception of the items in question has been attributed to, among other things, their perceptual non-saliency and their inaccessibility through semantic bootstrapping (cf. Pinker 1984).

Note, however, that this differentiation between *input* and *intake* shifts the triggering problem into the domain of perception. Again, theory-internal reasons for the delayed acquisition of functional items would be more valuable in terms of falsifiability and predictive power. An analysis along these lines requires a theory of lexical learning which could account for the asymmetry between lexical and functional categories. Unfortunately, a satisfactory theory encompassing these facts has not yet been developed. As shown in section 2.5 the interaction between lexicon and syntax has been mainly analysed with respect to lexical categories. If functional categories are not accessible through semantic bootstrapping, the question arises as to how they are learned at all.

The hypothesis that FCs are involved in grammatical processes raises a further problem pointed out by Verrips (1990:18):

> "... how can we be sure that syntax follows the lexical items and not the other way round? (...) The problem with the concept of lexical learning is that it is often hard to distinguish the syntactic properties of a lexical item that enable the child to set the parameter from the consequences of that parameter setting itself."

The Lexical Learning Hypothesis *qua item-to-rule* mapping approach has been further challenged by findings that some errors in early grammars, for example with respect to long-distance wh-movement and control structures, do not seem to result from a mis-analysis of lexical items (Weissenborn et al. 1992: 11).[75]

---

[75] Weissenborn et al. refer to the empirical evidence provided in Roeper and de Villiers (1992) and Goodluck and Behne (1992).

5.2.2 The syntactic learning approach

The syntactic learning approach put forward in Weissenborn (1990) states that the full target-like specification of FCs is dependent upon syntactic information. Weissenborn's analysis of the acquisition of German word order is based on two claims concerning the early German grammar (before Clahsen's *stage IV*), namely, (a) verb movement is general and (b) movement into COMP is available.

a. Evidence for general verb movement:

According to Weissenborn, empirical data show, contrary to Clahsen's claim, that verb movement also occurs for verbs which are neither intransitive nor *t*-marked. The position of postverbal adverbials, negation, subjects and objects in these structures is meant to indicate that verb movement has taken place. Utterances (7) - (10) illustrate this point.

(7) glaub   nich   B 25;07   (postverbal Neg)
    believe (1 pers. sg.) *not*

(8) suche   mal   S 22;20   (postverbal ADV)
    seek (1 pers. sg.) ADV

(9) kauft Angela   S 22;20   (postverbal subject)
    buys Angela

(10) malt   eier   S 22;20   (postverbal object)
    paints (3 pers. sg.) *eggs*

(ibid.: 196f., his transl.)

Weissenborn assumes that the acquisition of verb movement is independent of the acquisition of subject-verb agreement, the primary distinction being the one between finite and non-finite forms.[76] His argument is based on the following considerations:

---

[76] Cf. Weissenborn (1990: 18): "The claim of the primacy of finiteness over agreement in development is further supported independently by the finding that across languages finiteness develops before person/number agreement." Weissenborn further stresses that there is cross-linguistic variation with respect to whether both finiteness and agreement or only one of both is realised. Interestingly, Weissenborn argues that on learnability grounds the acquisition of the binary finiteness distinction is easier to acquire than the multiple person / number relations found in subject-verb agreement.

- There is no reason for the choice of the verb ending -*t* as a transitivity marker to the exclusion of all other endings.

- If -*t* was the only marker for low transitivity, overgeneralisation regardless of person and number should be expected, contrary to fact.

- In order to account for verbs in V1 and V2 position, it is assumed that all other endings acknowledged in the data have the feature [+ finite], as, in addition, nearly all infinitival forms occur in the final position. Weissenborn assumes that children already have subject-verb agreement (if not the full agreement paradigm) as the verb forms used agree with the subject.

- The prediction that verb movement should only occur with finite forms is borne out by the data.

As a consequence, both the development of verb movement and finiteness are held to be independent of the acquisition of subject-verb agreement. What serves as a trigger for the finiteness distinction under this hypothesis?
Weissenborn claims that the sentence negation element 'nicht' (*not*) plays a crucial role in this respect. He bases his assumption on the claim that the child is provided with a principle determining locality conditions for relations like modification and theta-role assigment and also for the relation between the negator and its argument, namely the *Adjunct Projection Principle* in (11):

(11) Adjunct Projection Principle
If some semantic type X" modifies some semantic type Y, and X and Y are syntactically realised as a and b, a is projected as adjacent either to b or to the head of b.
(op. cit.: 199, *pace* Sportiche 1988)

Weissenborn further assumes that the child has already determined the government direction in German as leftward. The child having been provided with these "tools" is believed to correctly conclude that the occurrence of a verb left to the negator must have moved from its underlying position.

b. Evidence for V-to-COMP movement

One of the crucial tenets underlying Weissenborn's analysis (and for that matter all other analyses within the framework of the Strong Continuity Hypothesis, see section 5.2.3) is that the presence of a particular X-bar position does not depend on its lexical realisation in the sense that

"... it is in the spirit of the logic of a modular theory of grammar that the projections of the X-bar tree are not uniquely defined by the possible occurrence of a particular type of lexical item." (op. cit.: 203)

Given that the COMP position in German may be lexically realised by a finite verb in matrix clauses, or by either a complementiser or a wh-phrase in embedded clauses, children may already project a C phrase before lexical complementisers become available.
Weissenborn believes that the availability of a CP in the early grammar is supported by the presence of the following structures in the empirical data (ibid., his transl.):

- preverbal elements other than subject, e.g.
  (12) 'bild   male   ich'   H 24;24
        picture paint I

- postverbal subjects, e.g.
  (13) 'baut   max   nich'   S 22;3
        builds Max   not

- wh-questions, e.g.
  (14) 'wo   is   der   ball'   S 22;20
        where is   the   ball ?

- tensed embedded clauses without overt complementisers, e.g.
  (15) 'papi sagt   (...)   schöne hose   anzieht hat'
        papi says   (that)   nice   pants put-on   has
                                                              H 25;18

According to Weissenborn the IP-analysis could not capture these data because

- elements in preverbal position other than subjects would be ruled out as the SpecI position is an A-position;
- it would be unclear how postverbal subjects received case;
- wh-operators in the wh-questions attested require an A-bar position.

Weissenborn's argument against the *unspecified-IP-proposal* (i.e. SpecI may function as both an A- and an A-bar-position) favoured among others by Clahsen (1990), Fritzenschaft et al. (1990) and Müller (1993) is based on the following considerations:

- It is unclear how the creation of a CP should be concurrent to a specification of IP.
- Given the IP analysis children may not find out the complementary distribution of verbs and complementisers in C.
- A grammar with an unspecified IP presupposes that non-subject elements in preverbal position should be evident from the beginning, contrary to fact. The preverbal position is initially reserved to the subject as expected if this position is an A-position.

As for the tensed embedded clauses without overt complementiser, Weissenborn assumes that the child grammar allows for a non-lexical realisation of C. His assumption is that the C position is realised by a feature indicating the sentence mode which prevents the finite verb from appearing in C in the cases indicated.
According to Weissenborn, error-free verb-final placement in embedded clauses further supports the assumption that V-to-C movement is available prior to the acquisition of lexical complementisers. Otherwise (i.e. V-to-I only) overgeneralisation of matrix clause V2 order to embedded clauses would be predicted as "*nothing would prevent the child from adding a new projection, namely CP, above IP*" (ibid.: 206).[77, 78]
Weissenborn notes that it would be unclear how the child could retreat from this assumption on the basis of positive evidence alone. Further, he argues that there is no evidence for productivity of embedded V2, main clause V3 and non-inverted wh-questions, which would be expected in such a case. Yet, Weissenborn acknowledges a main difference to the adult grammar based on the evidence that wh-phrases are the only A-bar elements occurring in preverbal position at this stage: up to the age of 24 months the child grammar has different analyses for declaratives (= IP) and wh-questions (= CP).
He assumes that after the 24th month children discover that German is a full V2 language in that matrix clauses also project to C. This change is claimed to follow from the *Structure Preserving Principle* (i.e. the child knows that a head has to move to a head position) and the correct selection of the head functioning as a landing site for this movement.
Prior to this change children will have correctly analysed questions as [+ C, - I] following the feature specification in (16).[79]

---

[77] Cf. also Hyams 1994.
[78] According to Weissenborn, V2 in embedded sentences and V3 structures - empirical data which could challenge this claim - only represent a minor percentage of the total data. In some recent studies, however, the relevance of these data has been acknowledged (see section 7.1.2 and 7.1.3).
[79] Weissenborn bases his analysis on Rizzi (1990).

(16) [+ C, - I] : a proposition, the CP of non-V-2 languages, which selects either operator (e.g. wh-phrase) or a trace belonging to an A-bar chain as possible elements for the specifier position.
(op. cit.: 207)

According to Weissenborn the target-like specification of C as the hybrid category [+ C, + I] following the specification in (17) follows from the correct analysis of topicalised [- wh/non-subject] elements in the specifier position of the verbal head in declarative clauses.[80]

(17) [+ C, + I] : the category of V-2 clauses in 'full' V-2 languages like German; qua [+ C] its specifier can contain wh-phrases or trace, qua [+ I] it can host a subject of the sentence.
(ibid.: 208)

From this analysis children will arrive to the conclusion that declaratives and wh-questions are projections of the same type, i.e. CPs.

5.2.3 Strong vs. Weak Continuity Hypothesis

Now, Weissenborn's analysis differs from Clahsen's not only with respect to the mechanisms assumed to trigger the target-like properties of German word order. Clahsen and Weissenborn also disagree on the question of whether all functional categories are available from the onset of language acquisition or not. The controversy centres on two different versions of the Continuity Hypothesis.
Under the *Strong Continuity Hypothesis*, the full structure tree (including both IP and CP) is available from the onset of language acquisition. Hyams (1994) thus calls this approach the *Full Clause Hypothesis*.[81] It is the presence of processes in which functional categories are involved, such as subject-verb agreement and case assignment as well as verb movement processes which is taken as empirical evidence for the assumption that all functional categories are in place from the onset of language acquisition (cf. Roeper 1992, Hyams 1994, Weissenborn 1990, among others). Weissenborn's analysis is representative in this respect.
Now, the assumption that children start out with the full structure tree raises two crucial questions:

---

[80] Weissenborn argues that the late recognition of [- wh/non-subject]-elements is due to the children not having yet acquired the necessary morphological case distinctions.

[81] Cf. also Poeppel and Wexler (1993) who term this hypothesis the *Full Competence Hypothesis*.

- How can it be that learner grammars represent possible grammars in terms of UG if they are devoid of language-specific information?
- How do learners arrive at the target grammar?

The traditional assumption (cf. Hyams 1986) is that children start out with a language particular tree specified in accordance with markedness considerations. As for movement constraints, for example, Hyams (1994) believes that V-to-C must be the unmarked option as in the opposite case (i.e. V-to-I = unmarked) negative evidence would be needed for the implementation of obligatory V-to-C. Note further that Hyams follows the tenets of the lexical learning approach regarding the question of how children acquire the missing functional items.

The problem with this analysis is that if initial structure trees are specified on the basis of markedness considerations, a large number of properties of the learner grammar would need to be revised upon contradicting evidence from the input. Hyams claims that this is in line with the learnability considerations implicit to markedness theory as conceived in GB theory.
What is unclear is how those parameters, which do not conform to markedness considerations, should be correctly set. In the case of the headedness parameter, for example, it is not plausible to argue for an unmarked option. For cases like this, additional learning principles would have to be invoked.
The hypothesis faces the empirical problem of explaining why children do not start out with unmarked hypotheses only (cf. Roeper 1992).

These problems may be contrasted with Poeppel and Wexler's (1993) claim that

> "[t]he Full Competence Hypothesis has no developmental question associated with it (except for the optional infinitive problem), whereas theories that assume less than full competence must explain how the missing or wrong properties are learned, or, alternatively, develop through maturation."
> (ibid.: 18)

Unfortunately, Poeppel and Wexler do not give an account of the learning problem, which children still face, even on the assumption of the Full Competence Hypothesis! Take, for example, the claim that the fixing of certain parameters must occur, in their terms, "quickly". Whatever this is intended to mean, it only shifts the learnability problem to an earlier acquisition phase. In view of these problems, Roeper (1992) proposes to distinguish between the *universal grammar* children would start out with and possible *adult grammars*. Roeper claims that initial phrase structure

trees are devoid of feature specifications of functional categories, directionality and other language-specific information.[82] The problem arises as to how these initial structure trees should be represented "*when all possible tree structures involve language-particular information*" (ibid.: 334).
Roeper assumes that the initial tree consists of dominance relations only (these are assumed to be universal), i.e. with the constraints in (18).

(18) UG: CP dominates IP, which dominates VP, which dominates NP (optional).
 (ibid.: 337)

Clearly, this syntactic *skeleton*-tree (cf. Müller 1993) needs to be fed with the necessary lexical and morphological information in order to become a *full blown* phrase structure tree of the adult or target grammar. But how how do children acquire this language particular information?
According to Roeper the selection of the elements relevant to the target grammar results from the "*interaction between the lexicon (with X-bar representations) and full syntactic trees (with functional categories IP and CP)*" (op. cit.: 340).
Roeper assumes that the paradigms created by the lexicon lead to a modification of syntactic trees on the basis of *the Principle of Joint Representation* in (19).

(19) Joint Representation
 Elements are expressed in Grammar when they are represented in two modules (at least).
 (ibid.: 335)

This allows for an explanation of the delay of the implementation of grammatical processes without resorting to a maturationally based explanation. Following Roeper's Principle of Joint Representation what has to come into play is the appropriate interaction of the modules making up grammar. The adjunction process plays a crucial role in this process, as elements unspecified for their syntactic status (and thus not yet fulfilling the requirement of the *Joint Modular Representation*) are first adjoined following the *Relevance Criterion* (ibid.: 342f.), which determines whether an element is of relevance to sentence grammar, i.e. receives a representation in one of the grammatical modules. Categorial identification

---

[82] In this sense the initial grammar is a "subgrammar" to the adult grammar and thus "... it is not, technically speaking, a possible adult grammar, since all adult grammars must set the Head Parameter" (ibid.: 334). Put differently, "the initial state cannot be both universal and a possible adult grammar" (ibid.: 336).

follows this step. Thus, the *skeleton*-tree children start out with allows for the presence of XP nodes as attachment sites "*prior to the point where their intrinsic content would be lexically expressed*" (ibid.: 339).[83]

Conversely, proponents of the *Weak Continuity Hypothesis* (cf. Clahsen et al. 1994) claim that it is the interaction between the principles of X-bar theory and the input data which determines the gradual development of phrase structure. Thus, learning is claimed to be conservative in nature (*pace* Pinker 1984, Lebeaux 1988). This approach presupposes that children will start out by projecting phrasal categories from lexical categories first, lexical categories being implemented via semantic bootstrapping.

Following findings regarding cross-linguistic variation with respect to the realisation and the specification of FCs it is claimed that functional heads will be posited only upon positive evidence in the input. A functional phrase structure position will only be posited if it is phonetically overt or if it is involved in some syntactic process, e.g. as a landing site for movement, in binding or in control processes. Furthermore, adjunct and specifier positions as opposed to complement positions (XPs universally contain a complement position) are only established through positive evidence. This allows for certain XPs not to have a specifier position (e.g. the PP, a lexical XP, or NEGP, a functional XP).

In this way, the Weak Continuity Hypothesis permits many of the descriptive problems encountered to be avoided when trying to account for the grammatical facts underlying German sentence structure. Consider, for example, Fritzenschaft et al. (1991: 66) who claim

> "... that the X-bar theory, which allows, in principle, that the X-bar schema be expanded again and again "telescopically" in terms of a new level, involves at the same time a meta-structural solution as to the problem of a descriptive decision regarding a certain amount of projection levels."[84]

---

[83] With respect to the acquisition of German word order Roeper agrees with the assumption that there is a relationship between the acquisition of the agreement paradigm and V2. Yet movement is not claimed to result from agreement (contrary to Clahsen). Rather it is the morphological recognition of the IP or the CP which serves as a trigger for the distributional analysis, which in turn determines the move-α module to become operative. According to Roeper, the presence of an agreement morpheme in a functional category indicates that movement from a non-functional position must have occurred, but it does not indicate the path of movement.

[84] The original reads as follows:
"... daß die X-bar-Theorie, die es im Prinzip gestattet, das X-bar-Schema immer wieder "teleskopartig" um eine weitere Stufe zu erweitern, in sich zugleich eine metastrukturelle Lösung hinsichtlich des Problems einer deskriptiven Entscheidung für eine bestimmte Menge von Projektionsstufen birgt."

Fritzenschaft et al. propose that the following principles play a crucial role in the acquisition of German word order regularities:

- Head Parameter:
  The position of heads has to be determined as either initial or final.
- Head Presence:
  Head positions should not be left empty at S-structure.
- Strict Structure Preservation:
  Movement has to be reconstruable via traces, heads may only move into head positions and maximal phrases only into positions which are also base-generated as such.

It is assumed that these principles guide the child in the acquisition of the German (complex) structure in the following way:

- Following the Principle of Head Presence children are expected to look out for heads and consequently discover lexical complementisers.
- Children should aim at fixing the Head Parameter to one of its values despite contradicting evidence in the input.
- As soon as children discover the difference between heads and maximal phrases the Principle of Structure Preservation is applied.[85]

In sum, the Weak Continuity Approach attempts to explain (a) why not all feature specifications of functional categories may be relevant during the initial stages of acquisition and (b) why children may not make full use of the complete sentence architecture from the very beginning.

5.3 Conclusion

We may summarise the preceding discussion by stating that the issue of determining the nature and the development of the early child grammar is far from uncontroversial. But we should also acknowledge that the controversy has been around for some time now, as pointed out by Weissenborn et al. (1992: 7; cf. also Hohenberger 1992, 1996), cf.

---

[85] For further details of their analysis of the acquisition of German complex structures see section 7.1.2.

"In some ways this current debate revives in new terminology the sort of debates about the nature of early grammars that have been going on since the early 1970s (...) and illustrates the extreme difficulty of accurately determining the nature of very early grammars."

Irrespective of the theoretical framework, the *telegraphic look* of early utterances has been interpreted, in some way or another, as evidence for some (more or less significant) differences between child language and the adult language.[86]

On the basis of UG theory, the question of whether there is any relevant difference between early child grammars and adult grammars is crucial. For one, UG theory states that universal constraints belong to the genetically determined *initial state*. If learner grammars are deficient in relation to adult or *end state* grammars, they should be so not only in predictable ways but also still in accordance with UG.

With the exception of Felix's Maturation Hypothesis the analyses presented above concur with the argument that learner grammars conform to the requirements imposed by UG, yet they disagree as to what extent the universal constraints may apply in the early grammar. The controversy centres around the question of whether children make full use of the range of FCs provided by the Functional Module or not.

What the proponents of both the VP-Hypothesis and the Weak Continuity Hypothesis have in common is that they are based on the assumption that the early grammar still awaits the full implementation of the lexical, morphological and syntactic properties of functional categories.

Both hypotheses differ as to their account of why the development of functional category systems is more time consuming than that of lexical categories.

It was pointed out that in terms of both falsifiability and predictive power grammar internal considerations have to be favoured. Cross-linguistic variation with respect to the relative order of emergence of functional categories may prove revealing in this respect.

Conversely, proponents of the Strong Continuity Hypothesis reduce the deficit of the early child grammar to a lexical one. The hypothesis implies in its strongest version that there is no developmental problem at all (cf. Poeppel and Wexler 1993). The following passage may serve as a further illustration of this point:

"What we mean when we say that the child is producing clause-like structures is that the utterances have the property of compositionality -

---

[86] As the attentive reader may have noticed the *Full Competence Hypothesis* (see section 5.2.3) represents one of the few exceptions.

that is, in some intuitive sense, the words combine in meaningful formal ways to form clauses. In short, the FCH says that, at the stage at which the child knows how to combine words to yield larger rule-governed meaningful units, she has full competence with respect to the principles and processes governing the clause. Therefore, on the Full Competence Hypothesis, it is impossible for the child who is producing significant combinations of words to be lacking the capacity to instantiate functional categories."
(op. cit.: 29)

There are a number of empirical problems which this version of the Continuity Hypothesis fails to explain.

Firstly, the data show that certain verb placement asymmetries occur during the initial stages. At least, these data suggest that some grammatical processes are optional up to a certain age. Consider, for example, V-to-C movement which is obligatory in German matrix clauses. If, as believed within the framework of the Strong Continuity Hypothesis, V-to-C movement is operative from early on, this should be so without exception, contrary to fact. There is no way of getting out of this dilemma under the Full Competence Hypothesis. Note that Weissenborn's analysis, which is also based upon the Strong Continuity Hypothesis, tries to account for the phenomenon in question on the basis of the claim that the CP system has not been correctly analysed yet.

What the empirical data analysed on both sides suggest is that the target-like specification of the CP system is delayed.

Interestingly, the explanatory controversy meets the descriptive problem of accounting for the German sentence structure (cf. Fritzenschaft et al. 1991, see section 2.6).

What needs to be mentioned as well is that the development in question takes place within short periods of time. In view of the fact that months or even weeks may be decisive with respect to a certain change in the learner grammar, it is the more striking that some of the accounts mentioned above are rather vague with respect to the age of the children analysed.

A further, much discussed issue concerns the question of how learners eventually determine language-specific properties of functional categories. As it seems the full implementation of functional category systems is only possible upon a correct syntactic analysis and this may only be possible once certain other properties of grammar are in place. What has to be determined additionally is in which way both lexical and syntactic learning may play a role in this process.

In summarising the ongoing discussion around the Developmental Problem, we may ask ourselves how it comes that similar data could be subject to such contradictory hypotheses. I would concede that in some ways each of them is *partially* true in the sense that we may regard continuity and discontinuity "*temporal variations on one and the same theme*" (Hohenberger 1996: 153). We may advance with Hohenberger that

> "[t]he proper question in language acquisition cannot be: "Continuity or discontinuity?", but must be: "When or, under which conditions, is language acquisition continuous, and when is it discontinuous?" (...) A language system as a whole may be in different regimes simultaneously, when one closer inspects the different time strata it operates on, viz. the phylogenetic or diachronic, the ontogenetic, and the actual genetic timescale, respectively; or, when one has the different modules in mind, viz. syntax, semantics, phonology and pragmatics, etc."
> (ibid.: 153/4)

In a similar way we may expect lexical and syntactic learning to *converge* and let grammar, *qua* complex system, "get organised" by means of its very own rules.

In sum, it seems that many of the dichotomies determining current hypotheses may reveal themselves as a mere by-product of too *linear* a perspective we will have to give up eventually. In chapter 7 I will discuss some recent proposals made in this respect. Before, however, we shall direct our attention to the intricate discussion around ASLA specific developmental problems.

6 The Developmental Problem of ASLA

As pointed out by Sharwood-Smith (1988) the observation that learner grammars are somehow deficient as opposed to adult or *end state* grammars applies to both adult and child language acquisition. Yet, the question arises as to whether adult learner grammars represent *subgrammars*, in the sense pointed out above, i.e. if they are UG constrained even though not yet possible target language grammars.

As for the various stages in the development of adult learner grammars, it is a matter of debate of whether all learner grammars develop in the direction of the target language norm and if this is the case, how this is achieved. Note that this issue, which Schwartz and Sprouse (1994) call the *Determinacy Problem of ASLA*, is specific to adult language acquisition. As for the differences between child and adult language development: can they be embraced by a UG-based learning theory? Consider, for example, Michael Sharwood-Smith's (1988: 178) argument that

> "... while it is still operating, the acquisition device works to make the developing grammar conform: the nonconformist aspects would be relatively more unstable than the conformist aspects."

Yet this view has been challenged in different ways. The following arguments have been put forward:

(a) The UG-is-lost-argument:
Adult learner grammars may never become proper target grammars (in the sense of UG) because access to UG is not possible after the critical period.

(b) The maturational-schedule-argument:
Language development in adulthood cannot be deterministic because determinism is given by the maturational schedule which is not available in adulthood.

(c) The no-functional-module-argument:
Development of adult learner grammars is different because the Functional Module is not accessible.

(d) The multicompetence-argument:
ASLA cannot be deterministic because L1 and L2 are related in the mind.

(e) The L1-carry-over-argument:
ASLA-specific learnability problems are the result of the L1

being part of the Initial State. Depending on whether the L1 is only partially or fully "carried over" development is characterised by structure-building or restructuring processes towards the L2 norm.

Note that arguments (a) to (c) maintain that there is a critical period whereby the mechanisms underlying determinism in child language acquisition are lost in adult language acquisition. Arguments (d) and (e), on the other hand, are based on the assumption that UG is operative in adulthood. (d) relates differences between adult and child language acquisition to the impossibility of learning a second language independently of the mother tongue knowledge. According to argument (e) the inter-relation of L1 and L2 varies in the course of the L2 development.

In the light of the hypotheses concerning the Developmental Problem in child language acquisition (a) to (e) may be related to either the Continuity or the Maturation Hypothesis as follows:

- Maturation Hypothesis and ASLA:
  All the implications following from maturation should be lacking in ASLA.
  If maturation pertains to *accessibility* as such, access to UG/the Functional Module should be impossible.
  If maturation pertains to the *timing of access*, access to UG/the Functional Module should be possible in principle.

- Continuity Hypothesis and ASLA:
  If access to UG is still possible in adulthood, adult learner grammars should also conform to UG. Differences between child and adult language acquisition may occur as adults may face different learnability problems due to their mother tongue knowledge.
  If access to UG is impossible after the critical period, adult L2 grammars are not grammars in the sense of UG theory.

The preceding considerations show how explanations of ASLA have been related to L1A accounts. Conversely, the possibility that ASLA research may also be involved in the evaluation of L1A theory, has received little attention even within the UG based approach to ASLA.[87] Consider, for example, empirical evidence from ASLA showing that there are similar developmental processes in both acquisition types. In such a

---

[87] Only a few authors, Suzanne Flynn (1988) among them, have pointed out that similarities in structural development rule out any account covering child development only, as is the case with the Maturation Hypothesis.

case, age-specific factors, such as a maturational schedule, would have to be ruled out as an exclusive explanatory basis for one acquisition form only.

The most obvious observation to be kept in mind when analysing ASLA on the background of the theoretical and empirical findings in the field of child LA is that all age-related explanations for L1A cannot be adopted in a theory of ASLA. Unfortunately, as the UG access debate shows, this has almost exclusively been interpreted in one way, namely, that in child LA everything is right because language acquisition in childhood is easy and always successful.
More often than not, it has been concluded that every theory which is suited to L1A cannot be so for ASLA because in ASLA practically nothing is easy and success is only an exotic phenomenon. Acquisition research in both fields shows neither of these hypotheses to be completely true.

6.1 Adult language acquisition devoid of maturation

As pointed out above, some researchers have sought to determine the implications following from the Maturation Hypothesis for ASLA.
If the maturational schedule *"tells the child where to look and what to do at what time"* (Felix 1991: 99), in other words, if it primarily determines the *temporal ordering* of universal principles (cf. Felix 1984, 1987, see section 5.1.1), then ASLA by being devoid of this ordering has to be characterised by random consultation of UG principles (cf. Felix 1991). Following this reasoning, adult L2 learners in having access to UG but no "guide" as to this access will have to find out "by themselves" among other things which developmental path to take or in which way input data could be of relevance.

As pointed out by Schwartz (1991: 301) the learnability problem in ASLA associated with the unavailability of the maturational schedule is further aggravated in that the mother tongue knowledge serves as a point of departure in the development of the L2, cf.

> "... not only do the correct values of parameters need to be acquired, not only do principles that are not activated in the L1 grammar have to be engaged, not only do principles that are available in the L1 but not relevant to the L2 have to be discarded, but the implicational relations among the relevant principles themselves need to be discovered. And indeed, this may be extraordinarily difficult..."

The critical question to be asked in this respect is whether there really is anything *extraordinary* in the degree of difficulty of the learnability task adults face, and if this is the case, in what respect is it *extraordinary*?

It is certainly not without irony that by being devoid of a maturational schedule adults are faced with a learnability task which would somehow be equivalent to the one the child is assumed to face under the Continuity Hypothesis.

Now, with respect to child language acquisition it was pointed out that the hard-headed interpretation of the Maturation Hypothesis lacks predictive power because any change in the learner grammar could be predicted to be the consequence of the maturational schedule.

We may advance a similar weakness regarding the considerations mentioned previously: any difference between adult and child language acquisition may be put down to the lack of the maturational schedule.

In view of these considerations we may ask about the implications following from the more restrictive VP- or Small-Clause-Hypothesis. Two possible hypotheses may be considered:

(a) If maturation temporarily determines the accessibility of the Functional Module, differences between child and adult LA occur because access to the Functional Module after the critical period is not possible.

(b) If maturation is the means for the emergence of the Functional Module its accessibility in ASLA should be possible in principle; differences between child and adult LA would result from children and adults facing different learnability tasks.

Clearly, hypothesis (a) is a revised version of the FDH. Yet, as will be shown shortly this hypothesis makes different predictions than the FDH. Hypothesis (b), on the other hand, restricts maturation effects to the processes underlying the emergence of the Functional Module without concluding, as done in (a), that emergence turns into loss after a critical period.

6.2 The No-Functional-Module Hypothesis

Ianthi Tsimpli and Anna Roussou (1991) are among the few authors who have explicitly dealt with the implications for ASLA from the assumption that successful language acquisition is tied to the maturation of the Functional Module.[88] They claim that the critical period pertains to the access to the Functional Module and not to UG on the whole. ASLA is predicted to differ from language learning in childhood in the following ways:

---

[88] See also Teresa Parodi (1990).

- L2 learners only have access to the parameter values realised in their mother tongue. Where L1 and L2 differ transfer errors are predicted to occur.

- Later restructurings of adult learner grammars towards the target language result from general mechanisms correctly analysing input data.

The authors find empirical support for these claims in the L2 German word order developmental sequence: that (parametric) lexical learning does not play a role in ASLA is understood to result from the unavailability of the target parametric values of the functional categories COMP and INFL.

On the other hand, given that L2 learners have access to UG, they argue (a) that learner grammars constitute possible languages in terms of UG and (b) that learners may resort to universal principles, which may be realised neither in the L1 nor in the L2, to try to adapt their learner grammar to the target. In other words, language acquisition is claimed to be UG-constrained, yet without the possibility of parameter resetting, as this would require access to the Functional Module.[89]
According to Tsimpli and Roussou these considerations are also borne out by their data of learners with a pro-drop L1 (Romance/Greek) acquiring a non-pro-drop L2 (English), which leads them to conclude that resetting of the pro-drop parameter is not possible.

Roughly, the data show that the L2 grammar allows for null subjects, especially expletive null subjects, and that-t violations, contrary to what is allowed in English. On the other hand, postverbal subjects are correctly excluded:

- According to Tsimpli and Roussou overt pronouns may identify null subjects as a result of a re-analysis of pronouns as agree-

---

[89] It is only fair to point out that an explanation of ASLA facts along these lines - yet within the traditional PP model - has also been considered by Clahsen and Muysken (1989). Clahsen and Muysken arrive at this conclusion after acknowledging compelling evidence from other studies that adult learner grammars conform to universal principles not subject to parametrisation. Roughly, the argument runs as follows: UG acts as a learning device in two ways. On one hand, UG provides a set of universal principles that hold cross-linguistically. Knowledge based on these principles may be accessed via the L1 in ASLA. On the other hand, UG consists of a set of parameterised options pertaining to language-specific grammatical properties. This latter part of the language acquisition device is claimed to be lacking in adulthood insofar as neither parameter-setting nor parameter-resetting is possible in adult language acquisition.

ment elements in AGR.[90] On the other hand, as null expletive elements need not be identified in pro-drop languages overt agreement features are not required.

- As for null subjects in the learner L2 system, it is argued that these are PROs occupying the specifier position of the TP.[91, 92] This latter property of the L2 is claimed to result from UG.

Clearly, Tsimpli and Roussou's model for ASLA is a more restrictive hypothesis of development and form of L2 learner systems. As opposed to the FDH[93] this is a hypothesis which attempts to define ASLA within the UG framework. Differences between L1A and ASLA are accounted for by a selective dysfunction - i.e. non-accessibility or non-availability - of one of the UG modules.

At first sight, the idea of correlating differences between child and adult acquisition with the dysfunction of one linguistic module may seem attractive because it is in line with present concepts of the modular nature of the human language faculty. Note further that similar considerations have been put forward with respect to pathologically motivated language disorders (cf. Ouhalla 1992, Grewendorf 1991). Roughly, agrammatical speech has been characterised as lacking functional categories and, in this way, resembling early child speech (cf. VP-hypothesis above). As a consequence, agrammatism also is understood to follow from the dysfunction of the Functional Module.

These correlations, however, face a number of problems. Note first that FCs are believed to be absent in agrammatical speech but not in ASLA. Recall that under Tsimpli and Roussou's analysis adult L2 learners have access to the FCs realised in their mother tongue, as the L1 structure is adopted in the L2 learner grammar. Now, the question to answer in this respect is: why do different implications follow from what in both cases is assumed to be the *loss* of the Functional Module?

---

[90] As Tsimpli and Roussou claim that there is no access to the Functional Module in ASLA, they argue that the re-analysis is a product of a strategy imposed on the learner grammar which is based upon L1 knowledge.

[91] In order for PRO to be ungoverned, the absence of Agreement is required. Only in this case will PRO lack a governing category which makes it possible for PRO to refer to an antecedent in the (discourse) context.

[92] Tsimpli and Roussou's account of that-t violations will not be discussed here. Roughly, learner errors are accounted for by the assumption that learners take over the mother tongue value of the Proper Government parameter.

[93] This applies to the general claims underlying the Fundamental Difference Hypothesis and not to the considerations put forward in Clahsen and Muysken (1989) as mentioned in footnote 89.

There is overall agreement in that the presence of the Functional Module is necessary for full language competence to be at work. Yet, how the Functional Module comes into play (= L1A), remains as part of the universal competence (= steady state) or is lost later - either as a source (= ASLA) or as a part of full competence (= agrammatism), is far from clear. In addition to these problems there is the question of how structural transfer or multilingual competence should be conceived of.

Note that it seems quite implausible to postulate various Functional Modules for the acquisition of various languages. It is also questionable to assume that the Functional Module becomes language-specific in the course of child language acquisition.
In other words, in order to maintain the assumption that adults have access to the functional categories realised in their mother tongue only, we have to reconsider the role of the Functional Module in the *steady state* of mother tongue knowledge.[94]

As it stands, the no-functional-module-argument for ASLA seems to imply that learners simply *relexify* their mother tongue structure. But how can it be that functional categories are "relexified" without taking into consideration their target-like grammatical properties?
Again, only if there was a satisfactory theory of lexical learning, could the ASLA specific failure be appropriately explained and the circularity of the no-functional-module-argument be avoided.
Tsimpli and Roussou do not address this issue. Yet they make an interesting claim when answering the question of how transferred structural knowledge may interact with UG and the L2 input. Contrary to other approaches (cf. Felix 1991, Schwartz 1991) UG consultation is not claimed to be random but rather determined by the *internal* properties of the learner system, i.e. it is assumed that learners may consult UG in order to make their system conform to universal constraints. In this way Tsimpli and Roussou draw attention to the relevance of grammar-internal mechanisms in language development.
We will see in chapter 7 that we need to reconsider the traditional concept of learning underlying the PP model. There I will show that the search for exclusively *external* (lexical or syntactic) triggers has to be given up in favour of an analysis of (UG constrained) *system-internal dynamics*.

---

[94] Note that a similar argument pertains to the assumption that adult learners may only access universal principles realised in their mother tongue. Somehow, considerations along these lines seem to imply that mother tongue knowledge is UG knowledge "frozen" into the form of a particular language. In many ways, this idea goes against the main tenets of the UG theory, i.e. UG is part of the steady state.

Tsimpli and Roussou still keep to the traditional concept of trigger, assuming that this is not valid in ASLA. Consequently, we are faced with contradictory claims regarding language development in ASLA. The prediction that "adaptions" of the L1 structure towards the L2 structure are UG-constrained is inconsistent with the more general assumption put forward with respect to the overall L2 development. Consider the following statement:

> "At the more advanced stages of L2 learning, where the L2 learner seems to adopt the correct parametric choice we will assume that this is the result of general learning mechanisms correctly analyzing the input data." (op. cit.: 152)

Unfortunately, no further specification of these latter mechanisms is given.[95]

It is thus unclear, why on the one side UG together with the L1 structure should account for the accommodation of PLD during the initial stages and on the other hand this interrelation should not guide the overall development and eventually lead to the target-like specification of functional categories.

In view of the fact that the authors do not analyse data of later stages their conclusions are speculative. Tsimpli and Roussou's position seems to be conditioned by the fact that access to the Functional Module in ASLA is excluded *a priori*. Their hypothesis suffers from the same problem as the FDH in that both claim that later grammars develop towards a kind of *L2 surrogate*. But, how should such a learner system be differentiated from one in which parameter resetting has actually taken place?[96]

In my view, such questions point to the necessity of reconsidering the traditional idea of parameter setting and, as mentioned above, of triggering. We will see in chapter 7 that this is much more necessary in the light of recent research in the domains of child language acquisition and of language change.

---

[95] Again, Tsimpli and Roussou's analysis agrees with Clahsen and Muysken's (1989). The latter claim that language development towards a further "resemblance" to the target is a result of cumulative learning rather than universally determined restructurings in child language acquisition.

[96] As pointed out in section 4.2 a hypothesis starting out with the assumption that parameter values are accessible in ASLA is more amenable to empirical testing because it is falsifiable. The alternative hypothesis is not: if parameter-(re-)setting is excluded a priori, changes in the learner system must be explained differently. In view of these considerations the assumption of a critical period pertaining to the Functional Module should only be considered if all other explanations fail to account for the empirical data.

Before, however, I will discuss current hypotheses which are based on the assumption that the Functional Module is present in ASLA.

6.3 Structure-building or restructuring in ASLA: The Initial State Debate

As opposed to the cognitivist account provided within the framework of the FDH (see section 3.3), Du Plessis et al.'s (1987) analysis initiated a research paradigm which has sought to show (a) that adult learner grammars conform to the constraints imposed by UG, and (b) that adult learner grammars, which are initially determined by the L1 grammar, develop towards the target L2 norm.
Recent studies in this framework have focused on the question of whether the structural properties of the L1 are fully or only partially transferred at the beginning of ASLA (thus the term *Initial State Debate*, cf. Eubank and Schwartz 1996). Consider, for example, Du Plessis et al. (1987) as well as Tomaselli and Schwartz (1990)[97] who affirm that adult learners with a Romance L1 start out with the underlying word order SIVO as a result of the L1 grammar defining the starting point of ASLA. Under this hypothesis, which we may term the *Full Transfer View*, ASLA is characterised by a number of *restructuring* processes of the pregiven L1 grammar, such as the resetting of parametric properties associated with FCs.
Vainikka and Young-Scholten (1994, 1995, 1996a, 1996b), on the other hand, claim that learners start out with L1 determined lexical projections only and that further *structure-building* will occur upon evidence in the L2 input. Thus they assume that the *Weak Continuity Hypothesis* applies also in ASLA (we will term this assumption the *Gradual Development View*).

We can see already that the determination of the initial state in ASLA is closely tied to the explanation of subsequent L2-*development*. So the denotation of *Initial State Debate* is somewhat misleading because it concentrates on one aspect of a discussion which is, in my view, primarily concerned with the account of how adult learners proceed on their way towards the L2 target. We shall now deal with the key elements of the debate.

---

[97] Cf. also Schwartz and Sprouse (1994), Müller (1993) and Eubank (1996).

6.3.1 The Full Transfer View

As we saw in section 5.2.3 proponents of the Strong Continuity Hypothesis claim that processes associated with FCs are in place from the very beginning. We can recall that one of the problems of this hypothesis is that it ignores the learnability problem associated with the parametric properties of the allegedly fully-fledged initial structure tree. Grammatical processes related to Germanic V2, for example, require that FCs be provided with some language-specific information which cannot be part of the initial state.

As we shall see next, the application of the Strong Continuity Hypothesis to ASLA raises similar questions. We may anticipate, however, that in ASLA the issue is more complex. Consider, for example, the assumption that in carrying over their fully-fledged L1 grammar adult learners make full use of it from the beginning. If this were the case we would expect universal constraints to apply and, in addition, language-specific properties. Consequently, we would predict that, for a certain period of time, adult learners simply "fill" their mother tongue syntax with L2 lexical elements irrespective of their L2-specific morpho-syntactic properties. But, when and how do learners restructure their L1 determined syntax? In what follows I will review some of the proposals made in this respect.

The assumption that adult learners make use of their full L1 grammar has been backed up by the empirical finding that verb raising is productive in the acquisition of L2 German from the beginning. The problem, however, is that this process seems to operate with a restricted set of verbs only. The relevant evidence concerns verb placement asymmetries in sequences with adverbs and negation elements (cf. Du Plessis et al. 1987, Tomaselli and Schwartz 1990, Eubank 1996).

Du Plessis et al. (1987) as well as Tomaselli and Schwartz (1990) point out that two different word order patterns occur in sequences with negation, namely (a) preverbal negation with main verbs and (b) postverbal negation with modal and auxiliary verbs, cf.

(1)   ich   nix   komme   in   Spanie
       I   nothing   come   in   Spain

'I don't come from Spain'

(Clahsen 1990b: 147, his transl.)

(2)   ich   kann   nich   eine   sache   machen
       I   can   not   a   thing   do

'I cannot do a [particular] thing'

(ibid.: 148, his transl.)

Tomaselli and Schwartz (1990) point out that the preverbal position of negators in the Romance L1 results from the fact that the negator is base-generated as a clitic in I, cliticising to the verb after this has moved into INFL. Thus the preverbal position of the negator with main verbs (cf. (1)) comes as no surprise. Postverbal negation with modal and auxiliary verbs (cf. (2)), however, is not expected.
According to Clahsen (1990b) the L2 negation data of this stage show that the L1-carry-over assumption cannot be maintained because "... *the system of Phase I cannot be just a relexification of the learner's L1 grammar.*" (op. cit.: 149). Instead, he takes these data as further evidence against UG-based analyses of ASLA.[98]
Tomaselli and Schwartz (1990), however, call for a more precise analysis of L1 Romance negation and the grammatical processes available at the beginning of ASLA. They argue that the Romance grammar provides a further position for the lexical negator left to the VP (cf. (3)). According to them this position is necessary for Romance discontinuous negative elements (e.g. Italian 'non ... mica', *not ... never*).

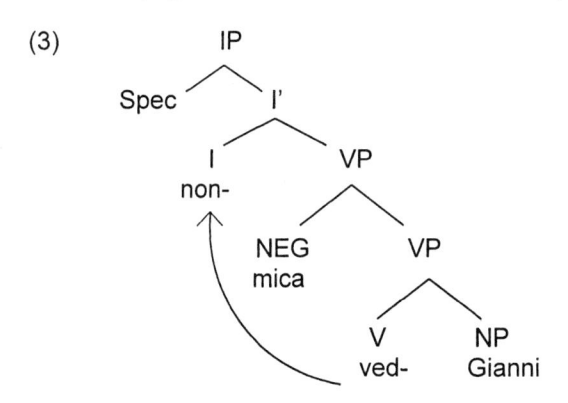

(3)

```
            IP
           /  \
        Spec   I'
              / \
             I   VP
           non- / \
              NEG  VP
              mica / \
                  V   NP
                 ved- Gianni
```

(Io) non   vedo   mica   Gianni.
(I)   not   see-I never John

'I never see John'

(ibid.: 9, their transl.)

---

[98] Clahsen (1984) adopts a different position. He stresses the similarity between child LA and adult SLA with respect to the development of negation:
"Some recent findings on the acquisition of German as a first language show that the sequence postulated above even holds for this acquisitional type, thus suggesting that the three stages can be said to represent general properties of the acquisition of German negation (...) It is most decisive that the children, similarly to the L2 learners, cannot initially separate the negator from the verb." (op. cit.: 237)

On the basis of this analysis Tomaselli and Schwartz assume that the verb placement asymmetry observed is the result of the learners not yet analysing the L2 main verb morphology. Unanalysed main verb forms are base-gerenated in V at this stage.[99] As there is no inflectional material in I main verbs do not raise to INFL (cf. also Eubank 1992),[100] the clitic negator has nothing to cliticise to and the sister-to-VP option is left as the position where NEG is base-generated.
Conversely, postverbal negation with non-thematic verbs proves that these verbs move to INFL. Tomaselli and Schwartz (1990) believe that non-thematic verbs are attracted to I due to their semantic properties. According to Eubank (1992) the asymmetry observed with respect to verb raising is due to the initial lack of a particular kind of language-specific information. Eubank starts from the premise that the functional projections in the L1-determined grammar are devoid of their morphologically-driven specification of associated features, i.e. AGR is only specified as [X-strong] and T as [X-tense] (cf. (4)).

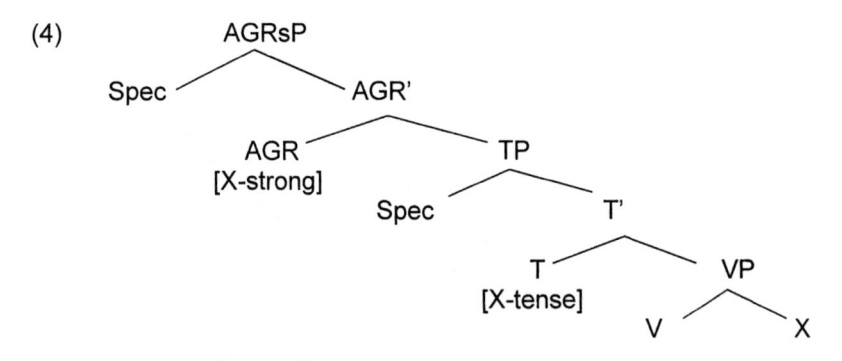

(4)
```
        AGRsP
       /     \
     Spec    AGR'
            /    \
          AGR    TP
       [X-strong]/  \
                Spec T'
                    / \
                   T   VP
               [X-tense] / \
                        V   X
```

According to Eubank the attested asymmetry with regard to verb movement respects the basic assumption that unspecified features classify along with the negative value of the feature in question.
Eubank's analysis assumes (*pace* Chomsky 1989, Pollock 1989) that verb movement is constrained by the Theta Criterion and further, that

---

[99] A similar phenomenon has been acknowledged in agrammatic speech by Ouhalla (1992), whereby the UG conformity of these forms is stressed:
"The presence of the agreement and case elements is forced by a conspiracy between the morphological requirements of the stem forms in the languages in question and the principle of UG which ensures morphological well-formedness." (ibid.: 16)

[100] Most of the traditional (non-UG based) analyses (cf. Klein 1986, Rieck 1989, Köpcke 1987) dealing with ASLA agree on the assumption that the early verbs are unanalysed forms, which do not correlate with the sentence subject on either semantic or grammatical grounds.

strong agreement is transparent to theta-role assigment as opposed to *weak* agreement. Verb movement into [X-strong] AGR at this stage will only be allowed for non-thematic verbs. Similarly, only non-thematic verbs move to the unspecified [X-tense].[101]

Eubank's conclusion that learners differentiate between the L1 properties they transfer needs to be substantiated. Why are the headedness values of FCs transferred and not the morphologically-driven feature specifications? Is this analysis valid irrespective of the L1-L2 constellation? According to Eubank the under-specification of functional projections results from the learner not yet having acquired the relevant *L2-specific* morphological information. If the initial L2 structure tree were designed as a *default structure* this would be plausible considering that target-like feature specifications *of any kind* occur only later, i.e. upon evidence in the input. But the structure tree Eubank assumes to be part of the initial state in ASLA is the L1 structure tree which is already provided with L1-specific information like headedness values for the projections in question. Eubank[102] seems to imply that learners disregard a particular kind of L1-specific information of functional projections because they *know* (a) that this information is language-specific and (b) that its determination depends on the target inflectional morphology they have not yet acquired. It is unclear, however, why this procedure is not applied in the case of other parameterised properties of the L1-grammar. Why do learners carry over the headedness values of functional projections but not their feature specification? This is even more surprising in view of Eubank's assumption that the eventual target-like specification of functional projections is concurrent to the resetting of their headedness values (see below).

We will turn our attention now to the account of the later stages of L2 German acquisition. Du Plessis et al. (1987) and Tomaselli and Schwartz (1990) agree that *Germanic V2* (see section 2.6) becomes firmly established after the implementation of VP final (which takes place at their *stage II*). Accordingly the *inversion effect* acknowledged in the utterances produced at (their) *stage III* (cf. (5) - (7)) results from the movement of some maximal constituent into SpecCOMP and concurrent verb-movement into empty COMP through INFL.

---

[101] Note that Eubank does not go into the details of negation in Romance (clitic negator vs. lexical negator, see Tomaselli and Schwartz 1990) but rather assumes that NEG is base-generated to the left of VP. This analysis is not uncontroversial, cf. Grewendorf (1990).

[102] Insofar as Tomaselli and Schwartz (1990) also propose a differentiation in terms of difficulty in the (lexical) filling of *functional* as opposed to lexical structure, the following considerations also pertain to their analysis.

(5) französisch kann ich auch noch heute (Pepe S.)
    French can I also still today
    'I still know French today'

(6) was lernt man in der literatur? (Maria S.)
    what learns one in the literature
    'what do you learn from literature'

(7) jetzt kann sie mir eine frage machen (Pietro I.)
    now can she me-dat. a question make
    'now you can ask me'
    (CMP 1983: 141, my transl.)

Eubank (1992), however, addresses the optional character of non-subject V2 at this stage. In his data he can identify the coexistence of ADV-V-S and Adv-S-V orders as well as verb-initial sequences. In view of this evidence he suggests that it is premature to conclude that learners have acquired the underlying processes of target V2.[103]

Eubank's findings are lent further support by previous research undertaken in Clahsen (1984). Clahsen pointed out that the relative order of acquisition of the so-called *permutation rules* INVERSION, PARTICLE and ADV-VP is not clear-cut. He further observed that the acquisition PARTICLE required less time than the acquisition of INVERSION, the acquisition of this rule proceeding only very slowly for some learners. Therefore he concluded that some learners initially acquire a "*preliminary version of the rule*" (ibid.: 228). Moreover, as pointed out by Clahsen (1984), CMP (1983) and Eubank (1992) the production of inverted structures co-varies with verb-initial utterances, in which the verb appears in sentence-initial position before the subject, which may either follow the verb as in (8) - (9) or appear sentence-finally as in (10).

(8) bin ich ein bißchen lang draus geblieben
    am I a bit long outside stayed
    'I stayed outside for quite some time'
    (CMP 1983: 142, my transl.)

---

[103] Under the analysis of Du Plessis et al. (1987) ADV-S-V sequences result from the adjunction parameter not having been set to the target value yet. If the adjunction parameter had been reset at this stage, fronting should only be possible through movement to SpecCP. Du Plessis et al. thus conclude that the adjunction parameter is reset at a later point, if at all.

(9) darf   er   auch noch nich in ne   firma   komm
    may   he   also yet   not   in an   enterprise come
    'he shall not yet get into an enterprise either'
    (ibid.: 142, my transl.)

(10) wohne   hier   viele Ausländer
     live   here   many   foreigners
     'many foreigners live here'
     (Clahsen 1984: 225, my transl.)

In some ways this evidence goes against the original idea of a clear-cut implicational scale which would account for more or less discrete acquisitional stages. As for the *inversion effect* acknowledged it seems that target-like and target-deviant forms coexist. Whatever the nature of the L2 grammar at this stage, we reckon that it is neither exclusively L1-determined anymore nor is it the L2 grammar. We may restate these observations in terms of *stability* and *instability*: the rather *stable* L1-determined initial grammar has turned into a rather *unstable* grammar in which alternative options coexist. Somehow it is *inbetween*. But these are concepts in the tenor of a more dynamic learning theory I will discuss in chapter 7. Here we are faced with the question of how proponents of the Full Transfer View cope with the data in question.

Eubank's (1992, 1994) account of the coexistence of both AdvSVO and AdvVSO orders as well as verb-initial sequences (VAdvSO) is as follows. According to Eubank (1992) the presence of perfect tense forms suggests that the feature under T is no longer unspecified. Thus he assumes that all verbs move to T. On the other hand he claims that subject-verb agreement morphology is not productive (with main verbs) yet. So it is unclear why thematic verbs should move to T at all. Furthermore, verb raising past the subject is not expected to occur if AGR is still unspecified.

Eubank considers the possibility that learners may identify the notion *uniformity* or *strength*[104] of verb inflection before they identify inflectional affixes per se

> "... and therefore exhibit the syntactic consequences of this recognition before the relevant inflectional material is observable in the acquisition data."
> (ibid.: 238)

---

[104] Cf. Jaeggli and Safir (1989).

It is unclear, however, how learners may recognise the syntactic consequences of verbal inflection by means of inflection elements without making consistent use of these elements. Consider Eubank's statements in this respect:

> "If an acquisition mechanism is to "strip" affixes from a stem, then it must presumably have some reason to do so. It follows, then, that the mechanism must first identify the criteria; in other words, it may, in fact, identify some notion like "uniformity" or "strength" even before the affixes have been identified *per se*. (...) José begins to recognize that there is a relationship between the various forms of the verbs and types of subjects. What one might expect here is that, depending on the exact hypothesis entertained at any one time, AGRo may sometimes carry the strong feature and at other times the weak feature. (...) What has not been determined at this stage is that the agreement relationship involves affixation. (...) The variation in the placement of thematic verbs would thus follow from José's attempt to determine the agreement relation."
> (ibid.: 238)

The apparent optionality of inversion is thus understood to be the result of AGR sometimes carrying the *strong* feature and sometimes the *weak* feature.[105] According to Eubank, subject-verb inversion may occur only in the former case. In Adv-SVO sequences, however, the verb moves only to T because AGR is *weak*.

We may restate Eubank's assumptions in terms of verb raising being dependent on the status of the verb form involved. What we do not know is whether the word order alternation is observed with the same verb (neither does Eubank explicitly remark that this was not the case). If both patterns were observed with the same verb, we would have to assume that the learner makes the respective choice depending on the status of the verb form in question. But Eubank implies that the alternation does not correlate with a difference in the verb endings (with or without agreement affixes) but rather with a variation regarding the specification of AGR. It is unclear how such a specification should only partly occur, if the specification refers to the morphological uniformity or strength of the verb in question.

According to Eubank (1992) the relationship between verb suffixes and subject-verb concord is established at a later stage (his *stage 3*), which

---

[105] In Eubank (1994) the optionality of inversion is related to the fact that the verbs have not yet been specified to <+tns>. Thus only when tense is acquired (which Eubank claims to become apparent with the appearance of preterite forms and not, as he did before, with perfect tense forms) verb raising is assumed to be obligatory.

is why the L2-grammar eventually undergoes a radical reorganisation along the following lines:

"The changes (...) are an indirect result of "stripping" the affixes from the finite verbs. Once this is accomplished, the learners are in a position to recognize that clause-final finite verbs in embedded clauses are, in fact, instantiations of AGRsP and TP. The result is that they adjust the headedness of both projections to head-final and therefore utilize the head of CP as a clause-initial landing site for the finite verb."
(ibid.: 240)

However, Eubank concedes that this analysis does not explain why verb-initial utterances increase at this point where inversion seems to have become obligatory. Do learners still lack the knowledge that verb raising must go along with the topicalisation of some XP into the specifier position of the position where V has been moved to?

All in all it seems Eubank is too preoccupied with his aim of proving that the *Lexical Learning Hypothesis* (whereby the acquisition of agreement morphology, verb raising and Germanic V2 should be acquired simultaneously) also applies in ASLA, if only in a somewhat delayed form. In doing so he ignores the possibility that L1-determined and L2-determined constraints on verb raising may coexist for a certain time in the L2 grammar in the form of alternating AdvSVO and AdvVSO orders. We may also have to consider the availability of the nominative case-checking mechanisms responsible for the generation of verb-subject sequences and placement-asymmetries resulting thereof, i.e. VOS *vs.* VSO orders.

In concluding, we may go back to our remarks at the beginning of this section. We anticipated the intricate learnability problem following from the assumption that adult learners carry over their full L1 grammar. The developmental process outlined in the preceding paragraphs restates the intricacy of the problem proponents of the Full Transfer View are faced with: in some areas the L1 grammar serves as the basis for L2 learning, in others this is not the case. Explanations for this differentiation are, however, not offered. Similarly, the reasons for the optional status of some phenomena which arises in the course of the L2 development and which is given up at a later stage remain vague.

Eubank's empirical research, however, is in itself important as his contradictory findings cannot be packaged in a neat succession of stages. I will comment on similar findings in my analysis of the L2 German of an adult Italian learner in chapter 8. And I will also show how L1 and L2 properties may sometimes converge and at other times possibly compete. We will see why we should leave aside the unfruitful dichotomy of lexical as opposed to syntactic learning to concentrate on a more dynamic understanding of the processes involved in grammar development.

6.3.2 The Gradual Development View

According to Vainikka and Young-Scholten (1994, 1995, 1996a, 1996b) ASLA is primarily determined by *structure-building*. Consequently, mother tongue influence is understood to play only a minor role in the development of the L2 grammar, i.e. the only L1-determined parametric property transferred is the headedness of the VP.

This assumption is related to Vainikka and Young-Scholten's claim that grammatical processes related to functional projections are lacking in the initial stage: auxiliaries, modals and the agreement paradigm being missing as well as complementisers and processes related to the CP such as wh-movement. In other words, in line with the VP- or Small-Clause Hypothesis (see section 5.1.2) the initial L2 grammar only consists of a VP. As opposed to this hypothesis, however, proponents of the *Weak Continuity Hypothesis* claim that functional projections develop gradually through the interaction of the input and X-bar theory (see section 5.2.3).

The authors find empirical support for their claim in the early data of adult learners of L2 German with Turkish or Romance L1. Vainikka and Young-Scholten observe that (a) early utterances only consist of a VP and (b) the headedness of the VP is determined by the mother tongue value. Their analysis reveals that in the data of learners with Turkish L1 60 % of the utterances are verb final (cf. (11) - (13)) at stage I.

(11) Hier   Jacke   ausmachen.   (Changsu #150)
     here   jacket   off.make

'here (you) took (your) jacket off.'

(12) Teekanne   die   Ofen   setzen.   (Aysel #24)
     teapot   the   oven   put

'(I) put the teapot (on) the stove.'

(13) Eine   Katze   Fisch   alle   essen.   (Changsu #150)
     a   cat   fish   entire   eat

'A cat ate the entire fish.'

(Vainikka and Young-Scholten 1994: 280, their transl.)

By contrast, early utterances of learners with a Romance L1 follow the SVO pattern indicating that the VP is head-initial. It is worth mentioning in this context that the contrast pointed out, i.e. L1-related initial L2 word order, goes against traditional cognitivist proposals. Recall that proponents of the Fundamental Difference Hypothesis found support for the validity of Operating Principles such as the COS (*Canonical Order Strategy*, see section 1.2.3) in the finding that adult learners of L2 German produce SVO order irrespective of whether this order was the basic order in their L1. It seems the empirical data deserved further scrutiny!

According to Vainikka and Young-Scholten, the absence of L1-determined functional projections in subsequent development as well as the similarities among learners with different L1s requires "*an explanation other than transfer of functional projections*" (Vainikka and Young-Scholten 1996a: 147).

In view of their finding that functional projections emerge successively they argue in favour of the Weak Continuity approach to ASLA, i.e. "*higher functional projections develop through the interaction of X-bar Theory with the input*" (Vainikka and Young-Scholten 1996b: 13).

Turning to the details of their analysis we can see that they claim that the resetting of the L1-determined VP-headedness, in case it differs from the L2, occurs already during the initial *VP-stage*. This assumption is based on empirical data of learners with a Romance L1 (cf. (14) - (17)).

(14) Ich immer nur eine Tag in de Woche gucken.
 I always only one day in the week look*-fin
 (Jose/5)
 'I always look one day in the week only.'

(15) Vielleicht Schule essen. (Salvatore/6)
 maybe school eat*-fin
 'Maybe (he/she) eats at school.'

(16) Ja sechszwanzig Tage arbeite. (Lina/6)
 yes six-twenty days work-1SG/*-fin
 'Yes (I) work(ed) twenty-six days.'

(17) Diese hier Tür zumache. (Antonio)
 this here door close*-fin
 'This (person) here closes the door.'

 (op. cit.: 161, their transl.)

According to Vainikka and Young-Scholten these four speakers with a Romance L1 produce a head-final VP at least 70% of the time. Note that this time lag in the production of head-final VPs is the only difference Vainikka and Young-Scholten find among learners with a different L1.

Subsequent to the VP-stage, Vainikka and Young-Scholten observe the emergence of an *underspecified* head-initial functional projection FP. The underspecification of this projection is related to absence of subject-verb agreement morphology (as a consequence agreement is ruled out as a trigger for verb raising, see section 6.3.3) and the optionality of subjects and of verb-raising. The availability of FP allows for the base-generation of auxiliaries and modals. The following utterances (all of them of learners with Romance L1) are quoted for further illustration of their findings.

(18) Mehr Deutsch lerne. (Maria)
more German learn-1SG/*-fin
'(I) learn more German.'

(19) Un dann nachher kommen die Sonne
and then afterwards come*-fin the sun
nochmal wieder.
yet again
(Maria)
'And then afterwards the sun comes out yet again.'

(20) Un anfang zu regnen. (Maria)
and begin to rain*-fin
'And (it) begins to rain.'

(21) Die Leute gucken sie mir so traurig.
the people look-1PL they me so sad
(Agapita)
'The people look at me so sad.'

(22) Un hier komm eine Junge mit eine Puppen
and here come-*1SG a boy with a doll
in de Hand. (Nieves)
in the hand
'And here comes a boy with a doll in his hand.'

(23) Ich geh immer in Winter. (Maria)
I go-1SG always in winter
'I always go in winter.'

(24) Gut mach ich ihm eine Cappuccino mit
good make-1SG I him a cappuccino with

    alles   voll.
    everything full
                                                    (Jose/7)
    'I make him a cappuccino with everything full.'
    (op. cit.: 167/169, their transl.)

At this stage processes which could be related to the CP are still rare. Utterances like (25) - (27), however, are analysed by Vainikka and Young-Scholten without resorting to a full CP analysis, i.e. they assume that the "*wh-phrase may remain in the subject position*" (ibid.: 171).

(25)   Wo   kenn?   (Agapita)
         where   meet-*1SG

         'Where (did you) meet (him)?'

(26)   Aber wann komm   einemal   (Jose/7)
         but   when come-*1SG a time

         'But when (subject) comes once...'

(27)   Und   wenn sie   alleine   kommen...   (Nieves)
         and   if   she   alone   come-fin

         'And if she comes alone...'
    (op. cit.: 171, their transl.)

Note that the implementation of a head-initial underspecified functional projection FP is argued to proceed similarly in child and in adult language acquisition. Therefore, Vainikka and Young-Scholten disregard the possibility that this functional projection is the result of mother tongue influence. Instead they argue that the projection of the FP results from the interaction between X-bar theory and the German input. The same holds at the subsequent stage (their *AGRP-stage*) where verb raising becomes obligatory concurrent to the re-analysis of FP as AGRP, which is still head-initial.

Unfortunately, the authors do not discuss the question of how learners acquire target-like word order in embedded clauses (i.e. the crucial *V2 asymmetry*, see section 2.6). It seems they did not find any relevant evidence for complex structures in their data (but see (27)). In view of the V2-asymmetry representing one of the decisive learnability tasks in the acquisition of German and the alleged L1 influence especially in the domain of subordinate clauses Vainikka and Young-Scholten's analysis suffers from a crucial shortcoming.

Another weakness of Vainikka and Young-Scholten's analysis is that it remains unresolved which mechanisms actually play a role in verb raising (optionally past the subject). Some of the sequences quoted above, which are intended as evidence for an underspecified functional projection do indeed suggest that the mechanisms for inversion are in place. The relevant sequences are repeated here for further illustration, cf.

(21)　Die Leute **gucken sie** mir so traurig.

(22)　Un hier **komm eine Junge** mit eine Puppen in de Hand.

(24)　Gut **mach ich** ihm eine Cappuccino mit alles voll.

(21) is an interesting case in point. The fact that the subject is realised twice (once as a full NP and once pronominally) suggests two possible analyses. Either (a) the pronominal subject is realised as a subject clitic left to the verb or (b) two structural positions are available for subjects to be case-checked. Unless we assume that subjects may be case-checked in SpecVP we would have to assume the availability of two projections FP and XP in the latter case (b).
In any case it is questionable whether utterance (21) belongs to the FP stage, subject-verb agreement being target-like in this case.
Utterances (22) and (24) pose similar problems as we must assume that the verb has been raised past the subject. If nominative case-checking is related to agreement it is unclear how this process may be satisfied by means of an *FP*-structure.
None of these issues are addressed by Vainikka and Young-Scholten. With the exception of (22) the verbs used agree with the subject. Learners may not yet master the full agreement paradigm, but they may already project an agreement phrase where necessary. As argued elsewhere (cf. Eubank 1994 *pace* Jaeggli and Safir 1989) this may already be the case as soon as learners master verb inflection for at least two persons. The optionality of the processes in question may thus have to be explained differently.
In claiming that the optionality of verb raising may result from competition between the former VP and the FP grammar Vainikka and Young-Scholten (1996a) depart from the traditional assumption of *discrete* stages in favour of an analysis based on the notion of "*competing grammars*" (ibid.: 13), cf.

> "Thus what we mean by, i.e. *being at the VP-stage* is that a VP-based grammar is the most robust one for the speaker; however, depending on the point in the development that data collection took place, the grammar of the subsequent stage (say, an IP-based grammar) may compete with the VP grammar."

This assumption, however, is not followed up. It is completely unclear how considerations like these should be compatible with the traditional learning concept underlying the PP model which they still favour (see section 6.3.3). More to the point, if one gives up the idea of discrete stages implicit in the notion of parameter-setting as conceived in the PP model, then one has to reconsider the notion of trigger. In other words, if we want to account for the dynamics underlying the development of learner grammars, then we have to embed our assumptions in the framework of a *dynamic* approach to language which overcomes traditional idealisations such as that of punctual parameter-setting or of triggers which would be valid across learners.

Furthermore, we need to consider the relevance of fossilisation in the data analysed. Recall that Vainikka and Young-Scholten's data collection is a compilation from cross-sectional and longitudinal studies. So at least for the cross-sectional data of learners which had been residing in Germany for quite some years we may speculate whether their respective L2-grammar has fossilised to an extent yet to be determined.

Therefore we have to be cautious with what is defined as a *transitory* learner grammar. What may be such when followed by later restructurings at later stages may as well be a *final* grammar in the absence of later changes. But our determination of such final fossilised grammars cannot be absolute either. What I have in mind is that we cannot know whether such a "final" grammar would not change in the future. We all know that, to a certain extent, this also holds true in language change. We will learn later (chapters 7 and 8) that *stability* is a relative concept and that what looks like an apparently stable state may well be a state at the edge of *instability*. Structure-building and failure to build structure, in ASLA we are faced with the task of explaining both possibilities. If we analyse the conditions under which the former is possible or necessary, we will be in the position of examining lack of success as a consequence of some learner systems not meeting the relevant conditions. Under the traditional PP theory one of the key issues is the determination of the triggers, i.e. *external* data, which are responsible for the system's changes. We could see in the preceding sections that the role of such triggers in ASLA is subject to a controversial debate. What has been ignored so far is the role of the system-internal conditions which need to be met for the relevant changes to take place. Fossilised properties of learner systems show a resistance to change which may as well be based on *internal* reasons.

In the next section we direct our attention towards Vainikka and Young-Scholten's proposals regarding ASLA-specific triggers. Considerations regarding the role of system-internal properties, however, I will discuss in the subsequent chapters.

6.3.3 The assumption of ASLA-specific triggers

Vainikka and Young-Scholten (1995: 5) adopt quite a "*general notion of trigger, namely any element which causes the grammar to be reorganised*". As they adopt the Weak Continuity Hypothesis this concept of trigger intends to embrace not only parameter setting but more general processes of structure-building or, in their terms, of "*tree growth*" (ibid.).
In line with the Functional Parametrisation Hypothesis they assume that parametric variation is allocated to functional elements which appear in functional projections. Functional elements are considered to act as triggers for development.

Vainikka and Young-Scholten conclude that the major difference between ASLA and L1A lies in the nature of the functional elements involved in the triggering of the target structure: while children would first acquire *bound* morphemes related to DP and IP, adults would only begin to master these after they have acquired *free* morphemes related to the functional projections in question.[106] I will discuss the details of their hypothesis following the chronological development they propose.

a. The VP-Stage:

- L1A:
  According to Vainikka and Young-Scholten, children acquire the target-like headedness of the VP by means of the stress pattern associated with the elements inside the VP phrase.[107]

- ASLA:
  As Vainikka and Young-Scholten assume that adult L2 learners filter

---

[106] In this respect they discuss Zobl and Liceras' (1994) findings regarding the review of the morpheme order studies carried out in the 1970s. Recall that these studies also intended to determine the similarities between L1A and ASLA. Zobl and Liceras also acknowledge a difference in the nature of the functional elements acquired first. Regarding the relative order of acquisition of DP and IP, they point out that IP is acquired prior to DP in ASLA whereas the DP precedes the IP in L1A. Zobl and Liceras' conclusion is that this finding further supports the assumption that in ASLA the full mother tongue structure is carried over. Vainikka and Young-Scholten, however, argue that this is no evidence against their structure-building approach to ASLA as no restriction on the relative order of acquisition is provided in syntactic theory.

[107] In this way they intend to solve the paradox implicit in the assumption that the fixing of the VP-headedness is related to the identification of the head-complement relation, which would presuppose that the child has already set the relevant parameter.

the L2 input through their L1 stress system, some other means of determining the VP headedness must be available in ASLA. It is believed that the transferred VP acts as a bootstrap for L2 syntax giving rise to reorganisation as soon as differences between L1 and L2 VP order are realised.

The problem with this analysis is that it restates the head-complement paradox (cf. footnote 107), this time for ASLA. If learners are in the position to "compare" their mother tongue VP order with the VP order of the L2 the alternative value must be available and thus it is unclear why they do not posit the correct order from the beginning.
As to the filtering of the L2 input through the L1 stress system, Vainikka and Young-Scholten do not provide any further specific implications. In the absence of a detailed analysis, however, any conclusion regarding learning theoretic differences between child and adult language acquisition remain speculative.

b. The FP-Stage:

- ASLA:
Vainikka and Young-Scholten argue that in ASLA modals act as triggers of the head of FP - i.e. the position they are base-generated in - rather than of verb raising. They assume that learners discover the option of verb raising upon the implementation of this functional category. As learners do not yet analyse inflectional morphology, verb raising at this stage also involves non-finite verb forms.

- L1A:
Conversely, it is believed that children are able to discover the relationship between agreement morphology and verb raising at the FP-stage. According to Vainikka and Young-Scholten, the first inflectional ending mastered, i.e. -*t*, acts as a trigger for verb raising.

A review of Vainikka and Young-Scholten's argument regarding modals *qua* triggers in ASLA reveals the inconsistency of their argumentation. Consider the following statements:

"A potential trigger for an FP projection is the modal *will* 'want' since it is often the first INFL-related element acquired (in our L2 data). A potential problem exists with modals being a trigger for verb raising: in the input data, modals are relatively less frequent in one of the two possible verb positions, namely the VP-internal position. An English-type analysis of German modals (i.e. base-generated in a functional head) would account for the majority of instances of modals. Thus, it appears that modals cannot function as robust triggers for verb raising in German. On the

129

other hand, modals would suffice as robust triggers for a functional head in which base-generated elements such as modals occur, without verb raising. Once such a functional head has been posited by the learner, the realization that the target language has verb raising becomes possible." (ibid.: 8f.)

This extended quotation illustrates some of the weaknesses of their argumentation. It is completely unclear why learners should posit an English-type analysis of German modals. We may rather conclude that this is an unfortunate *ad-hoc* assumption which is intended to circumvent the problem of explaining why modal verbs appear in a higher projection prior to main verbs. We could as well assume that modal verbs fulfill the finiteness distinction earlier by virtue of being the first tensed elements produced. So we would conclude that the availability of the structural basis for the realisation of the finiteness distinction occurs prior to the implementation of the inflection paradigm. Note that this line of reasoning may also be valid in the case of child LA where the verb ending *-t* is the only finite suffix produced for a certain period of time.

Considerations of this sort remind us of the questionable status of agreement-suffixes as triggers for Germanic V2 (see section 5.2.3). Recall further that the assumption of an underspecified projection FP is far from being unproblematic (see also section 5.2.3).

c. The AGRP-Stage:

- ASLA:
  Vainikka and Young-Scholten assume that the implementation of FP and the related realisation of verb raising allow for the acquisition of the agreement paradigm, which in turn results in the reanalysis of FP as AGRP. The authors believe that the forms of the copular paradigm, which are productive prior to main verb inflection, act as triggers for the acquisition of the agreement paradigm.

- L1A:
  As soon as they have acquired the agreement paradigm children posit a head-final AGRP.

Again, it is unclear to me how the suppletive forms of the German copular paradigm could fulfill the function of triggers for the acquisition of the agreement paradigm. Note that *qua* suppletives the copular forms are unrelated to the regular agreement morphology. At best it could be assumed that these forms undertake a pioneering function regarding the structural distribution of elements marked for agreement (cf. Tracy 1991). Following the Weak Continuity approach this would involve the projection of a functional projection related to agreement and tense.

d. The CP-stage:

- L1A:
  Vainikka and Young-Scholten advance the hypothesis that in L1A object clitics act as triggers for CP and for the recognition that in German complementisers and verbs occupy the same structural position. Object clitics may fulfill this function as they adjoin to C in matrix and embedded clauses.[108]

- ASLA:
  The triggering function of object clitics is ruled out in ASLA as they behave like bound morphemes. According to Vainikka and Young-Scholten complementisers are the trigger for CP in ASLA. Since complementisers are not directly related to verb raising an intermediate stage prior to the implementation of the V2 asymmetry is expected, whereby verbs do raise to the head-initial AGRP in embedded clauses also.

Regarding the triggers for the CP we can see that Vainikka and Young-Scholten do not propose an ASLA-specific trigger which would have similar implications as the L1A-specific trigger.
Leaving aside the question of whether object clitics are really more salient to child L1 learners than to adult L2 learners, what is at issue here again is the structural insight learners have to achieve, i.e. the acquisition of the target V2 asymmetry. The trigger proposed for L1A allegedly fulfills the function of triggering this structural insight which is related to the CP projection.
As for ASLA, however, only a trigger for the CP is considered without going into the details of how learners would reorganise their grammar so as to obey the target V2 asymmetry. Recall that the AGRP is still head-initial in the L2 grammar at this stage. We also know from other studies that SVO order in embedded clauses is quite commonly produced by adult learners of L2 German. So the question of how learners eventually achieve to produce target-like SOV embedded clauses is of crucial importance.

---

[108] The following sequences are given for further illustration of this phenomenon (op. cit.: 10, their translation):
  (i)   Ulrike kauft's   heute   in   der Stadt.
         Ulrike buy-3SG + it   today   in   the city
         'Ulrike is buying it today in the city'
  (ii)   Er fragte,   ob's   Ulrike heute   in   der Stadt   kauft.
         he ask-PAST/3SG   if + it   Ulrike today   in   the city   buy-3SG
         'He asked if Ulrike is buying it today in the city'

In concluding this brief overview of Vainikka and Young-Scholten's ASLA-specific triggers we may question their statement that in ASLA only free morphemes may function as triggers. Following this reasoning, the authors seem to be engaged in a somewhat "desparate" seek of free morphemes which could fulfill a similar function as bound morphemes in child LA. In doing so, however, Vainikka and Young-Scholten run into many conceptual and empirical problems they cannot solve.

Furthermore, if we take into account the problematic status of the triggers proposed for L1A, we can see that we are faced again with the shortcomings of the Lexical Learning Hypothesis. Recall that this hypothesis invokes a causal relationship between the acquisition of certain lexical items and structure-building and related parametric properties. However, the uni-directionality of this causal relationship needs to be questioned as it ignores the complex inter-relation of the different linguistic levels involved.

We will keep these considerations in mind and reconsider Vainikka and Young-Scholten's assumption that differences between L1A and ASLA result essentially from a difference in the nature of the triggers (bound morphemes vs. free morphemes). This in turn would be related to a critical period concerning the processing of complex morphology responsible for adults processing bound morphology in some other way than unimpaired children.[109]

Unfortunately, Vainikka and Young-Scholten do not expand on the predictions derivable from their assumptions. Does the critical period apply to all learners? If this is the case, then the successful processing of complex morphology in ASLA is ruled out. But, the authors acknowledge the acquisition of agreement morphology in ASLA, however delayed. Certainly, we have to account for individual differences but this is exactly what the assumption of a critical period cannot accomplish.

More to the point, we may restate the problems with Vainikka and Young-Scholten's analysis by asking whether the rapid and successful mastering of L2-morphology necessarily implies a successful acquisition of L2-syntax. There are many (obvious) reasons for why this statement cannot be taken at face value.

In this context it will be of interest to consider *Christopher* and some of his remarkable abilities...

---

[109] Interestingly, the authors also refer to the findings concerning language disorders in child language acquisition, which, as they claim, also involve morphosyntactic deficiencies.

6.3.4 Modularity revisited

There are a number of theoretical and empirical problems indicating that morphological properties alone "*are inadequate to characterize notions of 'strong' and 'weak' triggers in an account of language acquisition*" (Smith and Tsimpli 1995: 26). The original idea that the absence of functional categories correlates with the absence of their morphological realisation (cf. Radford 1990, among others) needs some revision in the light of the findings concerning the acquisition of languages with a rich morphology such as Greek and Spanish. The relevant empirical evidence suggests that (a) agreement morphology is available as soon as the first verb forms appear and (b) that aspectual distinctions in a number of learner grammars are marked in a similar way as in the adult grammars (cf. Smith and Tsimpli 1995).

In view of this evidence, do we have to conclude that Greek and Spanish children posit functional projections related to the functional elements they produce from the beginning? In such a case, we would have to dismiss any hypothesis which aims at being valid cross-linguistically, as, for example, the Maturation Hypothesis.

Smith and Tsimpli (1995) raise two further crucial questions related to the alleged triggering effect of rich morphology, namely

> "Is it a universal rule that rich morphology has particular syntactic consequences or is it the case that variation in syntactic terms is not necessarily reflected in morphological properties? (...) Further, should we expect languages like English, with almost non-existent agreement morphology, to exhibit patterns of acquisition parallel to those of morphologically similar but syntactically distinct languages?"
> (op. cit.: 26)

Smith and Tsimpli's rejection of the presupposed correlation between morphology and syntax is related to their claim that "*functional categories, on the one hand, and their morphological realization, on the other, belong to independent components of the grammar*" (op. cit.: 27). In other words, the development of the components need not occur concurrently. Furthermore, they assume that the morphological component constitutes an *interface level* responsible for the morphological realisation of both functional and substantive elements. At this level, concepts and conceptual structure are mapped onto words and the argument structure in a given language is assigned.

On the basis of these considerations Smith and Tsimpli analysed the linguistic behaviour of Christopher, a linguistic savant, who

> "... is institutionalized because he is unable to look after himself; he has difficulty in finding his way around; he has poor hand-eye co-ordination,

turning many everday tasks such as shaving or doing up buttons into a burdensome chore; but he can read, write and communicate in any of fifteen to twenty languages."
(ibid.: 1)

As regards the details of Christopher's medical and psychological profile, Tsimpli and Smith point out that Christopher was diagnosed as brain-damaged at the age of six weeks. At the age of twenty he was diagnosed as "*possibly having hydrocephalic brain damage and severe neurological impairment of his motor co-ordination, amounting to apraxia*" (O'Connor and Hermelin 1991: 675, quoted in ibid.: 4). However, the authors remark that there is insufficient evidence as regards Christopher's brain damage "*to allow any causal correlation with his psychological profile*" (ibid.). According to the authors, Christopher's low performance IQ contrasts with an average or above average verbal IQ.

His remarkable translation abilities, for example, show that his speed in translating contrasts with his failure in terms of sensitivity to contextual information and linguistic constraints. A similar observation pertains to Christopher's ability to acquire new languages after only a minimal exposure to new data.

Interestingly, Smith and Tsimpli remark a crucial difference with respect to (unimpaired) ASLA: in his acquisition of new languages Christopher always seems to reach a "cut-off point" in the development of the respective L2 grammar.

As far as his knowledge of English (his mother tongue) is concerned Smith and Tsimpli assert that it is "*identical to that of any other native speaker*" (op. cit.: 57). Thus they conclude that the linguistic phenomena Christopher does not master

> "... arise from processing difficulties which involve the interaction of his modular, linguistic faculty with central system operations."
> (op. cit.: 79)

In this respect, Christopher faces problems when confronted with syntactic structures requiring a high processing load. The performance of structures with topicalisation or extraposition is a case in point. In fact, Christopher rejects these structures and "corrects" them as illustrated in (28) - (29), where (a) represents the original sentence and (b) Christopher's correction.[110]

---

[110] With respect to structures with extraposition he only accepts co-reference between a pronoun and a CP if the pronoun is either in subject position or in object position followed by an adjective. The details of the grammatical analysis proposed by Smith and Tsimpli (op.cit.: 54f.) shall not be discussed here. Suffice it to say that, according to the authors, processes like dislocation, topicalisation and extraposition involve a further post-LF level.

(28) topicalisation:
a. I parked the car and went indoors. My keys I left in the car.
b. I left my keys in the car.

(29) extraposition:
a. I resent it that you eat biscuits.
b. I resent that you eat biscuits.

(op. cit.: 54)

According to Smith and Tsimpli the rejection of these sequences is a sign of processing problems with the structures in question. Low performance is predicted when the processing load is increased. As regards the nature of the processing strategy they reckon with the possibility that Christopher has problems whenever a constituent is not posited in its canonical position. Interestingly, he also rejects deviations from the SVO schema in other languages even though there these word orders do represent possible and even unmarked word orders, which would only require a low processing load.

However, as pointed out by the authors, Christopher obviously understands the sequences in question. So the alleged processing problems have to be restricted to the production level.

In turning to Christopher's behaviour regarding foreign languages, Smith and Tsimpli remark on his great interest in learning other languages as well has his extraordinary ability to register pairings of morphological and semantic content on minimal exposure.

The rule-governed nature of his ability is also apparent in cases of overgeneralisation of a particular rule for languages of which he knows very little (as, for example, in Berber, Hindi and Arabic). The authors assume that such overgeneralisations are "*mainly associated with information in the lexical component*" (op. cit.: 84) including processes of both derivational and inflectional morphology. According to them the acquisition of grammatical phenomena subject to parameter-setting is deterministic thus differing substantially from rule-governed learning processes. And this difference, they assume, lies at the heart of Christopher learning of foreign languages which they claim to be "*exceptional*" due to the

> "... 'enhanced' lexical sub-component, which appears to be constantly receptive to new input of the relevant kind: that is, he is sensitive to lexical rather than to sentential properties."
> (ibid.: 85)

This finding is in line with their assumption that lexical learning may well be dissociated from the acquisition of syntax, which can also open the way for domain-specific deficits: the presence of inflectional morphology does not have to correlate with the availability of the syntactic features of the functional category in question. Note that, so defined, lexical learning defers substantially from the notion of lexical learning underlying the Lexical Learning Hypothesis.

As regards the analysis of Christopher's L2 syntax[111] I already mentioned Smith and Tsimpli's finding that Christopher adheres to strict SVO order, apparently rejecting constructions that involve parametric choices not realised in his mother tongue.
According to Smith and Tsimpli, Christopher's L2 knowledge is basically lexical and morphological, syntactic judgements being influenced by his L1. The extent, however, to which his L2 syntax is determined by the L1 is unclear

> "... the degree to which his first language influences his judgments and the nature of this influence remain obscure and as yet unresolved issues. It may be (...) that the core of his second language knowledge is largely lexical and morphological so that the influence of his first language on his syntactic judgements is fairly direct. Alternatively, it could be that the grammatical representation of his (flawed) second language does include syntactic and semantic properties which are distinct from those of his first language (even including some instances of parameter-resetting), but that accessing this knowledge is inhibited, at any level beyond the purely lexical, by processing strategies that are based overwhelmingly on the first language".
> (ibid.: 118)

The authors further conclude that Christopher's remarkable speed in learning second languages as well as his (unproblematic) switching from one language to another is due to the modular nature of the processes underlying lexical access and selection. By contrast, he apparently faces problems in the integration of the output of the former. The deficit may thus lie in inter-active central processes. Consequently, the syntactic plateau-effect is related to problems in the processing of the L2 input. More specifically, Smith and Tsimpli assume that the L2 syntax imposes a higher processing load. They thus conclude that Christopher's L2 learning is different in nature from his L1 learning, as processing difficulties were not relevant in the latter case.

It is worth mentioning, however, that Christopher does not seem to face greater difficulties in understanding sequences deviating from the SVO order. This contrasts with his "correction" of such orders so that they

---

[111] Smith and Tsimpli analysed his judgements on word order, null subjects, that-trace effects, clitic doubling and clitic left dislocation in his L2 Modern Greek, French, Spanish and Italian.

conform to the SVO schema. Therefore, we have to ask whether his corrections result from a general (performative) preference of the SVO pattern or rather from a defective competence. According to Smith and Tsimpli both possibilities may be true. The former may be the case where his corrections produce an equally grammatical sentence, the latter may be in those cases where his correction results in an ungrammatical sentence.

In concluding this short insight into Smith and Tsimpli's study of Christopher's ability to learn second languages we may ask about the possible implications for unimpaired ASLA. Insofar as Christopher's flawed linguistic abilities as regards processing and metalinguistic awareness seem to interact with his second language learning, any explanation aiming to cover similarities between impaired and unimpaired ASLA remains purely speculative.
It appears that the differences between Christopher and unimpaired ASLs highlight some crucial issues to be considered in the study of (unimpaired) ASLA.
Christopher's remarkable speed in acquiring complex L2 morphology contrasts with the problems many adult learners have in the acquisition of the target morphology especially in untutored ASLA. Conversely, the rigidness of Christopher's syntax, while similar to the behaviour during the initial stages of ASLA, contrasts with the word order variety attested at later stages.

Clearly, successful language acquisition entails the interaction of the different sub-components of the language faculty.
It is thus the integration of knowledge drawn from different levels that marks the development in the acquisition process. If this is not the case, *plateau effects* on any of the levels involved may occur.
As Christopher's knowledge of L2 morphosyntactic properties seems not to bear on his L2 syntax in the expected way, the causal relationship between morphological elements and parameterised syntactic properties may be under question. For successful second language acquisition to happen more than the acquisition of morphological devices is needed. We should thus concentrate on explanatory models which seek to uncover the processes involved in the integration of the information of different linguistic levels. Smith and Tsimpli speculate on the possibility that Christopher's impairment may affect such processes. What needs further clarification, however, is how we have to conceive possible or impossible parameter-(re)setting in such a framework.
It seems that the singling out of (lexical) triggering elements is in no direct relationship to the mechanisms responsible for language development.

We will see in the next section how inter- and intra-individual variation in language acquisition further challenge traditional learning concepts of the PP theory. We will also address the issue of how variation in language development may provide us with some decisive cues as to the concept of the dynamic processes involved in the acquisition of a such complex system as language.

7 Language development and the mirror-world of chaos and order

> *It is therefore important that future studies develop the notion of individual variation in such a way that it goes beyond merely listing individual differences of all sorts. It must be determined in which way such differences relate to the functioning of man's language system, and in which way the various types of individual variation relate to each other.*

(Henning Wode 1981: 67)

7.1 Variation in child language acquisition

It is only recently that *variation* in child language acquisition has come under closer scrutiny. All the studies discussed so far are based on the idea that the development path is the same for every child (impairments apart). Therefore cross-sectional data were taken to be representative and variations among children to be too minimal to be taken into account. The uniformity assumption does not only have methodological implications, it also bears on much of the theoretical framework at hand. Both the Continuity and the Maturational Hypothesis in its various forms seek to determine a development path valid for every individual child.

Furthermore it was shown throughout the preceding sections that this main tenet is also relevant for the current understanding of ASLA. Variation in adult language acquisition as opposed to uniformity in child language acquisition is for quite a number of researchers the *fundamental* difference between both forms of acquisition. Predictability lies at the heart of the discussion, as it has been a crucial criterion for determining the explanatory power of the hypotheses.

Taken at face value the predictability criterion is satisfied by neither the continuity nor the maturational hypothesis. Recent research in the field of child language acquisition further challenges the idea of a (uniform) determinism on empiricial grounds.

7.1.1 Variation in the development of the early grammar

Take, for example, Tracy's (1991) detailed analysis of an extended data compilation of four children ('Julia', 'Stephanie', 'Mirko' and 'Florian') acquiring German. In short, her analysis follows the children's development from the onset of the acquisition process up to the emergence of complex structures. Her findings on inter-individual variation during this time span may be summed up as follows (cf. Tracy 1991: 402f.):

- Elementary structural domains:
  At the onset of syntactic development inter-individual differences pertain to the relative order of the available constituents: both Julia and Stephanie use rigid noun-verb order, yet only Stephanie permutes preverbal elements as shown in utterances (1) - (3), all uttered in the same context.

  (1) das   Papa   wieder neu machen
      that   Daddy   again   new make

  (2) Papa   das   machen
      Daddy that   make

  (3) das   wieder neu   Papa   machen
      that   again   new   Daddy   make

  'Daddy, do that again'

  (ibid.: 402, my transl.)

  A higher degree of word order variation was found in the data of the two other children, Mirko and Florian.[112]

- Differentiation of the left periphery:
  The development of elementary structural domains is followed by a further increase of structural heterogeneity and the emergence of verbal inflection. According to Tracy, there is no relation among these structural formats yet. The discovery of the meaning equivalence between VE verbs and those elements in initial positions (for example: "(da) [gehtə]" (*there goes-he*) and "Mama gehn" (*Mum go*), op. cit.: 420, my transl.) may lead to the realisation that these lexemes are to be handled equivalently on an abstract level as well.

- V2:
  Subsequent to this process Tracy observes V2 for all verbs in the data of three of the children (Julia, Stephanie and Mirko). The fourth child (Florian), on the other hand, seems to be working out

---

[112] Parallel to these elementary structural domains, utterances which may be characterised as lexicalised formulae were observed. On this assumption, children have not yet analysed these utterances as to the various levels of the adult system.

the agreement system first. At the same time modal and auxiliary constructions emerge. Julia, Stephanie and Mirko adjoin these elements at the left periphery. Florian, on the contrary, allocates these forms to the right of the main verb.
Concurrent to the convergence on the structure of the simple sentence single syntactic positions are developed paradigmatically. Subsequently, the left periphery is analysed for a second time. Sentence-initial deictic expressions appear as well as first complementisers with verbs on the right periphery.

Tracy's study draws two major conclusions with regard to the initial phases of language development, namely, (a) there is inter-individual variation in the development of structural domains and (b) development is crucially determined by system-internal principles of structural convergence. A more detailed discussion of such principles will be given in section 7.2.

7.1.2 Variation and the emergence of complex structures

Some further insight into the development of complex structures in the monolingual acquisition of German is given in Fritzenschaft et al. (1990). Their investigation is based on the longitudinal study of 5 children ('Paul', 'Max', 'Valle', 'Lisa' and 'Benny').
At the beginning of the study all of the five children produced V1 and V2 formats. Some of these V1 and V2 sequences occur with lexicalised deictic expressions such as "guckma" (*look-Adv*) and "schauma" (*look-Adv*) which involve verbs that may fit with complement clauses.[113] Furthermore, it was observed that the children resorted to *connecting strategies* in order to relate propositions, such as the use of lexical items like 'und' (*and*), 'dann' (*then*), 'wenn' (*when, if*) or a specific intonation contour. On the other hand, the children differ with regard to the way they acquire complex structures and the degree of differentiation of the available structures.
The following overview provides a short insight into the findings:

- 'Paul':
  Finite verbs appear in V1 and V2 position only. The appearance of complementisers is accompanied by stuttering, iteration or complete breaks and reverting to V2 structures (cf. (4) - (5)).

---

[113] These structures are considered as *precursor* structures in that they provide a special discourse pragmatic load to the pre-Vorfeld.

(4) samandu wiedəwieduwie warum is
    say-you how-you-how-you-how why is
    des ne uhr
    this a clock[114] Paul08 (3;6.27)
    'Tell me why is this a clock.'

(5) ənə ede we ne du du häls da fest
    FILLER if   you you hold there tight
    dəda geh lieg ich wieder runter
    then go fall I again down
    'If you hold tight there then I will fall down again.'
    (Gawlitzek-Maiwald et al. 1992: 144, their transl.)

Paul's problems to accommodate complementisers seem to result from only the IP with a head-initial landing-site being available to him. Subsequently, the differentiation of the types of subordinated structures goes along with finite verb placement in sentence-final position.

- 'Max':
  Max produces V1, V2 as well as finite and non-finite VE structures without correlating these orders with a particular sentence-type (cf. (6) - (8)).

  (6) soll ich nochmal machen/ Max07 (2;10.18)
      should I again do?
      'should I do that again?'

  (7) du hast ein bagger/ Max12 (3;1.7)
      you have an excavator?
      'do you have an excavator?'

  (8) hier fleisch gibt\ Max07 (2;10.18)
      here meat is
      'there is some meat here'
      (Fritzenschaft et al. 1990: 87/88, my transl.)

---

[114] Gawlitzek-Maiwald et al. (1992: 176, footnote 5) point out that they treat "sag mal du" as an idiomatic matrix expression.

According to the authors these structures may be analysed either as head-final VPs or as IPs with a mobile I-head.
Prior to the introduction of complementisers Max produces unintroduced finite VE structures (cf. (9)), which would require a subordinate clause construction in the target. Complementisers are introduced only a year later.

(9) interviewer: warum   gehört   des   so?
                   why   belongs that so
                   'why must it go like that?'

     Max: des   nicht rausfällt\   Max17 (3;4.3)
                   that   not   fall-out
                   '(so that) it does not fall out'

     (ibid.: 89, my transl.)

- 'Benny':
Variation on the left periphery: wh-elements appear in V2 and in VE sequences (cf. (10) - (11)). Benny also produces target-deviant V3 structures (cf. (12) - (13)).

(10) was   ist des/   Benny03 (2;6.25)
     what is   this?

(11) wo   da   hinko/ wi   des   da   hinkomm/
     where there go?   how that there go?
                                            Benny03 (2;6.25)
     'where does that get to? how does that get there?'

(12) was   ich kann MACHen/   Benny06 (2;11.26)
     what I   can   do?
     'what can I do?'

(13) warum weiter   geht   nich/   Benny06 (2;11.26)
     why   further goes   not?
     'why doesn't that go on?'
     (ibid.: 92/93, my transl.)

Shortly after he produces V1, V2 and VE formats with 'weil' (*because*) and some other complementisers. The authors assume that Benny projects a further level above the mobile IP. As these sequences also occur with topicalised non-subjects (e.g. "weiter"

143

in (13) and "schlumpf" in (14)) they consider the possibility that the subject stays in SpecVP in these cases.

(14)   der   auch   schlumpf   hat   mitbracht[115]
       this-one also   smurf   has   brought
       'he also brought a smurf'
       (ibid.: 95, my transl.)

Probably verbs and complementisers do not occupy the same position. Later on, V3 structures disappear but not in the case of wh-introduced V2 complement and relative clauses.

- 'Lisa' and 'Valle':
  Initially, wh-phrases appear only in finite VE structures (cf. (15) - (16)) even in contexts (direct questions) where the target would require V2.

(15)   wo   das   Haus   mit   dem   Feuer is\
       where the   house   with   the   fire is?
                                            Valle10 (2;2.25)

       'where is the house with the fire?'

(16)   was   du   machst/   Lisa03 (2;1.8)
       what   you   make?
       'what are you doing?'
       (ibid.: 102, my transl.)

Alternatively, the children produce *gap formats*, i.e. questions without a wh-phrase (cf. (17) - (18)).

(17)   das   lied   heißt/   Valle10 (2;2.25)
       that song   is-called?
       '(what's) the title of that song?'

(18)   das   sind/   Lisa03 (2;1.8)
       that are?
       'what's that?'
       (ibid.: 101, my transl.)

---

[115] The authors do not provide a corpus specification for this utterance.

Soon after introduced subordinate clauses appear. They coexist with target-deviant structures for some weeks.
The latter disappear only after complementiser introduced VE structures are well established.

This brief overview of Fritzenschaft et al.'s findings leads us to conclude that - against common belief - the acquisition of complex structures is *not* flawless. In view of the inter-individual variation highlighted in this study we need to reconsider many of the assumptions related to a development path which should be valid for all learners.
Firstly, we have to recognise that the development of complex structures may begin *before* the mastering of simple matrix clauses. We could see that some children produce embedded clauses despite having problems with the position of the finite verb, agreement and the position of wh-elements in matrix clauses. Furthermore, the way in which complementisers are integrated is related to the simple sentence structure available. In other words, the choice among the relevant system-internal mechanisms for the integration of complementisers depends on the respective learner grammar.
To conclude, the UG-based learning models we have discussed so far do not embrace the inter-individual variation. On the other hand, however, the relevant variation seems to be delimited to certain structural domains. As pointed out by Fritzenschaft et al. many of the problems children face correspond with the grammatical properties which also prove to be problematic in descriptive terms (see section 2.6).

7.1.3 Learner types

The third analysis to be mentioned in this context is the study of d'Avis and Gretsch (1994) who investigated the inter-individual variation in the acquisition of complementisers. Their study is based on the data of four of the children analysed in Fritzenschaft et al.'s study ('Valle', 'Benny', 'Paul' and 'Max'). According to d'Avis and Gretsch the acquisition of complementisers proceeds on different levels (among them the phonetic, the syntactic and the semantic level)

> "... with each successful developmental step consisting of the complete integration of the properties on the various levels involved."
> (op. cit.: 67)

For the eventual target-like determination of complementisers learners need to acquire both the target type and a set of related tokens.
D'Avis and Gretsch's differentiation of *learner types* is related to the way children acquire the features constituting the C head:

"Lexically oriented learners (bottom-up learners) initially acquire single tokens and generalize across them in the course of development in order to derive a type. Top-down learners, on the other hand, begin with a type where place holders for individual values have to be replaced by specific values."
(op. cit.: 69)

Additionally, they predict that bottom-up learners who abstract types from several tokens will take more time in the acquisition of complementisers because they acquire much redundant information. Conversely, top-down learners proceed faster: once they have recognised the relevant type they map the corresponding type information onto the information of the specific lexical items.

A case in point is the following characterisation of 'Valle' and 'Benny':

- 'Valle':
  Valle is characterised as a *type learner*. His precursor phase B[116] lasts three months. Initially he prefers a function dependent feature-form correlation of the structural types available to him: [+ w]-structures correlate with VE, and [- w]-structures with V1/V2. Target-like finite verb placement in embedded clauses is not expected to pose problems as Valle masters the verb-final position. The introduction of complementisers, however, occurs by means of the addition of complementiser tokens.

- 'Benny':
  Benny is considered to be a *token learner*. His precursor phase B lasts about 21 months. In his case no systematic connection between the VE pattern and complementiser introduced clauses could be observed. He produces several deviant patterns of matrix and embedded clauses.
  According to the authors Benny's orientation is primarily semantic as neither verb placement nor complementisers indicate the type of the construction. Before establishing the relevant type Benny is assumed to follow a token-by-token strategy.

We can see that feature-value matching may take place on any of the levels mentioned. Orientation towards the syntactic level results in the production of pre-conjunctional structures. A lexical learner, on the other hand, could start with the phonetic level, uttering single complementisers

---

[116] The *precursor phase* is the phase during which children produce "structures preparing for and accompanying the acquisition of complementisers" (op. cit.: 60). D'Avis and Gretsch's understanding of a precursor structure is related to the grammatical construction in question and to the respective learner system.

without taking into account either the semantics or the syntactic behaviour of the category.
Consequently, bootstrapping is not delimited to either the semantic or the syntactic level. Instead, d'Avis and Gretsch expect different developmental styles depending on the combination of *process orientation* (top-down vs. bottom-up) and *level orientation* along the following lines:

- Preconjunctional clauses with undifferentiated filler syllables at the left periphery or frequently used quotations are characteristic of a *phonetic orientation*.

- A *syntactic orientation* is reflected in the use of unintroduced preconjunctional syntactic structures and the acquisition of the VE pattern prior to the implementation of complementisers.

- A *semantic orientation* may be evident in the production of paratactic, complex structures with salient connections but without overt indices for subordinate clauses.

Note that a differentiation along these lines does not exclude the possibility of a combination of the different forms or even a change in the overall orientation. Consequently and as pointed out by d'Avis and Gretsch a clear-cut classification of the learners requires a "careful weighing" of the quantitative use of the respective strategies.
These considerations, however, show that generalisations in terms of learner types remain "*stereotypical and idealized characterization[s]*" (Hohenberger 1996: 62). Idealisations of this sort, however, cannot and should not replace the analysis of *individual* development paths. It makes no sense to explain variation by means of singling out learner groups because "*[t]here are no general types to abstract away from individuals*" (ibid.: 64).

Furthermore, we have to question d'Avis and Gretsch's assumptions regarding the *deterministic* and the *non-deterministic* dimensions of language acquisition. According to the authors, non-determinism holds with respect to interim grammars of phase B, whilst determinism holds at the level of complete developmental steps, i.e. at the level of *superordinate grammars*. But, these statements are insufficient, if not part of a learning model which would account for how such contradictory dimensions may, in fact, be part of one overall process (cf. also Hohenberger 1996).

7.1.4 Bilingual bootstrapping

The last study to be discussed in this section is the article of Gawlitzek-Maiwald and Tracy (1994) which deals with *bilingual bootstrapping*. In their analysis of the data of a bilingual child ('Hannah') acquiring English and German the authors concentrated on (a) the *developmental asynchrony* with respect to certain syntactic phenomena and (b) types of *language mixing* occurring for the duration of this asynchrony. Crucially, they address the issue of a possible *pooling of resources* (see below) at the syntactic level in bilingual acquisition.

Regarding intra-sentential language mixing Gawlitzek-Maiwald and Tracy distinguish two groups, i.e.

- lexically mixed structures, such as

    (19) ich habe gemade you much better   (2;4.17)
          I   have ge-made you much better
          (ibid.: 14, their transl.)

- potential literal translations or utterances with signs of interference, such as

    (20) ich   bin   falsch
          I   am   wrong   (adult German: Das ist falsch.)

    (21) ich   habe gegeben meine   löffel   zu dir (2;7)[117]
          I   have given   my   spoon(s) to you
          (ibid., their transl.)

As regards Hannah's use of the two languages the authors remark a preference for German, which she also uses when addressed in English.

The development of the two languages is characterised as follows:

- Initially, Hannah produces only propositions with one or two arguments. English utterances follow the VO order, German utter-

---

[117] As remarked by the authors such a classification is not unproblematic. The following passage illustrates their procedure:
"What justifies the assignment of individual examples to mixed utterances is the existence, in some cases, of sufficient numbers of comparable cases in the first group, i.e. *Ich hab gemacht dich nass* (Hannah 2;4.17) compares with *Ich hab gemade you much better*." (op. cit.: 14)

ances the OV order. Deviant word order is only found in lexically mixed utterances. There is no evidence for functional elements related to INFL.

- At the age of 2;4, V2 and the agreement paradigm are established in German. In her English, however, elements associated with the INFL projection are still absent.

- There is evidence of the availability of the IP in English as of the age of 2;9. At the age of 3;0 subordinate clauses appear in both languages, English wh-questions are now target-like.

Gawlitzek-Maiwald and Tracy point out that the development evident in Hannah's all-English or all-German utterances is not much unlike the findings in monolingual acquisition.
The analysis of the mixed utterances, however, reveals the faster progress in German, cf.

(22) Mama hat das fix it.
(23) Kannst du move a bit?
(24) Sie haben gone away.
  (ibid.: 18f.)

According to Gawilitzek-Maiwald and Tracy these sequences are the result of "*a mixing pattern where left periphery items of main clauses are taken from German*" (ibid.: 18). The assumption is thus that Hannah's English at this time consists of a VP only, wh-elements, auxiliaries and modals being *borrowed* from German, as illustrated in (25).

(25) [Germ Kannst du [Engl move a bit]]

Note that this kind of borrowing is not attested in Hannah's German utterances. According to Gawlitzek-Maiwald and Tracy, this kind of mixed utterances decrease as soon as the elements related to INFL are acquired. What needs further clarification is the question of how a child may be in the position of filling a gap which is apparently missing. In this respect, the child is assumed to know "*the equivalence at a very abstract level!*" (ibid.: 20), i.e. the universality of structure-building principles. The relevance of this knowledge is also considered in Tracy (1994/5: 484):

> "On a still more abstract level, children who are equipped with UG also 'know' that linguistic systems follow the same design anyway, so they will never conclude that they are dealing with totally different mental objects.

Language mixing, either temporarily as a help and bootstrapping mechanism in acquisition or as the permanent potential of the proficient bilingual is only a natural consequence of that (tacit) assumption."

As pointed out in Tracy (ibid.) bilinguals are thus in the position to resort to a strategy of language-borrowing where monolingual children would be left with other strategies such as the use of filler syllables as placeholders. Consider, for example, Gawlitzek-Maiwald and Tracy's (1994: 3) general definition of *bilingual bootstrapping*:

> "Something which has been acquired in language A fulfills a booster function in language B. In a weaker version, we would expect at least a temporary pooling of resources."

Developmental asynchronies in bilingual acquisition are also quite instructive as to the developmental problem: the evidence that some structures develop first in one language than in another clearly goes against the assumption that language development is determined by a maturational schedule. Put bluntly, it does not make much sense to assert that, for example, INFL matures earlier in one language than in another.

7.1.5 Implications for the Principles and Parameters theory

The studies discussed in this section generally show that language acquisition is crucially determined by processes of differentiation and integration of the different linguistic levels. In view of the modular nature of language the relevance of such processes comes as no surprise. By the same token, variation in language acquisition is only a natural consequence of the *freedom* implicit in the history of a complex system so designed. We are left to conclude that we have to do justice to these considerations also on a theoretical level. In view of the critical remarks we have put forward in the course of the preceding sections we can safely assume that the learning model underlying the PP theory has to be revised in the following terms:

- The ongoing discussion around the determination of *parameters* should benefit from research in the field of language development in its multiple forms when deciding among descriptive alternatives which cannot be decided only on theoretical grounds.

- The *instantaneous* model of language acquisition still rests on the concept of *parameter setting* as a punctual event. Parameter setting takes time, as manifested in the form of precursor structures.

- The idea that there are specific *triggers* which should be valid for all learners has to be given up in favour of a more global understanding of the mechanisms underlying the restructuring of (learner) grammars allowing for inter-individual variation. Triggers would be related to the respective development.

It goes without saying that the more *dynamic* model of language acquisition we envisage should encompass the creative unfolding of the modular nature of the human language faculty in *multiple forms* of language development. In other words, we expect research in different linguistic fields, such as language change, ASLA and language loss to be equally instructive in what we consider to be a common endeavour. And it is high time to take exceptions, structural variants and system-internal inconsistencies seriously (cf. also Hohenberger 1996, Tracy 1991). They have been ignored for too long. But they are returning into favour because they are likely outcomes of the creative potential of the human mind.

7.2 Linguistic variation and the theory of self-organisation: Preliminary considerations

7.2.1 The temporal dimensions of organisation

It is certainly not without irony that language acquisition research which has been devoted to the analysis of developmental regularities for decades is about to take up the challenge of explaining irregularities. It seems the reliance on regularities *qua* representatives of the laws underlying a linguistic system's development blinded us to the explanatory potential of what has been disregarded as irrelevant *noise*.
Today we know that we have to overcome this shortcoming if we are ever to understand the complexity of real-world phenomena. Consider Briggs and Peat's (1990: 14) statements in this respect:

"The world defined by science traditionally has been a world of almost Platonic purity. The equations and theories describing the rotation of the planets, the rise of water in a tube, the trajectory of a baseball, or the structure of genetic code contain a regularity and order, a clockworklike certainty, that we have come to associate with nature's laws. Scientists have long admitted, of course, that outside the laboratory our world is seldom as Euclidean as it seems in the mirror of those laws that we hold up to nature. Turbulence, irregularity, and unpredictability are everywhere, but it has always seemed fair to assume that this was "noise", a messiness that resulted from the way things in reality crowd into each other. Put another way, chaos has been thought to be the result of a complexity that in theory could be stripped down to its orderly underpinnings (...) Chaos, irregularity, unpredictability. Could it be that such things are not mere noise but have laws of their own? This is what some scientists are now learning (...) So a new breed of scientists has begun constructing a new mirror to hold up to nature: a turbulent mirror."

In fact, if we look at other scientific domains we can see that alleged contradictions such as continuity and discontinuity have been accommodated in the framework of a *dynamic theory of self-organisation* or *chaos theory*. Take mathematics, for example: In non-linear equations a small change in a variable may have an unexpected, possibly even *catastrophic* effect (ibid.: 24):

"Where correlations between the elements of an evolving system remain relatively constant for a large range of values, at some crucial point they split up and the equation describing the system rockets into a new behaviour."

Thus, depending on which point in time we look at the system we may be sufficiently convinced that the system will continuously remain constant. At some other point in time, however, we may be persuaded that the reverse is true...
So time plays a crucial role in our understanding of what we consider the subject of our analysis. Research in the field of chaos theory also teaches us to dismiss our (reductionist) belief that we could *predict* how processes unfold in time. In other words, in trying to understand or to explain non-linearity we may learn much about the way complex processes take shape, but we will not be in the position of determining exactly the future of such systems either on empirical or on conceptual grounds.

So far, linguistic research has been concerned mainly with the establishing of the format of language-specific universals and the relationship between these universals and the environment in the form of primary linguistic data. In the discussion on the developmental problem *change* is tied to external triggers, be they biological or specific linguistic items. The potential for change *inside* the language system, however, has not received much attention. Yet, if we focus on the internal organisation of the linguistic system we may restate the development problem as follows:

"[W]hat causes the system to change or, as a prerequisite, what sensitizes the system to novel stimuli that went unnoticed or at least remained without impact in the past... When is an organism sensitized to novelty, how are knowledge gaps recognized and, finally, what controls actual change and determines its direction?"
(Tracy 1994/5: 7)

It appears that we need to have a closer look at the cognitive capacities at the root of the *organisation* of the language system *qua* functionally complex system. Note that we use the concept of *organisation* in a double sense: on the one hand, organisation refers to the system's structure, on the other, it embraces the processes by which this structure comes into being (cf. Karpf 1990). So organisation has both a stable and an unstable moment. Traditionally, organisation has been tied to external factors which impose an order of whatever kind. But organisation may as well be a property of the system itself, i.e. in its potential for *self*-organisation. Under this view, we have to seek the reasons for continuity (or *stability*) and discontinuity (or *instability*) in the system itself.

In our discussion of recent studies on variation in child language acquisition we already came across some of the possible system-internal means a linguistic system may provide in terms of what Tracy considers as *UG-assisted self-regulation*:

> "With respect to linguistic levels of structure building, perceived conflicts, i.e. inconsistencies in the input, trigger self-regulating operations, which eventually leads to conflict resolution via the establishment of higher-level invariance, i.e. new and more abstract equivalence classes."
> (ibid.: 8)

We can see that the understanding of language development as an instance of self-organisation is based on such crucial concepts as structure, processes of differentiation and integration and non-linearity which are characteristic of dynamic systems.

7.2.2 The anticipatory and reconstructive potential of a structure

One of the basic concepts when studying organisation is that of a (complex) structure. Here I follow Tracy's (1991: 66) definition whereby a structure is a set of elements which can be set apart by means of its *internal regularity*. Note that, so defined, a structure has both an *anticipatory* and a *reconstructive* potential: any of its elements bears a relation to the whole, that is, any of the elements of a structure fulfills a *function* in this whole.[118]

This conception is highly relevant for language acquisition: one of the crucial tasks in language acquisition is that of discovering the functions linguistic elements fulfill. It has been mentioned previously that the com-

---

[118] As pointed out by Tracy (1991: 100) the definition of a function *qua "property of being a part of"* is intended primarily to overcome traditional problems in the field of language acquisition research regarding the causality between functions and the forms to be acquired.

plexity of the language system is reflected in any of its elements by virtue of being embedded in different structural contexts.

So in contrast to traditional functionalist assumptions (see section 1.2.1), it is not only the pragmatic or communicative function, which the learner has to determine. Rather, language learners are faced with the challenge of dealing with the *plurifunctionality* of linguistic elements (cf. also Tracy 1991). So we expect that in language acquisition the learner is equipped with something like Tracy's *Principle of Function Anticipation* ('Prinzip der Funktionserwartung') (cf. (26)) (ibid.).

(26) Principle of Function Anticipation
Once an element has been recognised as a part of a structural context, it may be assumed that it has a function related to this structure.[119]

Consider, in this respect, the alleged dichotomy of lexical and syntactic learning implicit in the discussion of the Developmental Problem. Language acquisition comprises many different processes on many different levels, lexical learning and structure-building among them. But there is no unidirectional, causal relationship between them. This is also reflected in the inter-individual variation outlined above. More to the point, the above-mentioned definition of a structure proves to be quite instructive: an element cannot anticipate anything unless embedded in a structure. By the same token, a structure only exists by virtue of its elements.

7.2.3 Differentiation and integration

There is a constant differentiation of the totality of knowledge into the parts and an integration of the parts back into the whole. This equilibrium between differentiation and integration plays a fundamental biological role.

(Piaget 1972: 17)

It is widely agreed that functionally complex systems select and evaluate the incoming data of the environment. As pointed out by Tracy (1991: 57) the selection of incoming data is preconditioned by the system's sensitivity to just these data. Furthermore, the processing of environmental

---

[119] The original reads as follows:
"Prinzip der Funktionserwartung
Sofern ein Element als Bestandteil eines strukturellen Kontextes erkannt wird, darf man diesem Element unterstellen, daß es eine Funktion in Bezug auf diese Struktur erfüllt."

data cannot only consist of a passive reception of stimuli, but rather of reconstruction processes.[120] We need to consider, additionally, that complex systems do not only strive for *stability* regarding their relation to the environment, *equilibration* is also sought in the relation

- among the subsystems of the system, and
- among the subsystems and the whole of which they are a part (cf. Piaget 1981).

We expect self-organisation to manifest itself in either one of the following ways (cf. Tracy 1991, Karpf 1990):

- Differentiation
  In order to maintain their stability complex systems may have to uncouple (competing) subparts by means of differentiation into further subsystems.
- Integration
  There must be principles of level congruence, which constrain the critical features of what may participate in the correlation across levels.

Among the relevant mechanisms in language acquisition we have to consider the cognitive capacities which allow the learner to recognise certain tokens as the realisation of the same type. Furthermore, variability in the input needs to be compensated. The principles in question have to allow for the possibility of higher level equivalences (cf. Tracy 1991). Linguistic principles like Structure Preservation or the Projection Principle conform to more general cognitive principles involved in the creation and in the guarantee of conceptual invariance (cf. Tracy 1994/5: 147).
In other words, if language processing implies the correlation of different linguistic levels insomuch as these cannot be reduced to each other, we expect the following processes to play a crucial role in language acquisition (cf. Tracy 1994/5):

- the reconstruction of the structural primitives on each level, and
- the establishment of correlations across levels.

For further illustration we may consider Tracy's (1991) observations regarding early child data (see section 7.1.1). According to her, the first process of convergence (after) the development of elementary structural

---

[120] As pointed out by Karpf (1990) these processes have been observed to play a role in the development of neuronal networks and the visual system.

domains is supposed to involve the differentiation of the left periphery. Tracy claims that the cracking of formulae like [da:zə] or [vo:zə] plays a crucial role in this process. In particular, the differentiation of the copula is followed by a series of (possibly) crucial structural consequences. Following the general assumption that learners already master consistent lexical representations of verbs (as to their phonological, categorial, subcategorisation and inherent features), Tracy claims that learners have a rudimentary Projection Principle telling them which arguments of a lexical item should be present in principle. This principle may guide the child in the "cracking" of yet unanalysed formulae such as [da:zə] as the child is to seek arguments of an already known thematic head (*Theta Seeking Strategy*, Tracy 1991: 418). Formulae like [da:zə] may further act as a basis for the discovery of the V2 phenomenon and the features of both AGR and INFL.

If much of what happens in the course of *monolingual* language acquisition is determined by the coexistence of different systems and their interaction, or, in Tracy's terms, by *contact situations*, the traditional contrast between monolingual and multilingual acquisition, i.e. the *"monolingual fiction"* (op. cit.: 13), has to given up in favour of a more general understanding of such contact situations in their multiple forms.

As it turns out, it is exactly at the point where the system seeks equilibration that developmental crises or *conflicts* may arise (cf. ibid.). We further anticipate that the potential for change unfolds in these very conflicts, where something new may *emerge* (cf. Hohenberger 1996), where self-organising principles come into play.
In language acquisition, such system-internal *conflicts* may arise in different situations, as, for example, in the mapping across representation levels, in the merging or linking of trees or in reconstructing a derivational relationship such as a path of movement (Tracy 1994/5: 147).[121] Tracy (1991: 113) observes that the potential for such conflicts emerges not only due to the coexistence of different levels but also because of the fact the levels cannot be reduced to each other. Actually, the modular nature of human language faculty bears much more creative potential than so far believed, if we only let modularity play a part.[122]
However, if functional complexity is the result of processes such as the ones described previously, the modularity hypothesis has to be weak-

---

[121] Consider, for example, the empirical data discussed in section 7.1 which reflected conflicts of this kind.

[122] As will be discussed shortly, this also implies that we have to allow for degrees of modularisation or, put differently, we have to allow for modularisation processes to take place in the course of language acquisition.

ened so as to capture the process of modularisation in the course of the developmental process.

7.2.4 Some preliminary conclusions on non-linearity and language development in its multiple forms

If the history of a system is characterised by the alternation of periods of relative stability or *convergence* and periods of instability, the traditional additive or linear concept of development has to be discarded. Development which manifests itself in the form of *crises* (Tracy 1994: 201, 1991) or *instabilities* allows for something *new* to emerge by means of self-organising principles. As it turns out, this creative potential of a dynamic system arises because of its very *non*-linear properties (Hohenberger 1996: 112).

Note that these processes need not affect all the sub-parts of the system at the same time. The coexistence of different structural levels allows for the modification of one level while leaving all other levels unchanged. Thus, the apparent contradiction of the continuity and the discontinuity aspect of language acquisition is only a natural progression.
As pointed out by Tracy (1991: 112), if a child erroneously assumed that 'geschwimmt' (instead of the target-like form 'geschwommen', *swum*) was the past tense form of the German verb 'schwimmen' (*to swim*) she will have to give it up at a certain point in the development without, however, changing all other representations of this lexical item. The theta-grid and the subcategorisation frame among other abstract representations will remain the same.
Note that these considerations extend to other forms of language acquisition such as bilingual acquisition in childhood (cf. Tracy 1994/5) or ASLA: the monolingual learner may be dealing with competing grammatical representations for a certain period of time, as much as the bilingual or adult learner of a second language may have to handle coexisting patterns.

It is worth keeping in mind that this creative aspect is also at the heart of inter-individual variation. There is no predetermined schedule which would provide information of when and where certain conflicts occur. Any individual development has a history of its own. In a certain way, similarities and differences among learners run parallel with processes of convergence or differentiation within one system: they are two sides of the same coin. Universal constraints determine the format of natural languages. As such they mark the limits of variation, for example, in the form of principles like Structure Preservation or the Projection Principle.

But they also allow for a degree of freedom regarding the path individual learners may take. We commonly agree that however non-deterministic or unpredictable the processes underlying language development may be, the guarantee for ultimate attainment in child language acquisition imposes itself by means of a determinism yet to be defined. At the same time this determinism needs to be relativised, for if this was not the case languages would never have evolved. In fact, more often than not, researchers in the field of language change have expressed their dissatisfaction with regard to "*an extremely static model*" of language acquisition which "*leave[s] little scope for the divergence of dialects and languages to occur*" (McMahon 1994: 44).

On the other hand, in the field of ASLA research variation has been subject to different interpretations: here variation or non-determinism have been either ignored or overinterpreted. The study of Clahsen, Meisel and Pienemann (1983) is certainly a remarkable exception. In its general outline the research program underlying their *multidimensional model* was certainly an ambitious one in that it intended to cover both the universal and the individual dimension of language acquisition, by means of determining both a *developmental sequence* and the spectrum of *variation*. The claim was that the invariant developmental sequence was determined by general processing mechanisms. As regards variation, it was assumed that inter-individual differences were related to socio-psychological variables. The theoretical framework, however, turned out to be insufficient for this ambitious project.

So far, the UG-based discussion of ASLA has focussed on the universal constraints at the base of a generally valid developmental sequence, if only in a weak sense because not every learner goes all the way. This aspect, in turn, has become one of the cornerstones of the UG-access debate.

Until recently, hardly any analysis has treated inter- and intra-individual variation in ASLA without concluding that variation cannot be captured by a UG-based learning theory. Generalising somewhat, variation in ASLA has always been interpreted as evidence for the lack of language-specific learning mechanisms of some sort, which are, conversely, present in child LA.[123] None of the studies, however, goes more deeply into the

---

[123] Felix's competition model is an important exception. But as discussed above, the competition hypothesis ultimately matches much of all other assumptions insofar as variation or for that matter failure regarding the ultimate attainment is ascribed to a restricted activity of the language-specific system. Put bluntly, what seems to be *more* (*two* processing systems) turns out to be *less* as competition manifests itself in the form of *suppression* of one of the cognitive capacities.

analysis of how learner grammars, their grade of development or of fossilisation, vary from one another.

Schwartz and Sprouse (1994) are among the first to explicitly address the issue of non-determinism in ASLA within the UG-paradigm.[124] And this they do by examining the history of a learner grammar along two main dimensions, i.e. its relationship with the input (increasing accommodation of incoming data) and its system-internal consistency (restructurings of the L1 grammar assumed to serve as a kind of default structure in ASLA and learnability problems arising thereof). In this way, Schwartz and Sprouse depict a development path which is crucially determined by system-internal requirements. According to Schwartz and Sprouse, there may be situations in which L1-knowledge in combination with UG may fail in such a way that some (target-deviant) properties of the learner grammar may not be unlearned. This is what Schwartz and Sprouse call the *Delearnability Problem* specific to ASLA.

We could restate their findings in terms of *conflicts* in the sense outlined above: the exposure to L2 input seems to yield certain system-internal conflicts which are overcome by means of restructurings of the respective interim grammar. On the other hand, we may revise remaining inconsistencies between the learner grammar and the L2 input in terms of *absent* conflicts. One of the crucial questions to ask is whether we could predict the presence or the absence of the relevant conflicts. We anticipate that we could do this only to a limited extent. Unlike traditional hypotheses which sought to determine learnability problems on the basis of (parametric) contrasts between the L1 and the L2, we are dealing here with the complexity of a system firmly embedded in a developmental process which we assume to be determined by self-organisation. In other words, L1-L2 differences or similarities are only part of the story. They do not tell us when and how they are accommodated in the learner grammar. Neither do they reveal why some learner grammars are more resistant to change than others.

In general terms, questions relating to the representation of the L2 have to consider both the autonomy of and the interaction among different linguistic systems. To the same extent as the bilingual child the adult learner of a second language may pool her resources in the manner outlined above. As the adult learner starts out with a fully-fledged system, the L1 may fulfill a kind of bootstrapping function in a stronger sense than the one acknowledged in bilingual acquisition. It remains to be seen

---

[124] The analysis of Schwartz and Sprouse is based on the longitudinal data of an adult learner of German with Turkish L1 ('Cevdet'). In the present context I will touch only upon some of the main conceptual ideas of this study. Some details of their empirical analysis will be mentioned in chapter 8.

whether there is also individual variation with regard to the extent to which the L1 system serves so.
In the course of ASLA processes of correlation and of differentiation will be of utmost importance (cf. Karpf 1990). Such processes may occur earlier for some parts of the L2 than for others. We also expect differences among learners in this respect.
The reasons for why learners' grammars may vary as to their resistance to such processes may be manifold. To date we know only very little about the interfaces between language-specific and extra-linguistic variables. Yet, the linguistic dimensions of what we may conceive of as a resistance to the challenge in the L2 input are intricate enough.
UG-based ASLA research has shown that L2 systems at any point in the developmental axis are constrained by UG. So extra-linguistic variables determine the form of a learner system only indirectly. They may drive the system forwards or even backwards, into one or the other direction: the linguistic analysis is concerned with the system's *reaction* to such impetus. Our understanding of triggering has to be revised accordingly in terms of

> "... the reaction of a given system to the introduction of new units able to multiply by taking part in the system's processes."
> (Prigonine and Stengers 1984: 189)

We will see in the next section that many of the apparent contradictions we have been dealing with in the preceding paragraphs have similar counterparts in other fields of scientific research. It is not without irony that *chaos* theory will provide us with the framework for analysing such similarities regarding regularities *and* irregularities.

7.3   Chaos theory and language development

> *Chaos is like a creature slumbering deep inside the perfectly ordered system. When the system reaches a critical value the sleeping monster sticks out its jagged tongue.*
> (Briggs and Peat 1990: 62)

7.3.1   The dynamics of chaos and order

7.3.1.1 Feedback, attractors and fractals

Everybody knows that if we put a microphone too close to a loudspeaker we will be confronted with a deafening sound. This results from an ampli-

fying process whereby the output signal of one level becomes the input signal at some other level (*positive* feedback coupling).
Today we know that *feedback processes* are elementary mechanisms in such different domains as ecology, society and mathematics and that they are the heart of the relation between order and chaos:

> "Feedback governs virtually every living process and can be ignored only in crude simplifications."
> (Cramer 1993: 138)

In mathematical terms the crucial observation is that the non-linear relation between X_n (= input) and X_{n+1} (= output) is dependent on the value C reentering the process during each iteration (ibid.: 138). The notion of *deterministic chaos* intends to explain the apparent paradox between the deterministic equations and the resulting chaotic itinerary of a system.
As regards the outcome of such feedback processes, Cramer (ibid.) distinguishes the following three possible situations:

> "First, the final value of X approaches a limiting value, which it ultimately attains, perhaps asymptotically (at infinity). This is the case of linear differentiation equations and integrable systems. Second, the process leads to harmonic oscillation. This case corresponds to the dynamics of the pendulum and the planetary orbits. Third, the outcome of the process is uncertain. Although the process is governed by its dynamics and the choice of initial conditions, its outcome is nonetheless unpredictable. All three situations are possible in physical and physiological reality."

We can see how feedback plays a crucial role either in a system reaching a new higher order or in a system being catapulted into chaos. Minimal disturbances may have major effects as exemplified in the much cited *butterfly effect* whereby

> "... a single flutter of a butterfly's wings can (but, of course, need not necessarily) result in a complete change in global weather patterns."
> (ibid.: 117)

In addition to feedback coupling we need to consider therefore the system's sensitivity to the initial conditions:

> "Potentially chaotic structures are always nonlinear structures that involve feedback coupling and are strongly dependent on initial conditions. The global structure arising during the process in question is influenced in an unpredictable way by the fine details of the initial situation."
> (ibid.)

In observing the non-linear behaviour of systems we get the impression that they are drawn or *attracted* into a certain state. Consider, for example, a landscape with valleys and mountains where quite a number of rocks roll down to the bottom. Independently of where the rocks started to fall down, they eventually land at the deepest point. In a similar way energy "valleys" attract natural systems. Research in the field of chaos theory has shown that there are infinitely many complex landscapes with multiple valleys or *attractors* and that these in turn may have different shapes:

> "The attractor is a powerful concept that spans the mirror-worlds of both order and chaos. An attractor is a region of phase space which exerts a "magnetic" appeal for a system, seemingly pulling the system toward it."
> (Briggs and Peat 1990: 36)

There is, for example, the possibility for mathematically describing an attractor underlying periodic motion. The circular path in the phase space of a simple oscillation is called a *limit cycle*. A mechanically driven pendulum, for example, will remain within the bounds of such a limit cycle. What is of interest here is that the system returns to its limit cycle in the case of a disturbance:

> "The ability of limit cycles to resist change through feedback is one of the paradoxes discovered by the science of change. More and more, researchers are appreciating the way nature has of coupling continuously changing things together in order to end up with systems that effectively *resist* change."
> (op. cit.: 37)

In many other cases, however, systems go through branchings or *bifurcations* leaving their original order. Such is the case when two separate limit cycles interact as observed in electric circuits or competing beast of prey-prey populations. Mathematically the coupling of two limit cycles derives a *torus* shaped attractor. In order to cover real world phenomena we have to assume multidimensional tori with multiple freedom grades. In analysing such systems we discover their *fractal* (Latin: frangere = break) nature: a torus splits into other tori, some of which are stable, others unstable. However small the scale subject to analysis, the *self-similarity* of the alternation of regularity and chaos imposes itself again and again. We can see how the simple encloses the complex, complexity in turn enclosing the simple.

Today we know that the notions of fractal dimensions and self-similarity which were conceived in mathematics also play a crucial role in our understanding of the processes whereby much of our organic and unorganic world came into being. It is important to stress that the fractal concept of complex systems differs radically from a *reductionist* point of view. While the latter derives complexity from the addition of simple parts, the former is based on the creative potential of every simple part engaged in the complexity. This relates on our understanding of evolution: instead of focusing on *quantitative* differences we have to determine the *qualitative* differences among complex systems. Consequently, we will also have to reconsider our understanding of time.

7.3.1.2 Bifurcations and the irreversibility of time

> *Bifurcation points are the milestones in the system's evolution;*
> *they crystallize the system's evolution.*
>
> (Briggs and Peat 1990: 144)

An apparently stable system may enter a chaotic phase and, after its transition through chaos, return to a new, possibly higher-level order imposed by the attractors. In this transition phase we encounter the system-internal potential which lies at the heart of the emergence of a new order. This is conceived as a process of *synchronisation*[125] (Hohenberger 1996) given by so-called *order parameters*:

> "The journey along the optimal developmental path (...) leading to an attractor (...) which pulls the variable local processes onto itself as a global parameter, gradually excludes all the other alternative paths and attractors or renders them increasingly improbable." [126]
> (Hohenberger 1996: 106)

As pointed out by Hohenberger, the circular causality implicit in these considerations is constitutive:

> "The attractor pulls the elements onto itself; yet, they themselves build up the attractor by virtue of their interactions."
> (op. cit.: 107)

Due to the dynamic relationship between chaos and order we can neither determine the direction of causality nor can we predict the effect of a cause:

> "Strictly deterministic initial conditions, even when all parameters are specified, do not allow predictions to be made about branch points. The result is indeterminism."
> (Cramer 1993: 107)

Consider that under certain circumstances, chaos appears as a kind of "intermittence". In other cases, by contrast, we regard order as a transitory phenomenon only.

---

[125] Hohenberger's concept is based on Haken's (1988) who uses the term *slaving* in his considerations about the emergence of new systemic states in the framework of synergetics.

[126] A selection along these lines has also been termed *symmetry breaking* (cf. Hohenberger 1996 among others).

This leads us to conclude that

> "... chaos is an intrinsic feature of natural systems. In other words, the basic structure of the world is nonlinear, even though islands of order, where the simple linear laws are still applicable, continually emerge out of deterministic chaos."
> (op. cit.: 142)

At a certain point in time we may observe a system's stability and expect that it remains in such a stable state forever. At some other point in time, however, we notice that the same system is not able to resist alternative attractors anymore leaving its stable state. We further acknowledge the state-dependency of dynamic systems as highlighted in Hohenberger (1996:71):

> "The system's state S_n depends on the system's state S_{n-1}, i.e. the state which the system was before."

The crucial importance of time evidences itself in the historic component of any system which has gone through phase transitions or bifurcations, which consists of deterministic and non-deterministic elements. What is more important: such histories are *irreversible* (cf. Prigonine and Stengers 1984, Cramer 1993).

The characterisation of a system as being *deterministic* is used in the literature in the double sense of "predetermined" and "predeterminable" (cf. Cramer 1993). This conception is based on classical dynamics where

> "... the general law then deduces from this "initial state" the series of states the system passes through as time progresses, just as logic deduces a conclusion from basic premises. The remarkable feature is that once the forces are unknown, any single state is sufficient to define the system completely, not only its future but also its past. At each instant therefore, everything is given."
> (Prigonine and Stengers 1984: 60)

Non-linear systems, by contrast, are *indeterministic* inasmuch as they are irreversible since they pass through bifurcation points.

We acknowledge the relevance of the system's bifurcations as the "milestones" in the history of its development: it is here that the variety of possibilities for change are displayed, it is here where a minimal influence will have its major effect (cf. Briggs and Peat 1990: 213). The intriguing aspect being that the transition through such bifurcations may throw the system into chaos but it might also render it into a stable state:

> "... the same nonlinearities may reproduce an order out of the chaos of elementary processes and still, under different circumstances, be responsible for the distinction of this same order, eventually producing a new coherence beyond another bifurcation."
> (Prigonine and Stengers 1984: 206)

The most fascinating aspect about bifurcations, however, is that they do not only reflect the irreversibility of time but also its *recapitulation* (cf. ibid.). Certainly, biological systems retain much of their stability. But they also allow for areas of major sensitivity wherever creativity and flexibility is needed. Briggs and Peat (1990) point to the increased sensitivity of the system at exactly the points at which the "memory" of such bifurcations crystallised. Again, it is precisely here that the constructive role of time becomes evident, breaking the symmetry of complex systems, making them irreversible and eventually unamenable to analysis:

> "Enfolded in all the shapes and processes that make us unique - in the chemical reaction of our cells and the shape of our nerve nets - are thousands upon thousands of bifurcation points constituting a living chronology of the choices by which we evolved as a system from the primordial single cell to our present form."
> (op. cit.: 144)

The sensitivity of a system at certain bifurcation points leading to so-called *catastrophes* has been modelled in terms of a *fold* in the phase space (cf. Briggs and Peat 1990). It is upon arrival at such a *catastrophy fold* that the system undergoes a dramatic change. Take, for example, a balloon. Depending on the air pressure, which is the *control variable* in this case, the state of the balloon will change. The increase of the air pressure leads the system near to the catastrophy fold. Beyond this fold the balloon will have exploded...

The issue becomes more complex in systems with more control variables where the effects of an increase of some of the control variables derives a topological "map" with multiple dimensions.

In the realm of synergetics such phase transitions have also been studied extensively.[127] Here we consider the case of a delayed phase transition or *hysteresis* (Hohenberger 1996: 175, *pace* Haken 1990) which is due to a

> "... bias or, metaphorically speaking, to a systemic conservation, that makes the system cling to an order parameter as long as possible, even when there is a coexisting and competing order parameter that will inevitably take over the attraction in the future. Hence, the transition is delayed and happens *later* than without this bias. Recall that *hysteron* means "later"."[128]

---

[127] See Hohenberger (1996) for further references.

[128] The phenomenon is illustrated by an example of visual perception: in a series of drawings a man's face is progressively distorted so as to represent a girl. As for the perception of either the man's face or the girl's it was observed that the relevant change takes place at different points depending on whether one begins to look at the pictures beginning with the man's face or with the girl's (cf. op. cit.: 173f. and Haken 1990)

The interesting aspect of hysteresis is that it illustrates the system's *overstability* or resistance towards an alternative attractor or order parameter. Despite its presence, the alternative attractor "*does not overtly exert any attraction*" (ibid.) until the system reaches a certain critical point - i.e. the end of the hysteresis region - where it switches to a new state. Again, we have to acknowledge the relevance of the system's previous state: whenever the system is in such a *hysteresis region* or *overlapping region* in which alternative attractors coexist it can be in either state depending on its direction.

In summarising the preceding considerations about bifurcations a final quotation of Briggs and Peat (1990: 143) which highlights the potential uncovered in any of a system's branching:

> "Like a momentary window into the whole, the amplification of bifurcations leads to order or to chaos."

As I remarked earlier our understanding of the theory of evolution needs to be reconsidered in terms of a dynamic theory. We cannot continue to regard evolution as the result of adaptation by means of variation and selection. Instead we have to allow for the emergence of something new as the result of "*a delicate interplay between chance and necessity*" (Prigonine and Stengers 1984: 176).

It is important to keep in mind that the dependency of a new state on the former state, on the one hand, and its non-reducibility to the former state, on the other hand - i.e. the apparent *paradox of emergence* (cf. Hohenberger 1996) - can only be solved in the framework of a dynamic model of emergence.

This hinges also on the controversial debate with regard to the question of whether development is continuous or discontinuous:

> "... this continuity of living systems is only apparent. At the branch points where something new emerges, disruptions of order are in fact necessary, abrupt changes occur. Indeed, the interplay of order and chaos constitutes the creative potential of nature."
> (Cramer 1993: 7)

I have already emphasised the relevance of these considerations for other research areas. In this respect, the study of the relevance of self-organisation in ontogeny is of special interest.

In her extended study about self-organisation and language acquisition, Hohenberger (1996) also touches upon our understanding of the genome. The emphasis is put on its self-organising or creative component of the genome relieving it from the blueprint character assumed in traditional analyses, which is reflected in the term *genetic envelope* (ibid.:

117).[129] Deterministic chaos is assumed to play a fundamental role in the brain:

> "[b]ecause of the genome it [the brain] is stable enough, because of self-organization *via* plastic synapsis it is flexible enough to optimally adapt to different environmental demands."
> (ibid.: 85)

I have also stressed the necessity of considering complex systems as a whole if we want to understand their behaviour or development. In this respect the creation of a new order on the basis of coincidence and feedback is closely related to communication and information.[130]

Following Prigonine and Stengers (1984) one of the fundamental characteristics of self-organising systems is their export of entropy. Self-organising systems with this property are called *dissipative* as opposed to *conservative* self-organising systems, which are subject to reversible structure-building processes:

> "We know that far from the equilibrium, new types of structures may originate spontaneously. In far-from-equilibrium conditions we may have transformation from disorder, from thermal chaos, into order. New dynamic states of matter may originate, states that reflect the interaction of a given system with its surroundings. We have called these new structures *dissipative structures* to emphasize the constructive role of dissipative processes in their formation."
> (op. cit.: 12)

Consider the role of the environment at the edge between order and chaos: dissipative systems maintain their relative stability by means of their import of energy and their production of entropy. As pointed out by Briggs and Peat (1990: 139),

> "[t]he name *dissipative structure* expresses a paradox central to Prigonine's vision. Dissipation suggests chaos and falling apart; structure is its

---

[129] The notion is used in the sense of "globally licensed by the genes but locally autonomously realized by the neuronal assemblies in the brain" (op. cit.: 88). Hohenberger concedes that this term is not unproblematic either: Whilst it is assumed that "[t]his conception is supposed to achieve a synthesis of the various contributing factors - the genes and the environment - on the basis of self-organisation" such proposals "run into the apory of infinite regress: who constrains the genetic envelope itself?" (ibid.: 124) The reader is referred to her study for an extended discussion of how a full-blown model of self-organisation may overcome this dilemma.

[130] As pointed out by Werner Ebeling (1991: 57) one of the major insights gained in physics was that the transmission of information was always related to energy and entropy transmission without being identical to these two factors. Furthermore, it was understood that information was only relevant in systems with more states. Eventually, information would only work in a state of non-balance.

opposite. Dissipative structures are systems capable of maintaining their identity only by remaining continually open to the flux and flow of their environment."

We can now elaborate our considerations about self-organisation outlined above in the broader temporal dimension of evolution. If self-organisation is the elemental process of evolution, our understanding of evolutionary processes requires the consideration of the interwovenness of the underlying self-organising processes (cf. Ebeling 1991: 17).
This enhances our non-linear understanding of evolution: apart from bifurcations and enhancements which create new laws we need to consider the interaction of the sub-parts:

> "A system far from the equilibrium may be described as organized not because it realizes a plan alien to elementary activities, or transcending them, but, on the contrary, because amplification of a microscopic fluctuation occurring at the "right moment" resulted in favouring one reaction path over a number of other equally possible paths. Under certain circumstances, therefore, the role played by individual behaviour can be decisive. The more general "overall" behaviour cannot in general be taken as dominating in any way the elementary constituting it."
> (Prigonine and Stengers 1984: 176)

Any scientific analysis of nature seeking a linear and hierarchical causality misses the point. Living systems are 'autopoietic' (*Greek: self-creating*) and subject to a kind of paradox: they are self-creative and autonomous whilst embedded in their environment in quite a complex way (cf. Briggs and Peat 1990).

7.3.2 Dynamic conceptions of language development

By means of the preceding insight into the field of chaos theory we have familiarised ourselves with some notions which have proven to be of crucial importance in our understanding of many organic and unorganic phenomena. Certainly, terms such as fractal dimension or bifurcation originate from mathematics and were originally used in natural sciences' modelling of such diverse phenomena as the motion of a pendulum or the reaction of chemical solutions. During the course of the preceding decades, however, theories of dynamic systems or self-organisation have had a major impact in such different scientific fields as biology, neurology or sociology. The "impact" has been rather "smooth" in linguistics. We could see in section 7.2 that self-organisation in linguistic development is a topic which has only recently received due attention and research in these terms has not yet gone all the way long (but see Hohenberger 1996). It goes without saying that the endeavour of providing such a full-blown model of language acquisition along these lines would also go beyond the scope of this analysis. Instead, we will explore the relevance of chaotic dynamics and self-organisation for a theory of ASLA. In the preceding sections I highlighted some of the implications following from this framework for our understanding of development on different time scales. We may anticipate that a similar procedure will be quite fruitful in the domain of language. In section 7.2.4 I already discussed some preliminaries about the relevance of self-organisation in language development. We will now enrich these considerations with what we learned in the preceding sections about the *mirror-world* (Briggs and Peat 1990) of dynamic systems. Firstly, we will have a look at some assumptions put forward in this regard in the fields of language change and child language acquisition respectively. We will then draw our attention to the field of ASLA and consider some general implications before proceeding to the detailed analysis of an adult learner's L2 German.

7.3.2.1 Gradualness, catastrophes and language change

In his study about parameter-setting and diachronic language change Lightfoot (1991) already highlighted the fractal dimension of changes in the history of a language:

> "Large-scale changes that one can perceive over centuries reflect, in some way, smaller changes."
> (ibid.: 157)

We all know that any living language is subject to perpetual change as much as we, *qua* individual speakers of a language, are "*exposed to different forms of that language through changes of circumstances*" (ibid.). As pointed out by Lightfoot research in the field of language change has been bound to the gradualness of this development. Interestingly, this gradualness was understood to be deterministic as much as child language acquisition. A critical review of findings along these lines reveals, however, that

> "... the commitment to the gradual acquisition of the new harmonic properties was much more an article of faith than an empirical result based on investigation."
> (ibid.: 159)

In other words, many of the studies suffer from basic empirical shortcomings, i.e. in many cases the assumed gradual steps of development would not coincide with the actual change. In this respect Lightfoot envisages a more promising approach, namely, the delimitation of gradualness on the basis of generative grammar as conceived in GB theory:

"If grammars assign different structures to expressions from one generation to the next, then at least some changes will be abrupt: if syntactic structures are topological entities, as assumed here, they are not generally amenable to incremental modification. However, the triggering experience and grammars may change gradually in certain ways."
(ibid.: 160)

Following this reasoning, gradualness pertains to performance of speakers. And up to a certain (critical) point such minor changes do not affect the (internal) grammar. Thus Lightfoot's claim is essentially that *abrupt* changes only take place at particular points and this they do through the *triggering experience*. The intricacy of the issue is further related to the concept of grammar as conceived in the Principles and Parameters model:

"Because grammars are abstract objects, grammars with quite different structural properties might generate sets of sentences which were more similar to each other, and grammars differing in just one parametric setting might generate wildly different outputs."
(ibid.: 161)

Lightfoot further considers the possibility that gradualness may characterise the implementation of a new parameter-setting as it may happen at an individual level before affecting the whole speech community. Such a view is based on the premise that an individual's speech may change in the course of his life (ibid.: 162):

"As somebody adopts a new parameter setting, say a new verb-object order, the output of that person's grammar often differs from that of other people's. This in turn affects the linguistic environment, which may then be more likely to trigger the new parameter setting in younger people. Thus a chain reaction may be created, which may gradually permeate the speech community."

According to Lightfoot continuity and discontinuity in language change can be modelled by means of a logistic growth curve. Such S-shaped curves illustrate how abrupt changes are preceded by a gradual instability of the system. But it is only at a critical point that dramatic changes come in, for example, in the form of parameter-resettings:

"... the change may be foreshadowed in various ways, but there is a short period of rapid change, followed by a longer period where occasional residual forms gradually disappear."
(ibid.: 168)

In general, Lightfoot argues that languages are in a "*punctuated equilibrium*" (ibid.: 173), a notion which aims at uncovering how language is subject to both constancy as well as to structural changes. In analogy to other dynamic systems, Lightfoot also speaks of *catastrophes* in such cases. He also assumes that the "catastrophic" nature of parameter-resetting is reflected in the clustering effects or even chain reactions following such changes. Thus the Principles and Parameters model is necessary and insurpassable regarding the explanation of such dramatic changes and the course they take.

On the other hand, however, linguistic research has to realise the impossibility of determining the temporal dimension of such changes:

> "The theory of grammars cannot prescribe a universal path for language to slide along at various rates, acquiring properties in a predestined order; it cannot prophesy what changes a language will undergo in the future, because it cannot predict which chance factors will operate or when."
> (ibid.: 166)

Lightfoot considers various possibilities, i.e. "*chance or nongrammatical factors*" (ibid.: 170), which would lie at the heart of the gradual shifts in the triggering experience, such as "*environmental changes (...) induced by contact with other languages and dialects or introduced for stylistic reasons*" (ibid.: 169). Such factors, however, which may initially be considered as being just random, are not amenable to a systematic analysis, since

> "... in contrast with new parameter settings, they do not necessarily cast light on grammatical theory, and they properly remain beyond grammatical explanation."
> (ibid.: 171)

Largely compatible with our considerations in section 7.2.4 regarding the role of external factors in ASLA Lightfoot argues that the linguist's concern should lie in the analysis of the linguistic system's internal processes, how they constrain the limits of variation and potential change. We need to discern the quantity and the quality of the experience needed for a change in parameter-setting to happen.

7.3.2.2 The tripartite algorithm of language acquisition

In her study about self-organisation in language acquisition Hohenberger (1996) puts forward a model of language acquisition which aims at uncovering the relevance of the unstable or *liminal* states *qua* transition phases in the development of complex dynamic systems.

Hohenberger's considerations about this *fractal* algorithm are a subpart of a more general tripartite model of change, which is based on the anthropological studies of V. W. Turner (cf. op. cit. for further references). As its denomination already reveals, the model comprises three crucial phases, namely, (a) a *pre-liminal*, (b) a *liminal* and (c) a *post-liminal* phase (ibid.: 67). As pointed out by Hohenberger this differentiation of

the sub-phases of change of state runs parallel with the concepts of initial grammar, interim grammar and target grammar or initial state, interim states and steady state respectively in the field of linguistics.
Hohenberger, however, goes a step further and embeds this algorithm in the framework of a dynamic theory of language acquisition. Basically, the application of the tripartite algorithm to language acquisition runs as follows (cf. op. cit.: 68):

- Preliminal state A:
  Initial state: stable and coherent grammar
- Liminal unstable state B:
  Interim state: unstable grammar allowing for (restricted) variation
- Post-liminal state C:
  Steady state: stable and presumably more complex grammar

Due to the fractal dimension of the algorithm it

> "... is assumed to apply repeatedly, not only once, leading to an increasing dissolution and refinement on several scales of magnitude and time (...) Yet, on any such scale the system looks self-similar."
> (ibid.: 68f.)

As for language development, we believe that the *liminal states* will be decisive as much as *catastrophy folds* or *bifurcations* in deterministic chaos. Individual trajectories are expected to manifest themselves especially in such liminal states. Subsequently, however, in the stable post-liminal or steady state liminal diversity will converge on to the target *qua* attractor. On the basis of the Principles and Parameters model the target "attractor" is a cover term for the language-specific instantiation of the universally constrained parametric options:

> "If one understands parameters as attractors, i.e. ordered states in the whole parameter space, then the attraction is directed towards only few dimensions, i.e. the many possibilities are compressed to only few solutions (...), but not just one. As the attraction is as intricate as a meander, there is ample phenomenological variability."
> (ibid.: 146)

If we further consider Hohenberger's claim that the initial or pre-liminal state need not be "*equi-initial, i.e. the same for every subject*" (ibid.: 141), we are left with a picture of language acquisition determined by the possibility of variation with the exception of the end state which is *equi-final* (ibid.: 145).
Consequently, language acquisition research should be aware of the relevance of the fractal character of individual developments or trajectories:

> "... the acknowledgement of interindividual variance directly leads to the **reflected idiomatic method** as the dynamic method of choice (...) Given the dynamic equations, a multitude of differing trajectories is simultaneously available. Every singular path "fits" the equations equally well, so no extra measure, like the arithmetic mean etc., is in fact needed."
> (ibid.: 147, her emphasis)

In addition, we need to look at the variation which takes place intra-individually. Such variations may be quite revealing with regard to the dynamics underlying the determination of the target-like language properties such as parameter-setting qua *bifurcations*. In this respect, Hohenberger pays special attention to the emergence of functional categories. The following passage highlights some of the fundamental assumptions underlying Hohenberger's analysis:

> "The system is supposed to show new qualitative properties once a critical threshold of complexity is passed. The idea is that what we usually call functional properties are emergent properties of the lexical ones or that functional projections are the appropriate emergent spell-out of lexical projections under respective conditions. After the lexicon has reached a certain volume, i.e. the child has acquired a certain number of lexical items, and after the child's phrase marker has reached a respective size, too, a spontaneous bifurcation takes place: Functional Categories and with them phrasal syntax emerge."
> (ibid.: 193)

Following this line of reasoning, her dynamic approach intends to overcome the shortcomings of the Continuity and the Maturation Hypothesis we acknowledged in chapter 5.

As regards parameter setting and triggers, we are left with a model of change that embraces the system-internal potential which will allow for the triggering experience to induce the desired effect at exactly the points at which the system's sensitivity is at its peak:

> "It is also at these critical points of bifurcation that the trigger applies. Here, on the *limen*, it can almost effortlessly guide the system from one attractor that has become unstable into a new stable one."
> (ibid.: 150)

7.3.3 Conclusion and preliminary outlook at a dynamic approach to ASLA

Far from opposing "chance" and "necessity",
we now see both aspects as essential in the description
of non-linear systems far from equilibrium.

(Prigonine and Stengers 1984: 14)

It is plausible to assume that *sensitive bifurcation points* will be relevant on the different temporal scales of linguistic analysis. We already came across Lightfoot's considerations regarding language change. We could see that a dynamic approach proves to be quite revealing as to the interplay of continuity and discontinuity in diachronic language development. It seems languages are prone to relative stability until they are pushed into the vicinity of "catastrophy folds" where their sensitivity to change is crucially increased as much as other complex systems when they are far from the equilibrium:

> "... in equilibrium matter is "blind", but in far-from-equilibrium conditions it begins to be able to perceive, to "take into account", in its way of functioning, differences in the external world (...)."
> (Prigonine and Stengers 1984: 14)

Lightfoot explores the possibility of a gradual change in linguistic performance. Ultimately, however, the relevant "abrupt" changes take place due to grammar-internal reasons. The linguistic system simply cannot accommodate contradictory evidence in the input anymore and is forced to undergo reorganisation. For a certain period of time we expect a *hysteresis effect* especially wherever the input is amenable to an ambiguous analysis: the system may oscillate between alternative "attractors" during a chaotic or *liminal* phase.

In general terms, the overall aim of striving for stability (recall the above mentioned dimensions of equilibration in self-organising systems) also holds in the case of human language faculty: universal constraints ensure that language systems remain within the universal bounds. We may further enrich our understanding of the Principles and Parameters model once we acknowledge that the bifurcations language undergoes are recapitulated in what we may term the "parametric memory" of grammar, namely, functional categories.

If we take the fractal nature of language seriously, we expect the preceding considerations to be of relevance also in ASLA. In somewhat preliminary terms we anticipate that the aquisition of a language in adulthood, i.e. at a point where we fully master (at least) one language (our L1), should show some similarities to the processes taking place in diachronic language change. This consideration entails the possibility that the L1 is part of the initial state to an extent yet to be determined. Such similarities should be most evident at the non-equilibrium states where the system oscillates among alternative attractors. As much as in language change we do not know whether or when the L2 interim sytem will be eventually drawn onto the L2 target grammar or *L2-attractor*. Note that in this case also the L2-attractor is a cover term for a specific constellation of parametric choices or attractors. As opposed to child language acquisition we cannot rely on the assumption of equi-finality in the case of ASLA. In view of diachronic changes we should however concede a certain relativity of this deterministic uniformity. Nevertheless, it seems variation in any of the sub-states of change and especially as regards the end state is more evident in ASLA.

In the course of the present investigation we have come across many different hypotheses which state that failure to reach the ultimate attainment marks the fundamental difference between language acquisition in childhood and language acquisition in adulthood. For decades (!) variability was assumed to be of relevance only in ASLA. And it remained an unresolved problem in every theoretical framework. On the basis of the theory of self-organising dynamic systems one of the fundamental implications for our work in the field of ASLA or language development in general should be that our world and the way it has evolved in the course of time is by no means as linear or as predictable as the reductionistic scientific tradition made us believe (cf. Briggs and Peat 1990, Cramer 1993 among others). Once we realise that this also applies to language and its acquisition or development, non-linearity and variability should cease to be regarded as exotic phenomena. As regards ASLA, I would like to argue here that in many ways language acquisition in adulthood will prove to be quite instructive as regards our dynamic language faculty. Following this line of reasoning, anyone of the individual trajectories needs to be taken seriously since any case may evidence some of the different aspects of the underlying dynamics.

Following Cramer's initial differentiation among the possible situations regarding feedback processes (see section 7.3.1.1) we may at this preliminary stage consider the following possibilities for ASLA:

- The L2 interim grammar reaches the final value X or target "L2 attractor". This possibility would amount to successful ASLA.

- The L2 interim grammar oscillates in the bounds of a "limit cycle" consisting of the L1 and the L2 attractor. In the case of a "fossilised" learner grammar the learner would end up with a hybrid grammar. On a smaller time-scale such a situation is similar to the hysteresis effect described above.

- The L2 interim grammar evolves in an unpredictable way. Neither the L1 nor the L2 seem do exert their necessary influence so as to draw the system onto their attractors.

As much as in the physical and physiological reality we expect these possibilities to manifest themselves in hybrid cases in ASLA. In other words, as there are many decisions to be taken, we expect that the above-mentioned possibilities may be relevant in different situations. One of the main tenets in chaos theory is that dynamic systems are especially sensitive to initial conditions. Among the conditions which may play a role in the dynamics underlying the individual trajectories we may consider the respective L1-L2 constellation or the exposure to L2 input. If the L1 system is part of the initial state in ASLA the decisive question will be in which way the L2 input will challenge the apparent "structural stability". We expect that considerations similar to the ones outlined in Prigonine and Stengers (1984: 189/190) will hold, cf.

> "... the new constituents, introduced in small quantities, lead to a new set of reactions among the system's components. This new set of reactions then enters into competition with the system's previous mode of functioning. If the system is "structurally stable" as far as this intrusion is concerned, the new mode of functioning will be unable to establish itself and the "innovators" will not survive. If, however, the structural fluctuation successfully imposes itself - if, for example, the kinetics whereby the "innovators" multiply is fast enough for the latter to invade the system instead of being destroyed - the whole system will adopt a new mode of functioning: its activity will be governed by a new "syntax"."

And after all these remarks on "chance", where would the deterministic aspect of ASLA come into play? Certainly, what comes to mind immediately is the developmental sequence which has been subject to controversial discussion over the last decade. The very possibility of such a sequence *qua* rough characterisation of the developmental milestones in ASLA illustrates that the range of variation is limited. More technically, processes of structure-building or restructuring are constrained by UG. Learners do not construct grammars which would be impossible in terms of UG. The choice among universal parametric options is universally limited. This is also evident in language change. Furthermore, for those learners who progress towards the target, the sequential determination of the target-like properties also follows grammar-internal reasons. Self-organisation draws upon the system-internal potential. In ASLA, the unfolding of this UG-constrained potential is probably conditioned by the L1 knowledge adult learners are equipped with and the ways in which the "intruding" elements of the L2 input impose themselves.

In concluding, we anticipate that research in the field of ASLA will undoubtedly profit from a dynamic approach to language. In the following sections we will discuss some of the milestones of one such individual trajectory in ASLA and discuss the implications for a theory along the lines proposed.

8 Intra-individual variation in ASLA: A case study

aber ich brauch vergessen meine sprache für lernen die deutsch
'but I need to forget my language in order to learn German'
(Bruno, file 11: 261)

8.1 Preliminary considerations

In the following sections I will discuss the acquisition of L2 German word order by *Bruno*, an adult learner with L1 Italian. Bruno arrived in Germany in 1978 at the age of 16. The analysis is based on the data collection undertaken in the framework of the ZISA project mentioned in section 1.2.3. The data comprise the transcripts of 29 recorded interviews (henceforth *files*) which were held on a regular basis (approx. every fortnight) over a period of about two and a half years.
Following our previous assumptions regarding a dynamic approach to language development I will pay special attention to the *linguistic bifurcations* and the *far-from-equilibrium* states Bruno's L2 German undergoes. In doing so I aim at providing further empirical insight into the question of how chance and necessity interact in ASLA. I will focus on the dynamics underlying parameter (re-)setting or triggering in ASLA and reconsider the traditional opposition of lexical as opposed to syntactic learning.

The analysis will be restricted to structural areas of contrast between Italian and German which are commonly believed to be related to universally constrained parametric choices. The appropriate descriptive analysis of these areas of contrast are still subject to some controversy. Wherever the ongoing discussion is of relevance for the present study I will take pains to highlight the current proposals. The analysis will be based on the following parametric differences between Italian and German:

- VP-headedness
  L1 Italian: VP-initial
  L2 German: VP-final

- Nominative case-checking
  L1 Italian: under spec-head agreement
  L2 German: under government

- IP-headedness
  L1 Italian: IP-initial
  L2 German: IP-final

If the assumption of the fractal nature of language is correct, the individual developmental path should be regarded as an instance of self-similarity applying to the multiple time-scales at which language development manifests itself. Therefore, I will also consider findings from the domain of language change or language acquisition in childhood.
In sum, I believe we are well-equipped and ready to embark on our trip through Bruno's L2 German development.

8.2 Developmental milestones

8.2.1 VP headedness

8.2.1.1 VP initial

The analysis of the data in files 1-4 reveals that the underlying word order of Bruno's incipient L2 German is SVO. In parametric terms this means that the headedness of the VP is set at the value "initial".
The strict adherence to the verb-object pattern is especially evident in constructions with periphrastic verb forms[131] and *für*-introduced infinitive clauses, where the object always follows the infinitive (cf. (1) - (7)).[132]

(1) [3-131] jetze   da   ich   **habe gebringte** keine person
              now   there I   have brought   no   person
     'I have not taken anybody there now'

---

[131] It is certainly striking that similar utterances also occur in bilingual LA, if only randomly. See, for example, Müller (1993: 180), where the following sequences are quoted (my transl.):
  (i)   Ivar 2:6, 6   woll lesen ein buch   (*want read a book*)
  (ii)   Ivar 2:9, 18   ich i will reiten mit du   (*I want ride with you*)
  (iii) Ivar 2:9, 18   i muß zumachen meine   (*I must close my*)
  (iv)   Pascal 2:9, 28   ich will machen das   (*I want make that*)
  (v)   Pascal 3:0, 17   ich will verstecken das   (*I want hide that*)
  (vi)   Pascal 3:2, 23   aber du mußt fangen   (*but you must catch*
                          den gelben auto   the yellow car*)
Note, however, that the question of why children also produce VO orders, if only randomly, is not treated any further.

[132] The number in square brackets follow the indications in the transcripts provided to me: the first number specifies the number of the transcript or file, the second the number of the utterance. Every utterance is followed by a word-to-word translation. For ease of understanding I also supply a free translation.

(2) [4-28] eine person **muß studieren** eine sprache
a person *must study* a *language*
'you have to study a language'

(3) [4-31] meine wenn du **hast gesprochen** mit
mean-1S when you have spoken with
die andere personen wenn ich war krank
the other people when I was ill
'I mean, when you spoke to other people, when I was ill'

(4) [4-41] **biste gewesen** mite deutsche kinder
have-[you] been with German children
für lernen die literatur
for learn the literature
'have you been with German children in order to study the literature?'

(5) [4-85f.] eine person **für matte** eine schöne
a person *for make* a nice
foto von eine person **muß matten**
picture of a person *must make*
zehn foto für eine foto mehr gut
ten pictures for a *picture more good*
'in order to make a nice picture of somebody a person must make 10 pictures, for a better picture'

(6) [4-100] ich habe gesehn wenn er **hat gehab** barbiere
I have seen when he has had beard
'I saw him when he had a beard'

(7) [4-197] ich **habe vergessen** meine schuhe zu arbeit
I have forgotten my shoes to work
'I forgot to take my shoes to work'

In files 1 and 2 the finite and the non-finite verb are not interrupted by another syntactic constituent with the exception of the adverb 'schon' (*already, yet*) (as of file 2) (cf. (8) - (11)). Note that the possibility of allowing adverbs inside the verb bracket, if only restrictively, is given in VO languages as in Bruno's mother tongue Italian (cf. Belletti 1990).

179

(8) [2-2] isch habe schon versteh
         I   have already understood
         'I have understood already'

(9) [2-21] isch bin schon   gegangen
          I   have already gone
          'I have gone already'

(10) [2-43] isch habe schon gesagt
           I   have already said
           'I have said already'

(11) [2-175] ich habe schon gegessen
            I   have already eaten
            'I have eaten already'

Case-marked pronominals occur inside the verb bracket as soon as they appear (as of file 3), cf.

(12) [3-103] jetzt hat mir gesagt das lehrerin
            now   has me   told   the teacher
            fotomontage
            photo-montage
            'now the teacher showed me the photo-montage'

(13) [3-142] nein aber eine person hat mir gesagt eh
            no   but a   person has me   told   eh
            'no, but a person told me...'

(14) [3-153] eine mädche hat mir gesatte das
            a   girl   has me   told   that
            'a girl told me that'

(15) [4-99] ich habe **ihn** gesehn mura von   letzte male
           I   have him   seen   mura of   last   time
           'I have seen him, mura, [the one] from last time'

(16) [4-129] ich habe **dir** gesagt
            I   have you   told
            'I told you'

(17) [4-138] meine mutter hat eh **mir** gesatte
my mother has eh me told
'my mother told me'

The position of case-marked pronominals is especially interesting as regards the target-like determination of the VP-headedness. For one, the position of these pronominals is target-like, i.e. left to the non-finite case assigning verb[133] (cf. also (18) - (20)).

(18) [3-95] wenn **mir** gesagt
when me told
'when he told me'

(19) [3-134] **mir** sagen ja bringst eine turke hier
me tell yes bring a turk here
'[she] told me, yes, next time you come along with a turk'

(20) [4-99] ich habe **ihn** gesehn mura von letzte male
I have him seen mura of last time
'I have seen him, Mura, [the one] from last time'

Note that the correct determination of their position must be input-driven. In Bruno's mother tongue, Italian, the pronominal would occur as a clitic left to the finite verb, be it an auxiliary or a main verb. Furthermore, these pronominals are the only overtly case-marked elements so far.

Recall that in German case is assigned to the left (as well as theta-role assignment), which in turn bears on the underlying object-verb order. Consequently, it seems plausible to assume that case-marked pronominals have a pioneering function in Bruno's determination of the target-like direction of theta-role and case assignment. (Note that I explicitly do not regard them as triggering elements!)

With respect to the distribution of object NPs and pronominalised objects utterance (20) is further revealing. In this sequence the direct object occurs twice, the pronominalised version inside the verb bracket, the object NP right to the non-finite verb. This distribution indicates that the position inside the verb bracket is restricted, for the time being, to overtly

---

[133] There is, however, one exception, namely
(i) [4-340] meine bruder immer gewonnen mir
my brother always won me
'my brother always beat me'
where the status of the verb is unclear. In target German this form corresponds to the participle, but it could well be that Bruno uses this form as a finite verb form.

case-marked elements which are somehow "light" as opposed to "heavy", non-overtly case marked object NPs. So whilst the target-like underlying object position seems to have been discovered the position right to the verb is still being used. In the light of subsequent development, (20) is instructive as to Bruno's extended use of alternative structural possibilities.

8.2.1.2 Restructuring of the VP headedness

Object NPs start to show up inside the verb bracket, i.e. between the auxiliary and the non-finite main verb, from file 6 onwards (cf. (21) - (27)).

(21) [6-24] ich **habe** da alle meine schule **gemacht**
I have there all my school made
'I had there all my school education'

(22) [6-35] ich **habe** viel arbeit **gemacht**
I have much work done
'I have done a lot of work'

(23) [7-70] seine vater **hat** eine fehler **gemacht**
his father has a mistake made
'his father made a mistake'

(24) [7-79] in akzehn jahren **hast** du nicht gute
in eighteen years have you not good
freunde **gehabt**
friends had
'for eighteen years you did not have good friends'

(25) [7-81] jetzt **hat** seine vater eine fehler **gemacht**
now has his father a mistake made
'his father has made a mistake now'

(26) [7-109] ich **habe** mit eine spiele von worte **gesatt**
I have with a game of words said
'with a play on words I said'

(27) [7-113] ich **habe** auch eine diskussion mit eine
I have also a discussion with a

182

           prätre **gematt**
           priest made
           'I also had a discussion with a priest'

But target-like OV is not obeyed across the board (cf. (28) - (31)).

(28)   [6-105]   isch   **habe gehabet** keine lust
                 I   have had   no   inclination
                 'I was not in the mood'

(29)   [7-68]   aber ich   **habe gehört** viele problematische
                 but I   have heard   many   problematic
                 diskussion von alfio
                 discussion of   alfio
                 'but I heard many problematic discussions of Alfio'

(30)   [7-108]   ein kollege   **hat** mir **gesagt** andere worte
                 a   colleague has   me   said   other   words
                 'a colleague said other words to me'

(31)   [7-134]   oweh   wir **haben** schon   **gehabt** viele
                 oh-dear we   have   already   had   many
                 fragen
                 questions
                 'oh dear, we have had many questions already'

Furthermore, we can see that both orders occur with the same verbs and even with the same object NPs as illustrated in the following (utterances (31), (24), (30) and (26) are repeated here for convenience).

(31)   [7-134]   oweh wir **haben** schon **gehabt** viele fragen
(24)   [7-79]   in 18 jahren **hast** du nicht gute freunde **gehabt**

(30)   [7-108]   ein kollege **hat** mir **gesagt** andere worte
(26)   [7-109]   ich **habe** mit eine spiele von worte **gesatt**

There are also sequences in which adverbs, prepositional phrases and object NPs are "distributed" over the positions left and right of the non-finite verb (cf. (32) - (35)).

(32) [6-43] nach isch **habe** eine jahre **gemacht**
afterwards I have a year made
fotograf
photograph
'Afterwards I made photography for a year'

(33) [8-69] ich **habe** alfio **gesehn** mit eine renault grün
I have Alfio seen with a Renault green
'I have seen Alfio in a green Renault'

(34) [8-205] ich **bin** schon da **gegangen** in schweiz
I have already there gone to Switzerland
'I have already been to Switzerland'

(35) [9-129] ich **habe** alle nummer **gelernt** ganz perfekt
I have all numbers learned quite perfect
'I learned all the numbers very perfectly'

Figure 8.1 shows that the orders non-finite verb - object and object - non-finite verb alternate in files 6 to 11.

Percent

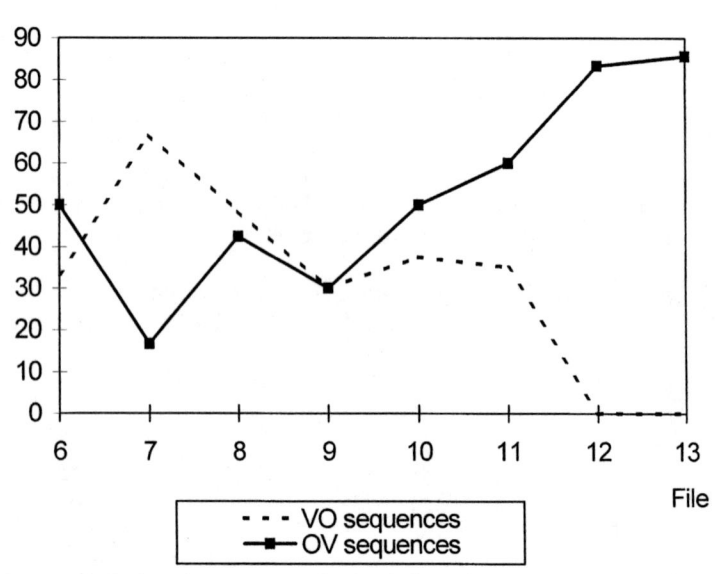

Figure 8.1 Relative frequency of target-like OV and target-deviant VO sequences

184

It is certainly striking that both orders are used alternatively, i.e. there is no apparent reason for why and when one option is chosen over the other. Note that VO and OV orders occur equally frequently from file 8 to file 11. As of file 12, however, VO orders disappear, indicating that the target-like parametric option has been implemented.

On the assumption that what is at issue here is the simultaneous availability of two alternative structural positions, the fact that the same variation can be observed with particle verbs, which are used with increasing frequency, comes as no surprise (cf. (36) - (41)).

(36) [8-205] ich **bin** schon *da* **gegangen** in schweiz
             I   have already there gone   to Switzerland
             'I have been to Switzerland already'

(37) [8-212] **bist** du schon **gewesen** *da*
             have you already been   there
             'have you been there already?'

(38) [8-275] **bine**   **gegange** *unter*
             [I] have gone   under
             'I sank'

(39) [9-42] wenn ich **habe** wieder *unter* **gelassen**
            when I   have   again under   let
            'when I let it go down again'

(40) [11-44] und wie lange **machst** du *leer* eine
             and how long make   you empty a
             flasche so
             bottle so
             'and how long does it take you to empty a bottle?'

(41) [11-45] in wie lange **machst** du eine flasche
             in how long   make   you a   bottle
             so *leer*
             so empty
             'and how long does it take you to empty a bottle?'

Furthermore, we need to consider modal verb constructions which also become productive at this time. Note that modal verb inflection morphology is deviant at the beginning in contrast to auxiliary verb forms, which correctly agree with the sentence subject from the beginning. As the following sequences show, some of the deviant forms of the modal verb 'wollen' (*to want*) and 'müssen' (*to have to*) result from the overgeneralisation of main verb inflection morphology (I will deal with this issue below). As for the relative order of modal and non-finite verb the same development as with auxiliary and particle verbs can be observed: there is a period of time in which we observe an alternation between the orders modal - non-finite verb - object and modal - object - non-finite verb, as well as the apparent "distribution" of adverbs, prepositional phrases and object NPs over the positions left and right of the non-finite verb (cf. (42) – (56)). The target-like order is implemented as of file 12. [134]

(42) [7-23] ich **wolle**   **kommen** mit   dir
             I   want   come   with   you
             'I want to come with you'

(43) [7-29] ich **musse**   **sache**   ein   was
             I   must   say   a   something
             'I have to say something'

(44) [8-44] eine person   **muß**   **sprechen**   natürlich
             a   person   must   speak   naturally
             'you have to speak naturally'

---

[134] Note that initially Bruno erroneously uses the verb 'brauchen' (*to need*) in the sense of 'müssen' (*to have to*).
 (i) [11-22]   momente   ich   brauche   überlegen
               moment   I   need   think
               'one moment, I have to think [about it]'
 (ii) [11-26] ich   brauche   die   stuhle   richtig   legen
               I   need   the   chair   correctly   lie
               'I have to put the chairs correctly'
 (iii) [11-75] und   brauchst du   immer   vorsicht   machen
               and   need   you   always   carefully   make
               'and you have to do it always carefully'
 (iv) [11-261] aber   ich   brauche   vergessen meine   sprache   für
               but   I   need   forget   my   language for
               lernen   die   deutsch
               learn   the   German
               'but I have to forget my language in order to learn German'
But there are, on the other hand, also target-like sequences like the following.
 (v) [11-103] aber   braucht   nicht   ganz   perfekt   sein
               but   need   not   completely perfect   be
               'but it need not be completely perfect'
Interestingly, the erroneous usage disappears as of file 12, i.e. at the point where target-like OV is implemented.

(45) [8-130] ich **muß** sofort die dusche **machen**
I must immediately the shower make
'I have to take a shower immediately'

(46) [8-146] **muß** heute oder morgen **kommen**
must today or tomorrow come
'[he] should be coming today or tomorrow'

(47) [8-262] was **willst** du **machen** in spanien
what want you make in Spain?
'what do you want to do in Spain?'

(48) [9-66] du **mußt** mehr vorsichtig **machen**
you have-to more carefully make
'you have to do it more carefully'

(49) [9-67] dann du **mußt** **sagen** deine probleme zu
then you must say your problems to
de chef
the chef
'then you must tell your problems to the chef'

(50) [9-127] ich **muß** jeden tag **sagen** auf italienisch
I must every day say on Italian
'every day I must say in Italian'

(51) [9-147] ich **kann** nicht **bringen** mit de zug zwanzig
I can not bring with the train twenty
apparade
cameras
'I cannot take twenty cameras in the train'

(52) [9-241] **muß** andrea **sein**
must andrea be
'it must be Andrea'

(53) [10-35] a aber ich **kann** niche so schnelle **lesen**
but I can not so fast read
eine wort so
a word so

187

'but I cannot read a word as fast'

(54) [11-6] **willst** du vielleicht auch so eine steine
want you perhaps also such a stone
so mit eine loch dadrin **haben**
so with a hole there-inside have
'would you also like to have such a stone with a hole'

(55) [11-140] ich **kann** dir **bringen** wo wo sind
I can you bring where where are
die schlechte haus für ausländer
the bad house for foreigners
'I can take you to the bad places for foreigners'

(56) [11-187] aber wenne die expositione
but if the "expositione" [= Ital. exposure (Phot)]
da ist nicht wichtig **kannst** du auch
there is not important can you also
scheiß **machen**
shit make
'but if the exposure is irrelevant there you may as well mess it up'

The eventual implementation of target-like OV is also evident in infinitive clauses. Interestingly, the frequency of constructions with infinitive clauses increases considerably from file 12 onwards, cf.

(57) [12-16] ich habe dir schon verstanden brauchs nich
I have you already understood need not
mehr zu zeigen
more to show
'I have understood you already, you do not have to show me more'

(58) [12-27] ich habe dir schon lange gekannt brauch
I have you already long known need
nich zu sagen
not to say
'I do not have to say that I know you for a long time'

(59) [12-164] | normale | ein | italiener | wenne | mache | im
| --- | --- | --- | --- | --- | ---
| *normally* | *an* | *Italian* | *when* | *make* | *in-the*
| fernseh | eine | spielfilm | hate | viel zu | lerne
| *television* | *a* | *film* | *has* | *much to* | *learn*
| so | wie | wir | hame sonntag | gemachte |
| *so* | *as* | *we* | *have Sunday* | *made* |

'normally an Italian has a lot to learn when they show a film on TV, as we did on Sunday'

(60) [14-40] | ich | habe | nie | etwas | zu | machen
| --- | --- | --- | --- | --- | ---
| *I* | *have* | *never* | *something* | *to* | *make*

'I never have something to do'

(61) [15-61] | das | hat | nicht | zu tun | mit -
| --- | --- | --- | --- | ---
| *that* | *has* | *not* | *to do* | *with*

'that has nothing to do with...'

(62) [15-106] | er | versucht | ein | paar | fragen | zu | machen
| --- | --- | --- | --- | --- | --- | ---
| *he* | *tries* | *a* | *couple* | *questions* | *to* | *make*

'he tries to ask a couple of questions'

(63) [16-17] | ich | habe | telefon | da | liegen | gelassen
| --- | --- | --- | --- | --- | ---
| *I* | *have* | *telephone* | *there* | *lie* | *let*

'I let the telephone there'

(64) [16-45] | das | ist | kompliziert | zu | erklären
| --- | --- | --- | --- | ---
| *that* | *is* | *complex* | *to* | *explain*

'that is difficult to explain'

(65) [16-110] | die | können | schon | beginnen | eine
| --- | --- | --- | --- | ---
| *that-ones* | *can* | *already* | *begin* | *a*
| wohnung | zu | finden | | |
| *flat* | *to* | *find* | | |

'they may already begin to find a flat'

(66) [16-186] | also | ich | habe | nie | gelebt | eine
| --- | --- | --- | --- | --- | ---
| *so* | *I* | *have* | *never* | *lived* | *a*
| programme | machen | | | | |
| *program* | *make* | | | | |

'I have not had the experience of making a program'

189

(67) [17-117] wir   haben   noch   zeit   sie   zu   kennen
              we   have   still time   her   to   know
       'we still have time to know her'

(68) [17-121] jeder   hat   immer   etwas   zu   lernen
              everybody has   always   something   to   learn
       'everybody has always got something to learn'

(69) [17-141] zum   beispiele   er   beginnt   eine   kopfschmerz
              for   example   he   begins   a   headache
              zu   haben   und   dann   zwei   drei   tablette
              to   have   and   then   two   three   pills
       'for example, he gets a headache, then he takes two, three pills'

(70) [17-216] mein   bruder   hat   gar   nichts   mehr   zu
              my   brother   has   at-all   nothing   more   to
              sagen
              say
       'it isn't for my brother to say anything anymore'

Furthermore, we can observe the target-like specification of the VP headedness in Bruno's *für*-introduced infinite embedded clauses (cf. (71) - (73)). It is worth mentioning that the replacement of 'für' (*for*) by the target-like 'um... zu' (*in order to*) only takes place at a later point in time. As will be discussed below it is certainly striking that the introduction of the correct conjunction occurs exactly at the point where Bruno is involved in restructuring his grammar so as to generate target-like verb-final embedded clauses.

(71) [12-15] normal   für   eine   persone   besser   eine
             normally   for   a   person   better   a
             ausländer   versteh[135]
             foreigner   understand
       'normally for a person to better understand a foreigner...'

(72) [13-65] wieviel   geld   brauchst   du   für   in
             how-much   money   need   you   for   in

---

[135] The forms "versteh" in (71) and "fahre" in (72) are taken to be the non-finite forms. See section 8.2.2 below for a discussion of agreement morphology in Bruno's L2 German.

190

>   spanien   fahre
>   *Spain   go*
>   'how much money do you need for going to Spain'

(73) [16-172]

aber	normale	die	emigrante	in	deutschland
but	*normally*	*the*	*emigrants*	*in*	*Germany*
normal	die	kommen	hier	für +n	bißchen
normally	*they*	*come*	*here*	*for +a*	*bit*
geld	verdienen	und	auch	für +n	bißchen
money	*earn*	*and*	*also*	*for +a*	*bit*

sparen
save

'but normally the emigrants come to Germany in order to earn and save a bit of money'

8.2.1.3 Conclusion

The most striking aspect about Bruno's development as regards the target-like determination of the VP-headedness is that it challenges the traditional idea that parameter (re-)setting must occur somewhat *instantaneously*. Instead, the data show that the implementation of the target-like parametric option only occurs after a phase, which we regard as a *transition phase*, in which target-deviant and target-like options coexist. Note that the alleged transitory character of the intermediate phase is due to the target-like parametric option being subsequently implemented. Furthermore, it is worth noting that each of the phases seems to be well-delimited: from a certain point in time target-like and target-deviant sequences are produced alternatively and from a certain point in time target-deviant sequences disappear. How do we account for such a development?

The sub-division of the process which seems to underly parameter-(re-)setting reminds us of the *tripartite model of change* put forward in Hohenberger (1996, see section 7.3.2.2): Bruno's acquisition of the target-like VP-headedness value also commences with a *pre-liminal state* in which VP is initial. His subsequent use of alternative orders would reflect an unstable *liminal state* which is eventually superseded by the stabilisation of the target-like parametric value in the so-called *post-liminal state*.

Apart from Müller (1993, 1996), who also discusses Bruno's acquisition of L2 German, no-one else has reported the details of this development before. According to Müller, Bruno introduces the alternative object-verb

order by means of lexical learning which affects the thematic structure associated with every single verb. Note that here "lexical learning" means learning in an *item-by-item manner* and not lexical learning in the sense of Clahsen (see section 3.1), i.e. the learning of lexical items which then trigger correct parameter fixation.
Unfortunately, the conceptual differentiation which would be necessary in view of the ambiguous use of the notion of *lexical* learning is not taken any further. Müller bases her argument of an item-by-item learning on the observation that some verbs start to appear in alternative positions prior to other verbs. In my view this assumption has to be refuted on several grounds. We could see that the use of the two alternative options only occurs during the course of a well-delimited time-span (which we have called *transition phase*). On this background the time-lag regarding the realisation of the structural alternation with some lexical items becomes nearly insignificant. Thus the broader temporal context delimits the availability of structural alternatives, the use of which may well be related to the productivity of the respective verb.
Therefore it seems implausible to assume that Bruno treats the target-like direction of case and theta-role assignment as a lexical idiosyncrasy. This is not to say that some lexical items may not be involved earlier in the realisation of a new structural option thereby fulfilling a kind of bootstrapping effect... But once the structural alternatives are in place, i.e. the two *coexisting* grammatical analyses of the VP-headedness, Bruno does not have to learn that these apply to every verb. As mentioned above the assumption that for a certain period of time Bruno freely exploits alternative structural options is further supported by his usage of these alternatives in all relevant constructions, such as sequences with particle verbs, with auxiliary and modal verbs as well as with infinitive complements.
To a certain extent Müller is right in her rejection of adopting the common trigger concept as an explanatory basis of Bruno's target-like determination of the VP-headedness. But, this is not a shortcoming on the part of Bruno. In my opinion, what is at issue here is the conceptual shortcoming of the traditional conception of parameter-setting. In chapter 7 we discussed empirical findings showing inter-individual as well as intra-individual variation in child language acquisition. We concluded that self-organising principles allow for the possibility of individual ways of tackling the learnability problems at issue. We also looked into the creative potential underlying the processes responsible for intra-individual variation and the ensuing conflicts.

Furthermore, if we take into consideration the alleged properties and evolution of dynamic systems, we arrive at the striking conclusion that Bruno's German VP obeys the turbulent laws of deterministic chaos as it passes from stability to stability through instability. Similar to many dynamic systems it goes through a bifurcation or catastrophy fold as if opening a "window" onto the whole...

From language change we know that such "windows", to continue with the metaphor, are also opened on the diachronic time-scale. Note, for example, that the coexistence of VP-final and VP-initial structures has also been observed by researchers working in the field of language change. Kiparsky (1995: 152 *pace* Pintzuk 1991), maintains that Old English at a certain stage *"acquired two competing basic word orders, reflecting the coexistence of left- and rightheaded VP and IP."* This conclusion is based on findings that the orders (a) S Vfin O V and (b) S Vfin V O alternate in the Old English data (cf. also Lightfoot 1991). These findings support our previous considerations regarding the self-similarity of language development on different time-scales.

We are thus left with the question of what *tilts* the decision in favour of one option over the other, if structural alternatives are balanced in certain interim systems. Self-organising principles may come into play here, conforming to universal constraints requiring that a decision needs be taken. So what may look like peaceful coexistence can in reality reveal itself as a period of initial *instability* (contrasting with a system in which one option is settled) and of subsequent *competition* (among different options) and *differentiation* (in which one option succeeds and is established)...

8.2.2 Verb raising

8.2.2.1 Subject-verb agreement and verb raising

The analysis of Bruno's early L2 German verb forms shows that, surprisingly enough, periphrastic verb forms appear from the very beginning in Bruno's data.[136] In fact, the verb 'haben' (*to have*) and the copula

---

[136] To my knowledge it is fairly uncommon to find periphrastic verb forms at such an early point in adult L2 development. According to CMP (1983) their longitudinal study provides evidence for the acquisition of the different verb forms in the following order: 1.) main verbs, 2.) copula, 3.) auxiliaries / modal verbs (whereby auxiliaries are acquired prior to modal verbs). Recall that Bruno is one of the subjects studied in the framework of the ZISA project. In somewhat speculative terms we may assume that Bruno's early use of perfect tense forms was enhanced by his attending some German lessons upon his arrival to Germany. Apparently he did so only at the beginning and not on a regular basis. Unfortunately, I received no further details regarding this issue. In addition, recall that Vainikka and Young-Scholten's (1994, 1996a, 1996b) claim of an initial VP-phase is also based on the finding that periphrastic verb forms are absent in early ASLA (see section 6.3.2).

'sein' (*to be*), which also function as auxiliaries, are inflected (nearly) without error from the beginning, cf.

(74) [1-44]
isch	bin -	isch	**bin**	**gekomm**	hier	mit
I	*am*	*I*	*am*	*come*	*here*	*with*

er zusamm
he together

'I have come here with him'

(75) [1-58]
isch	**bin** -	eh	isch	**hab** -	isch	**habe**	sekzeh
I	*am*	*eh*	*I*	*have*	*I*	*have*	*sixteen*

jahr
years

'I am sixteen years old'

(76) [1-64]
isch	**bin**	in	geller
I	*am*	*in*	*cellar*

'I am in the cellar'

(77) [1-72]
sind	viel	italienische
are	*much*	*Italian*

'there are many Italians'

(78) [1-104]
nein	ich	habe	ver -	ich	**habe**	**geversteh**
no	*I*	*have*	*[suffix]*	*I*	*have*	*understood*

'no, I have understood'

(79) [1-121]
eeh	der	deutschlande	**hate**	eeh	conditioné
eeh	*the*	*Germany*	*has*	*eeh*	*"conditioné"*

			meine	sprache	franzosisch
[= French: *conditioned*]			*my*	*language*	*French*

'German has influenced my French'

(80) [1-123]
ich	**habe**	**geler**	franzosisch	drei	jahr
I	*have*	*learned*	*French*	*three*	*years*

'I learned French for three years'

(81) [2-40]
ich	**habe**	kein	geld	für	kamera
I	*have*	*no*	*money*	*for*	*camera*

'I do not have money for buying a camera'

(82) [2-42] eine reflex **ist** gut für mich ja hier
              a   *reflex* *is*   *good* *for* *me* *yes* *here*
              'in my opinion a Reflex(-camera) is good for me'

(83) [2-90] isch **bin** alleine in das kurs
              I   *am*   *alone*   *in* *the* *course*
              'I am alone in the course'

(84) [2-103] ich **habe** eine idee
              I   *have*   *an*   *idea*
              'I have an idea'

Note though that the 2nd person singular or plural verb forms of these verbs are not productive during files 1 and 2.[137] Main verb agreement morphology, however, is not yet productive. In (85) I provide an overview of the relevant suffixes in the target for ease of comprehension.[138]

(85)

Person	number	suffix	example	
1st	singular	-e/-0	ich spiel-*e*	(*I play*)
2nd	singular	-st	du spiel-*st*	(*you play*)
3rd	singular	-t	sie spiel-*t*	(*she plays*)
1st	plural	-n	wir spiel-*e-n*	(*we play*)
2nd	plural	-t	ihr spiel-*t*	(*you play*)
3rd	plural	-n	sie spiel-*e-n*	(*they play*)

In (86) a comprehensive overview of the main verb forms in files 1 and 2 is given. We can see that Bruno uses the endings *-0*, *-e* or *-en* irrespective of the grammatical person and number of the subject.[139, 140]

---

[137] There are only two instances of these forms which Bruno gives upon prompting by the interviewer (cf. (184) and (186) below).

[138] The table gives an overview of the person/number distinctions relevant for present purposes. We will leave aside the mood/inflection paradigm as well as more intricate formation rules such as changes in the root vowel.

[139] Note that there are only two instances of 3rd person singular *–t* (cf. (i) and (ii)). The 2nd person singular verb ending *–st* occurs twice in (iii). However, as we can deduce from the context, Bruno simply repeats a part of the interviewer's question which he did not understand.
(i) [1-149] wenn dies geht kaputt das
            if   *this* *goes* *broken* *this*
            'if it gets broken, this'
(ii) [1-150] nicht funktioniert flash
             not   *works*   *flash*
             'the flash does not work'

(86) Overview of main verb forms in files 1 and 2[141]

File 1:

pers. / no.	subject	- verb form	file-no.
1s	ich	- heiße	1-4
	isch	- komme	1-11
	isch	- arbeite	1-36
	ische	- spreche	1-37
	isch	- arbeit	1-51
	isch	- spreche	1-87
2s	tu	- komme	1-33
	du	- verstehn	1-77
3s	meine bruder	- geh	1-33
	meine bruder	- komm	1-42
	(er)	- hilfe	1-99
	dies	- geht	1-149
	flash	- funktioniert	1-151
1p	-		
2p	-		
3p	zwanzisch mädsche	- arbeite	1-79
	alles persone	- spreche	1-100
	sie	- spreche	1-111

(iii) [2-5] *Interviewer:*
Bruno, glaubst du denn, daß der journalist
Bruno, think you ADV that the journalist
etwas machen kann
something do can
'Bruno, do you think that the journalist can do something?'
Bruno:
bitte glaubst du glaubst du
please think you think you
'please, what does "glaubst du" mean'
Interviewer: pensare [=Italian: *to think*]
Bruno: ahso [= ach so] 'I see'

[140] Interestingly, the choice of one of these options sometimes conforms to the target or to some dialectal version of it. The drop of the consonant -*n* for 3rd person plural, for example, is quite productive in some regional variants of colloquial German, so the utterance
(i) [1-110] sie spreche französisch
'they speak French'
would not be deviant in this respect.

[141] Some of the verb forms appear in utterances in which the subject is omitted. For ease of understanding I provide the corresponding subject pronoun in brackets.

File 2:

pers. / no.	subject	- verb form	file-no.
1s	isch	- versteh	2-1
	isch	- mach	2-7
	i[ch]	- weiß	2-28
	ische	- weiß	2-31
	isch	- gehe	2-36
	ich	- rauch	2-88
	ich	- möchte	2-89
	(ich)	- gucke	2-107/1
	ich	- versteh	2-107/2
	isch	- bringen	2-137
	ich	- mache	2-138
	(ich)	- versteh	2-164
	ich	- versteh	2-193
	ich	- versteh	2-198
2s	(du)	- versteh	2-239
	(du)	- versteh	2-240
	du	- versteh	2-253
3s	er	- sprechen	2-31
	er	- bringe	2-128
	er	- bringen	2-136
	das turkisch	- arbeite	2-168
	er	- versteh	2-251
1p	wir	- verstehn	2-97
2p	-		
3p	barbare	- wohnen	2-245
	diese wickinge	- kommen	2-247

The following utterances further illustrate (a) Bruno's use of the same verb ending for different grammatical person/number constellations and (b) Bruno's use of different verb endings for the same grammatical person/number.

(87) [1-33] bruno **tu** **komme** mit mir germania
 Bruno you come with me germania
 'Bruno you will go with me to Germany'

(88) [1-42] **meine** **bruder** nein eh - agoste meine
 my brother no eh August my
 bruda for ferie **komm** in sizilie
 brother for holiday come in Sicily
 'my brother came to Sicily in August'

197

(89) [1-87] ein wenig **ische** **spreche** mit sie deutschland
a little *I* *speak* with they Germany
'I speak a little German with them'

(90) [1-100] **alles** **persone** **spreche** italienisch in
all *people* *speak* Italian in
deutschland
Germany
'everybody speaks Italian in Germany'

(91) [1-110] sie **spreche** französisch
they *speak* French
'they speak French'

(92) [2-31] er **sprechen** etwas das i-**ische** schon
he *speak* something that *I* already
weiß
know
'he said something I already know'

(93) [2-128] er **bringe** negativ
he *bring* negative
'he brought a negative'

(94) [2-137] **isch** **bringen** negativ da
I *bring* negative there
'I will take a negative there'

(95) [2-247] und **diese** **wickinge** - **kommen** von norwegia
and *these* *Vikings* *come* from Norway
'and these Vikings came from Norway'

(96) [2-245] barbare sind eeh franzosich primitiv
Barbarians are eeh French primitive
franzosische und eeh **wohnen** ein moment
French and eeh *live* a moment
wohnden **wohnden** ine france
live *live* in France
'the primitive French were the so-called Barbarians that lived in France'

198

(97) [2-193] **isch versteh** gut danke
	I understand well thanks
	'I understand well, thank you'

(98) [2-251] moment er **versteh** französisch spreche
	moment he understand French speak
	eeh schuldigung
	eh sorry
	'one moment, he understands - he speaks French, sorry'

(99) [2-253] du **versteh** construction
	you understand "construction" [=French *construction*]
	'do you understand the word 'construction'?'

In the light of these findings we can conclude that in Bruno's early L2 German subject-verb agreement appears only restrictively, i.e. with non-thematic verbs[142] and with the exception of the 2nd person forms. These findings run in unison with the restricted (unambiguous) evidence for verb raising in files 1 and 2. The placement of sentence-internal adverbs is a case in point. As mentioned above, the adverb 'schon' (*already, yet*) appears inside the verb bracket in constructions with periphrastic verb forms (as of file 2), indicating thus, that the auxiliary has been raised to a position outside the VP (utterances (8) - (11) are repeated here for convenience).

(8) [2-2] isch habe **schon** versteh
	I have already understood
	'I have understood already'

(9) [2-21] isch bin **schon** gegangen
	I am already gone
	'I have gone already'

(10) [2-43] isch habe **schon** gesagt
	I have already said
	'I have said already'

(11) [2-175] ich habe **schon** gegessen
	I have already eaten
	'I have eaten already'

---

[142] With the exception of 'haben' (*to have*) which is also used as a main verb.

Conversely, the few negation data are not particularly useful in this respect as there is no instance of negation in constructions with periphrastic verb forms. The following comprehensive overview of constructions with a negator shows that the negator is placed before the negated element (be it a verb or a noun) across the board, cf.

(100) [1-54] **kein** arbeit
              no   *work*
              'no work'

(101) [1-58] **nix** akkord
              no   *piecework*
              'I do not do piecework'

(102) [1-77] **nicht** verstand , du **nicht** verstehn
              not   *understood* *you* *not* *understand*
              'you did not understand?'

(103) [1-151] **nicht** funktioniert flash
              not   *works*   *flash*
              'the flash does not work'

(104) [1-164] getroffen kennengelernt **nich** versteh
              met   *known*   *not* *understand*
              'I do not understand 'getroffen', 'kennengelernt'...'

(105) [2-136] aso er   **nix** bringen negativ **nix** brings –
              ah he *not* *bring* *negative* *not* *bring*
              bring(te) negativ
              brought *negative*
              'ah, he did not bring a negative'

(106) [2-243] Interviewer:
              ich weiß **nich**.
              I know not
              'I do not know'
              Bruno:
              nich weiß
              not   *know*
              'I do not know'

200

If the main verbs do not raise to a projection outside the VP at this time, as is claimed here, preverbal negation comes as no surprise. But note that a "target-minded" perspective depends on this issue insofar as postverbal negation is expected on the basis of target L2 German.
As the negator would appear in a position prior to the raised verb in Romance, the utterances in question are ambiguous.
Note further that there is no instance of negation with auxiliaries or the copula, which could further decide on the question of whether verb raising applies only in these cases.

Constructions in which the subject appears sentence-finally and a non-subject in sentence-initial position are equally ambiguous.
On the basis of the L2 grammar utterances in which the verb appears before the subject would indicate verb raising past the subject. In L1 Romance, on the other hand, the sentence-final position of the subject in utterances like (107) is a base-generated one (cf. Burzio 1986: 21).[143]

(107) Arriveranno molti esperti.
will arrive many experts
'Many experts will arrive.'

So an utterance like (108) below is ambiguous with respect to verb raising because there is no further indicator such as inflection morphology, for example, which could decide on this issue.

(108) [1-78f.] in ganzes fabrica arbeite zwanzisch mädsche
in whole fabrica work twenty girls
italienisch in ganze fabrica
Italian in whole fabrica [= Ital. *factory*]
'there are twenty Italian girls working in the whole factory'

(109) below is the second utterance of the only two sequences with main verb-subject order in files 1 and 2. In this case the verb is correctly marked for subject-verb agreement, indicating that the verb has raised out of the VP. But this comes as no surprise as it is the case of 'haben' (*to have*), exactly one of the two verbs, which are correctly inflected as of file 1.

---

[143] This analysis applies in the case of ergative verbs such as 'arrivare' (*to arrive*). For further details regarding the analysis of non-ergative verbs see Burzio (1986) and Rizzi (1982).

(109) [1-142] für   unterhalten hat+s   hier in deutschland din
               for   entertain   has-it   here in Germany   din
               'for entertainment you have 'din' here in Germany' [144]

Sentence-final subjects in copular constructions are quite productive (cf. (110) - (114)). Since Bruno masters the suppletive forms of the copular paradigm as of file 1 (with the exception of the second person sing./plural forms) these verb forms are likely to appear in a functional projection above the VP.

(110) [1-21]   eeh   akzeh   kilometer   iste   paterno
               eeh   eighteen   km   is   paterno
               'Paterno is at eighteen km distance'

(111) [1-22]   hier   ist eeh   catania
               here   is   eeh   catania
               'Catania is here'

(112) [1-24]   ach- achte   (undtse)   kilometra   ist   paterno
               eight-eight   and-ten   km   is   Paterno
               'Paterno is at 18 km distance'

(113) [1-72f.] in   meister   eeh   sind   eeh   viel   italienische -
               in   master   eeh   are   eeh   much   Italian
               junge
               young
               'there are many young Italian working at the master's'

(114) [2-98]   in   das   kors   in das   korse   sind   sechs
               in   the   course   in the   course   are   six
               okay   fünf   deutsch   und   ich
               okay   five   Germans   and   I
               'there are six, no, five Germans and me in the course'

In sum, the present findings suggest that verb raising is operative with exactly the restricted class of verbs which are correctly inflected, i.e. non-

---

[144] Note that the English version of this utterance is a word-for-word translation. I am not sure, however, whether I fully grasped what Bruno intended to say. I must admit that the utterance does not make much sense to me. Unfortunately, the context is not much revealing either.

thematic verbs.[145] In the light of subsequent development this early phase, however short-lived, offers some important insights into the interrelation of grammatical processes such as subject-verb agreement, finiteness and verb raising in Bruno's L2 German.

8.2.2.2 The finiteness distinction and the implementation of the inflectional paradigm

As we will see subsequently, the introduction of target-like inflection morphology in Bruno's L2 German is quite instructive as to the role of self-organising principles described in section 7.2.3. The apparent "chaotic" behaviour underlying the simultaneous productivity of target-like inflected verb forms, contracted verb forms and the interference of mother tongue Italian phonology reveals the relevance of processes of integration and differentiation in the development of the L2 grammar.

Target-like inflection morphology as well as generalised verb raising of main verbs are introduced in the course of files 3 and 4.[146] The verb ending -*st* (or variations thereof like -*s*, -*se*) for 2nd person singular verb forms is already used in file 3 nearly without error, whilst the 3rd person singular -*t* appears with less regularity, cf.

(115) [3-42] eine   deutsche   kolleg   sage   ihr
              a   German   colleague   says   you [= plural]
              alle   persone
              all   people
              'a German colleague addresses everybody with 'ihr''

(116) [3-81] wenne   ma**st**   das
              when   make   that
              'when you make that'

---

[145] The analysis falls into line with the studies of other proponents of the UG Hypothesis of ASLA discussed in previous sections (cf. Du Plessis et al. 1987, Tomaselli and Schwartz 1991, Eubank 1992, 1994, not so Müller 1996, see below).

[146] The fact that 2p pronoun 'ihr' (*you*) as well as the corresponding verb ending only appear as of file 13 raises the question as to whether this delay is due to pragmatic factors (interview situation) or whether the morphological specification of this grammatical person is not mastered until a very late point in time. As far as I can see, this phenomenon does not have any relevant effect on the development under discussion. It is thus not given any further importance.

(117) [3-97] wenn du   trink**st**
              when you drink
              'when you drink'

(118) [3-106] wenn isch gehe da   bring**et** mir eine film
              when I   go   there bring   me   a   film
              'when I go there [she] brings me a film'

(119) [3-134] mir   sagen ja   bring**st** eine turke hier
              me   say   yes bring   a   turk   here
              '[she] said to me, yes, come along with a Turk'

(120) [3-144] matassa   jakati heiß**te**   das da   das eeh
              matassa   jakati is-called   the there the eh
              lehrerin ne   jakati
              teacher   ne   jakati
              'the teacher is called matassa jakati'

(121) [4-272] geh**st** du   hier nicht hier
              go   you her   not   here
              'you (have to) go here, not there'

The first imperative forms appear in file 4 (cf. (122) - (123)).

(122) [4-223] **nimm** besser da
              take   better that
              'you should better take that'

(123) [4-270] oder **guck** mal hier hier da
              or   look   ADV here here there
              'or look here'

Bruno also produces some verb forms which are equivalent to colloquial German contracted verb forms. Sequences (124) - (131) show, however, that Bruno's use of these forms does not always conform to the target.[147]

(124) [4-41] bi**ste**   gewesen mite deutsche kinder
              are(-you)   been   with German   children

---

[147] Verb endings in bold letters indicate the contracted forms.

		für	lernen	die	literatur		
		for	*learn*	*the*	*literature*		

'have you been with German children in order to study the literature'

(125) [4-82]
		wann	ha**ste**	gemacht	da
		when	*have(-you)*	*made*	*that*

'when have you made that'

(126) [4-89f.]
		aber	das	<eh> -	wenn	du	machs	so
		but	*that*	*eh*	*when*	*you*	*make*	*such*
		eine	fotografie		wie	eine	person	das
		a	*photography*		*as*	*a*	*person*	*that*
		hatte	geld	wenn	du	bist	fotograf	
		has	*money*	*when*	*you*	*are*	*photographer*	
		un	mach**se**	fotografie	<eh>	fotografie		
		and	*make(-you)*	*photography*	*eh*	*photography*		
		fotografie	ein	andere	person	für	arbeit	
		photography	*an*	*other*	*person*	*for*	*work*	
		dann	mach**se**	zehn	negativ			
		then	*make(-you)*	*ten*	*negative*			

'when you make a photography as a person that has money; when you are a photographer and you make photographies of somebody as a job, then you make ten negatives'

(127) [4-171]
		meine	schwager	hat	gesagt	du	holest
		my	*brother-in-law*	*has*	*said*	*you*	*take*
		da	ein	apparat	und	dann	mach**ste**
		there	*a*	*camera*	*and*	*then*	*make(-you)*
		deine	profession[148]				
		your	*profession*				

'my brother-in-law told me that I should take a camera and practise my profession'

(128) [4-226]
		für	eine	stunde	ha**ste**	freie	nase
		for	*one*	*hour*	*have(-you)*	*free*	*nose*

---

[148] Bruno's expression "apparat" is a reduced form of German 'Photoapparat' (*camera*).

ungefähr
approximately

'you will have a free nose for approximately an hour'

(129) [4-224] bring**ste**   drei
               bring(-you)   *three*

'you bring three'

(130) [4-262] iß**te**   besser   du   jetzt
               eat(-you)   *better*   *you*   *now*

'you should better eat now'

(131) [4-356] bringe**ste**   gebe**ste**   mir   ein   küchenmesser
               bring(-you)   *give(-you)* *me*   *a*   *kitchen-knife*

               zu   große
               too big

'you are giving me too big a kitchen-knife'

Firstly, as exemplified in (130), the apparent contracted forms occur simultaneously with the regular subject pronoun. Secondly, we can see in (126) that Bruno omits the "*t*" which is constitutive of 2nd person singular *-st* even when contracted. If we contrast (126) with (127), we can see that Bruno also produces the target-like form "machste". Thirdly, we need to consider possible interference of mother tongue phonology in the form of schwa *-e*. As illustrated in (132), however, schwa *-e* is not used throughout.

(132)

[4-196] ich binne gegangen mit *I have gone with* eine kalte fuß *a cold foot* 'I went with cold feet'	[4-183] eine mal ich bin gegangen *one time I was gone* mit das freund *with the friend* 'I went once with a friend'
[4-221] nur das iste für trinken *only that is for drink* 'this you have to drink'	[4-222] das ist gut *this is good* 'this is alright'

[4-182]	[4-285]
sinde schon zwei monate *are already two months* ich geh da nich *I go there not* 'I did not go there for two months'	die sind zu klein *they are too small* 'they are too small'

[4-41]	[4-67]
biste gewesen mit *were been with* deutsche kinder für *German children for* lernen die literatur *learn the literature* 'have you been with German children in order to study the literature'	bist du zu schön *are you too beautiful* 'you are too beautiful'

[4-90]	[4-279]
du sachse persone... *you say people* 'you tell the people...'	du sagst deine männer *you tell your men* wo gehen *where go* 'you tell your men where to go'

In this context we may consider Young-Scholten's (1993) detailed analysis of such contracted verb forms, which she understands to be *clitic groups*. According to her, the clitic group is "*a syntactically defined domain in which postlexical resyllabification occurs*" (ibid.: 113). Note that this process occurs in informal speech only. What is important for the present context is Young-Scholten's remark that

> "[t]he acquisition of clitization presupposes that the learner is able to analyze the morphological components of the clitical group into stems, affixes and clitics."
> (ibid.: 115)

Following this reasoning she distinguishes three steps in the acquisition of these constructions, which are also valid for children and for uninstructed adult L2 learners, namely (cf. ibid.: 118, her examples and her transl.):

(a) production of unanalysed chunks,
    e.g. deine frau   bistdu   gehen   karstadt
         your wife   are-you   going   karstadt
         'My wife was going to Karstadt'

(b) treatment of clitics as agreement suffixes,
    e.g. ich   weiss-ich   nicht
         I   know- I   not
         'I don't know'

(c) disappearance of pronominal copying upon the productivity of target-like agreement on main verbs.

Interestingly, Young-Scholten mentions Bruno's development as an exceptional case which would question the validity of (c) as he produces sequences with pronominal copying at a time when he has already acquired agreement.
As Young-Scholten still adheres to a linear conception of language development the intra-individual variation evident in Bruno's data does not fit into her model. Under a dynamic account, however, the coexistence of alternative options bears a potential for change. So the developmental steps proposed by Young-Scholten have to be reconsidered in terms of correlation processes in the sense outlined in section 7.2.3 above.
The data show that the introduction of the inflection paradigm is related to processes of reorganisation on the phonological, morphological and syntactic level. As will be discussed below pronominal copying takes place at a time when the government option for nominative case-assignment is introduced in Bruno's L2 German, which is, in turn, concurrent with the implementation of target-like subject-verb agreement. So the morphological analysis of contracted verb forms converges with a structural analysis of target German. Related processes of overgeneralisation or partial misanalysis should be regarded only as a natural consequence of the instabilities we believe to be characteristic of dynamic processes (cf. also Karpf 1993). This holds equally with respect to Bruno's acquisition of the L2 inflection paradigm.

The assumption that Bruno masters the inflection paradigm is not to say that verbs are inflected without error in files 3 and 4. But the overall rate of errors decreases quite rapidly in subsequent files. Presently, the following considerations can be made with regard to the errors:

- Target-like inflection endings alternate with the endings -e, -en, -0:

(133) [4-211] eine   robot **arbeite**   akkord (-> arbeitet) [149]
               a   robot works   piece-work
               'a robot does piece-work'

(134) [4-215] **arbeit**   ohne   kopfs   (-> arbeitet)
               works   without   head
               '[he] works without thinking'

(135) [4-134] mir **sagen**   ja   bringst   eine   turke   hier
               me say   yes   bring   a   Turk   here
                                                             (-> sagt)
               '[she] said to me, yes, come along with a Turk'

(136) [4-169] meine   schwager   **sagt**   das   ist   gut
               my   brother-in-law   says   that   is   good
               'my brother-in-law says that that is good'

(137) [4-263] immer   zwei   ich   **eß**
               always   two   I   eat
               'I always eat two'

(138) [4-268] jetzt   ich   **esse**   eine   mal
               now   I   eat   one   time
               'now I will eat once'

(139) [4-284] hier   mit   diese   ich   nicht   **essen**   das
               here   with   this   I   not   eat   that
                                                               (-> esse)
               'with this I cannot eat that'

(140) [4-323] ich   **kennen**   sie   nicht   das   auch   in
               I   know   they   not   that   also   in
               italien[150]
               Italy

---

[149] For further illustration I will indicate the target-like verb form in brackets in the case of target-deviant forms.

[150] As you can deduce from the translation I take "sie" (*they*) to be the subject of this sequence. If one took "ich" to be the subject, the correct verb form would be "kenne". See subsequent remarks.

'they do not know that either in Italy'

(141) [4-352]　aber　ich　**kenn**　sie　nich　schach
　　　　　　　but　 I　 know　they　not　chess
　　　　　　　'but I do not know to play chess'

(142) [4-354]　eine　person　ich　**kenn**
　　　　　　　a　 person　 I　 know
　　　　　　　'I know somebody'

(143) [4-254]　ich　**sakrifizieren**　eine　für　essen
　　　　　　　 I　 sacrify　 one　 for　eat
　　　　　　　　　　　　　　　　　　(-> sakrifiziere)
　　　　　　　'I will sacrify one for eating'

I take (139) as a "key" for interpreting similar examples as instances of the verb remaining in its base position. At a point where the negator is correctly placed postverbally with inflected verbs - note that there is no instance of a postverbal negator with a verb with the ending -*en* - sequences with preverbal negators indicate that the verb in these sequences has the infinite status.
Utterance (140), however, is ambiguous as to whether "ich" (*I*) or "sie" (*they*) should be taken as the subject ("kennen" (*know*) would be target-like with 3rd pers.pl. 'sie').
In (141) the verb agrees with the subject "ich", here the problem lies in the analysis of "sie" (erroneous choice of object pronoun?). Alternatively, it could be assumed that "ich kenn(en) sie nich" is still a partially lexicalised sequence which has not yet been properly analysed.

- Some verb forms are invariantly carried over for a long period of time:
  In my view, these forms do not challenge the assumption that Bruno masters the inflection paradigm.[151] The verbs in question are used in some invariant form although only for a certain period of time. This is the case with verbs like verbs 'gefallen' (*to please*) and 'sich erinnern' (*to remember*).
  'Gefallen' is an interesting case in point: Bruno uses "gefäll(e) mir nicht" (*pleases me not*, in the sense of *I do not like*) irrespective of which subject is used. In the cases quoted below the target-like form would be 'gefallen' (= 3rd pers. pl.). Note though that the

---

[151] But see Müller (1996) for the opposite claim.

relative order of verb, pronominal and negator is target-like which supports the assumption that these are lexicalised chunks. Probably, one of the reasons for the delayed analysis of this verb lies in the fact that it is irregularly inflected (vowel change).

(144) [4-311] gefälle   mir   nicht - gefälle   mir   nicht
               please *me* *not*   *please* *me* *not*
               diese
               these
               'I do not like these'

(145) [4-314] in   generale   alle   blume   gefälle   mir
               in *general* *all* *flowers* *please* *me*
               nicht   zu   haus
               not   *at* *home*
               'in general I do not like flowers at home'

(146) [6-134] aber   viele   freunde   haben   mir   gesatt
               but   *many*   *friends*   *have*   *me*   *said*
               deutsche   gefäll   mir   nicht
               Germans   *please*   *me*   *not*
               'many friends told me that they do not like Germans'

As late as of file 17 Bruno still seems to have some difficulty regarding the analysis of some (colloquial) forms of this verb, cf.

(147) [17-49] ich   habe   schon   probiert   mit   elektrisch
               I   *have*   *already*   *tried*   *with* *electric*
               aber   gefällst   mir   nicht
               but   *pleases*   *me*   *not*
               'I already tried the electric [shaver] but I do not like it'

Note that (147) occurs at a time where impersonal 'es' (*it*) makes its appearance also in its clitic form '*s*. If we consider, additionally, the alternation of the forms 'gibs', 'gibt es' and 'gibts' (*there is*) (see section 8.2.4.2) we can assume that Bruno is engaged in *cracking* these forms. As mentioned previously, Bruno's use of the verb 'erinnern' (*to remember*) is also an interesting case in point. Consider, in this respect, the following utterance:

(148) [8-84] aber   so   wie jetzt isch mich nicht
              but   so   as   now   I   me   not

              erinnern eine worte
              remind   one   word

              'like now, I cannot remember the word now'

Note that the correspondent target-like order would be 'ich erinner mich nicht', i.e. negator and pronominal would follow the finite verb. In (148), however, the verb is non-finite and appears preceded by the relevant elements. But, as the following passage illustrates, Bruno is aware of the target-deviant nature of "ich mich nicht erinnern":

(149) [10-120] (...) ich nicht erinn - ich mich nicht
                     I   not   remind   I   me   not

              erinnern   die   worte   gleich
              remind   the   words   immediately

              'I do not remember immediately the words'

(150) [10-121] <hahaha> ist schon   falsch
               ...   is   already wrong

              'this was wrong already'

(151) [10-122] *Interviewer:*
              aber erinnern ist gut   hast du
              but   remember is   good have you

              dir gut   gemerkt -
              you good remembered

              'but "erinnern" is good, you remembered well'

              Bruno:
              und dann ich mich erinner   nicht
              and then I   me   remember not

              iste korrekt
              is   correct

              'then "ich mich erinner nicht" is correct?'

(152) [10-123] *Interviewer:*
              fast ne?
              'nearly, isn't it?'

212

Bruno:
fast
'nearly'

Interviewer:
ja   ist   egale   mach mal nicht
yes is   the-same   do   ADV not
zu   kompliziert
too   complicated
'yes, it does not matter, don't complicate it'

(153) [10-125] aber   ganz   korrekt iste ich mich
                but   completely   correct is   I   me
                nicht erinnern   oder ich erinnern
                not   remember   or   I   remember
                mich nicht
                me   not
                'but [what] is really correct ...?'

Eventually, the target-like verb form is used alongside the correct order as utterances (154) and (155) illustrate:

(154) [12-150] erinner   mich nicht
                remind   me   not
                'I do not remember'

(155) [14-8]   erinner   ich mich ganz genau
                remind   I   me   very exactly
                'I exactly remember'

- Main verb agreement morphology is overgeneralised to modal verb forms, cf.

(156) [7-23]   ich **wolle**   kommen mit   dir   (-> will)
                I   want   come   with you
                'I want to come with you'

(157) [7-29]   ich **musse**   sachen ein was   (-> muß)
                I   must   say   a   something
                'I must say something'

213

(158) [8-298] vielleicht **willt** auch urlaub auch er
              perhaps   want   also   holiday also he
                                                      (-> will)
              'maybe he also wants a holiday'

The overgeneralisation of main verb agreement endings shows that Bruno's acquisition of agreement morphology is rule-derived.[152]

- Inflectional endings which unequivocally mark a finite form do not appear in non-finite contexts.
  There is, in fact, no instance of *-t* or *-st* marked verbs occurring in non-finite contexts.

The preceding considerations permit us to conclude that Bruno masters the inflection paradigm in the sense that he knows the relevant forms and uses them, in general, in the appropriate contexts.

8.2.2.3 Conclusion

In general terms, our insight into the data proves that Bruno's acquisition of agreement morphology and his application of the finiteness distinction can be described as a progression from a restricted to a generalised application of the relevant universal constraints.
Thus the analysis proposed here contrasts with Müller's (1996: 23, emphasis mine) argument that

> "... Bruno does not seem to use the inflection suffixes productively, which means that **agreement does not have an independent lexical entry**. He rather starts out with **word-specific paradigms**."

In my view, this is an overinterpretation of the above mentioned lexicalised chunks which does not correctly mirror the empirical facts. Recall that there are only a few such cases compared with the vast amount of correctly inflected verb forms. If subject-verb agreement morphology was acquired via word-specific paradigms much more variation would be expected. Instead, we witness some cases of overgeneralisation as with modal verbs, which shows that inflection is acquired as a rule-governed process. It goes without saying that we do not expect the acquisition of agreement morphology to occur instantaneously and its production to be

---

[152] Cf. Karpf (1990, 1993) for some interesting insights into morphological development in child LA and ASLA on the basis of a dynamic approach to language development.

error-free from the beginning. So we can conclude with Karpf (1993: 12) that

"... the acquisition of systems is subject to fluctuations in the applications of rules and brings about a continuous reduction of non-analyzed chunks."

Bruno's temporary production of alternating target-deviant and target-like sequences reminds us of the optionality of verb raising in ASLA discussed in section 6.3.1. We can recall that the problem of explaining apparent optional verb raising is only restated in Eubank's account in terms of alternating feature specifications of FCs. More to the point, any hypothesis working on the basis of the traditional Principles and Parameters model conceptions fails to account for intra-individual variation in the form of the alleged optionality of grammatical processes.

According to the analysis proposed here, such intra-individual variation is quite instructive as to the dynamics underlying language development. Recall Vainikka and Young-Scholten's (1996a: 13f.) recent statements on similar findings:[153]

"... the grammar of an earlier stage *competes* with the grammar of a later stage, and signs of both stages can be observed in the data (...) Furthermore, we take Wexler's (1994) Optional Infinitive Stage (proposed for L1 acquisition) to reflect a situation where a VP grammar (giving rise to non-finite matrix clauses without verb raising) competes with an IP grammar (giving rise to verb raising); under this view, the notion of *competing grammars* is responsible for the illusion of optional verb raising."

We can see that Vainikka and Young-Scholten, too, restate the apparent optionality, i.e. the coexistence of "old" and "new" structures, in terms of competing grammars. Note, however, that we have to explicitly admit that the alleged competition is an interpretation of the coexistence observed which hinges on subsequent development. This remark is especially relevant in view of the well-known possibility that adult interim L2 grammars may "fossilise". On the other hand, we have to allow for target-deviant forms to occur even at a point where the target-like constraints are well implemented. In such a case the unanalysed forms represent, in dynamic terms, *minor* oscillations.

In the following sections we will discuss whether and if so to what extent Bruno acquires the grammatical properties which qualify German as a so-called V2 language. I will focus especially on the following subjects:

---

[153] Interestingly, Vainikka and Young-Scholten also draw upon the present discussion in the field of language change. Note, however, that these considerations are still embedded in the framework of the traditional Principles and Parameters learning model (see section 6.3.2).

- nominative case-checking
- non-subject topicalisation
- word order in embedded clauses (IP-headedness)

8.2.3 Nominative case checking

One of the grammatical phenomena to be considered when analysing cross-linguistic word order variation is nominative case-checking. As already mentioned (see section 2.5.4) nominative case-checking is subject to parametrisation. In this respect Italian and German differ as follows:

- Italian: nominative case-checking under spec-head agreement
- German: nominative case-checking under government

Consider in this respect the following sequences (cf. also Vikner 1995).

(159) Quale   film   ha   visto   Paolo?
      which   film   has   seen   Paolo

(160) *Quale   film   ha   Paolo   visto?
      which   film   has   Paolo   seen

(161) Welchen Film   hat   Paolo   gesehen?
      which   film   has   Paolo   seen

(162) *Welchen Film   hat   gesehen Paolo?
      which   film   has   seen   Paolo

(163) Paolo   ha   visto il   film.
      Paolo   has   seen the   film

(164) *Il   film   ha   Paolo   visto.
      the   film   has   Paolo   seen

(165) Ha   visto   il   film   Paolo.
      has   seen   the   film   Paolo

(166) Paolo   hat   den   Film   gesehen.
      Paolo   has   the   film   seen

(167) Den   Film   hat   Paolo   gesehen.
      the   film   has   Paolo   seen

(168) *Hat   gesehen den   Film   Paolo.
      has   seen   the   film   Paolo

The ungrammaticality of (160) and (164) results from the unavailability of the government option in Italian. Nominative case-checking in Italian subject-verb inversion (i.e. the so-called *free inversion*) (cf. (165)) occurs under spec-head agreement to a *pro* in the preverbal position which is coindexed with the postverbal subject.
As (168) proves this possibility is not given in German, in which the postverbal subject has to immediately follow the verb (see (161) and (167)). (166) and (167) show that the preverbal position can be occupied either by the subject or by any other XP.
On the basis of these observations, we will now elaborate on Bruno's acquisition of nominative case-checking under government.

8.2.3.1 Restricted verb raising and nominative case-checking

The following comprehensive overview of the interrogation sequences[154] in files 1 and 2 shows that Bruno does not yet master target-like question formation.[155] This comes as no surprise in the light of our previous conclusion that verb raising is not operative at this point. If we compare these utterances with the interrogative sentences in files 3 and 4, we can draw the conclusion that in addition to the implementation of verb raising we have to study the introduction of nominative case-checking under government.

Interrogative sentences in file 1:

(169) [1-77] du   nicht verstehn
              you   not   understand
              'you did not understand?'

(170) [1-77] nisch verstand
              not   understand
              'you did not understand?'

(171) [1-118] der   deutschland   aad   hate   conditioné
              the   Germany   has   has   "conditioné"

---

[154] In the transcripts of the inverviews provided to me no details as to the intonation contour nor the status of the main clause were given. Thus the utterances were classified according to the context and the relevant syntactic cues.

[155] There are are two exceptions - the interview passages (179) - (184) and (186) - which show that Bruno is in the position to produce target-like word order whenever prompted by the input. However, unlike Müller, I do not take this to show that target V2 is productive from the beginning.

conditioné lingua -
[= French: *conditioned*] "lingua" [= Italian: *language*]

meine	sprake	ne	franzosische	verstand
my	*language*	*no*	*French*	*understand*

'German has influenced my French, do you understand?'

(172) [1-18] *Interviewer:*

kannst	du	mal	catania	zeigen	ungefähr?
can	*you*	*ADV*	*Catania*	*show*	*approximately*

'can you show me where Catania is approximately?'

Bruno:

sizilie	catania	wo	ist
Sicily	*Catania*	*where*	*is*

'where in Sicily is Catania?'

(173) [1-36] *Interviewer:*

ja	und	hat	der	schon	arbeit	gehabt
yes	*and*	*has*	*this-one*	*already*	*work*	*had*

für	dich	bruno	oder?
for	*you*	*bruno*	*or?*

'yes, and did he already have a job for you?'

Bruno:

wo	isch	arbeite
where	*I*	*work*

'where I do work?'

Interrogative sentences in file 2:

(174) [2-5f.] *Interviewer:*

Bruno	glaubst	du	denn,	daß	der	journalist
Bruno	*think*	*you*	*ADV*	*that*	*the*	*journalist*

etwas	machen	kann?
something	*make*	*can*

'Bruno, do you think that the journalist can do something?'

Bruno:

bitte	glaubst	du	glaubst	du
please	*think*	*you*	*think*	*you*

'please, what does "glaubst du" mean?'

                Interviewer:
                pensare
                [= Italian: *to think*]
                Bruno:
                aso   [= ach so]
                'I see'

(175) [2-23]   versteh   oder   nein
                understand or   no
                'do you understand or not?'

(176) [2-217] und   das   was   iste
                and   this   what   is
                'and what is this?'

(177) [2-138f.] Bruno:
                was   ische machte
                what   I   did
                'what I did?'

                Interviewer:
                mache   [= present tense]
                'do'

(178) [2-140] mache mit   ohne   negativ
                do   with without   negative
                'what I do without a negative?'

(179) [2-172] *Interviewer:*
                ich gestern   auch italienisch   gegessen ... war
                I   yesterday   also Italian   eaten   was
                lecker
                nice
                'I ate at an Italian restaurant yesterday ... it was delicious'
                Bruno:
                was   haben   sie   gegessen
                what   have   you [= formal] *eaten*
                'What did you eat'

(180) [2-173] *Interviewer:*
                was   hast   du   gegessen
                what   have   you [= informal] *eaten*

'what did you eat'

Bruno:
was haben sie gegessen
what have you [= formal] eaten

'what did you eat'

(181) [2-174] *Interviewer:*
nee was hast du gegessen mußt du sagen
no what have you eaten have you say

'No, you have to say "what have you eaten"'

Bruno:
isch erste -
I firstly

'Firstly, I...'

(182) [2-175] *Interviewer:*
ja wenn du mit mir sprichst, sagst
yes when you with me speak say

du was hast du gegessen
you what have you eaten

'Yes, when you speak to me, you have to say "was hast du gegessen"'

Bruno:
isch habe gegessen -
I have eaten

'I ate'

(183) [2-177] *Interviewer:*
nicht lei sondern
'not "lei" [= Italian: *you* (formal)] but

tu
"tu" [= Italian: *you* (informal)]

Bruno:
isch - aso
'I' 'I see'

(184) [2-179] was was hast du - was hast du gegessen
what what have you what have you eaten

'What have you eaten?'

220

(185) [2-188] wieviele   fisch
               how-many   fish
               'How many fish?'

(186) [2-202] *Interviewer* (asking a third person, 'Alfio'):
               und   was   hast   du   gemacht   in   der   letzten
               and what   have   you   done   in   the   last
               woche?
               week
               'And what did you do last week?'
               Bruno:
               was   hast   du   gemachte   in   arbeit
               what have   you   done   in   work
               'What have you done at work?'

(187) [2-217] und   das   was   iste
               and   that   what   is
               'and what is that?'

(188) [2-239] versteh   oder   nein
               understand   or   not
               'do you understand or not?'

(189) [2-251] was   war   dein   nome   dein   name
               what was   your   name   your   name
               'what is your name?'

(190) [2-253] du   versteh   construction
               you   understand   "construction" [= French *construction*]
               'do you understand "construction"?'

Interrogative sentences in file 3:

(191) [3-67]   wie   heißt   das   aber   das
               how   is-called   that   but   that
               'but how do you call that?'

(192) [3-79]   was   ist   das
               what is   that
               'what is that?'

221

(193) [3-152] und was machst du
and what do you
'and what do you do?'

Interrogative sentences in file 4:

(194) [4-41] biste gewesen mite deutsche kinder für
were been with German children for
lernen die literatur
learn the literature
'have you been with German children in order to study the literature?'

(195) [4-101] wie heißt eine nur eine
how is-called one only one
'and how do you call only one?'

(196) [4-106] was sinde diese vier haaren
what are these four hairs
'and what are these four hairs?'

(197) [4-116] wann iste nekste lezhio von schule
when is next lesson of school
'when is the next school lesson?'

(198) [4-164] hast du einmal gesehn
have you once seen
'did you see once?'

(199) [4-228] kennst du das spiele
know you the game
'do you know this game?'

(200) [4-332] was hast du hier gemacht
what do you here done
'what have you done here?'

As regards word order in declarative clauses we could see in section 8.2.2.1 that verb raising in files 1 and 2 applies only restrictedly. In sequences in which the verb is not raised (= VP-structures) there is also no nominative case assignment.

222

As already seen in section 5.1.2 word order variation in such VP-structures is only a natural consequence of the fact that the relevant functional categories do not figure in these structures. From the data of files 1 and 2 it is apparent that sequences with verb raising follow the SVO pattern. Germanic subject-verb inversion is not productive.[156] In keeping with our previous observations we conclude that in Bruno's early L2 German nominative case-checking occurs under spec-head agreement.

8.2.3.2 Implementation of the government option

Verb-subject orders appear in Bruno's L2 German as of file 3 concurrently with the implementation of main verb agreement morphology and generalised verb raising. This convergence was brought to light in section 8.2.2.2 in the case of apparent contracted verb forms.

A closer look at the data reveals, however, that the position of the subject in sequences with postverbal subjects depends initially on whether the subject is realised as a pronoun (cf. (201) – (205)) or as an NP (cf. (206) – (210)). In sequences with complex verbs, subject pronouns appear inside the verb bracket. By contrast, subject NPs follow the verb complex. In constructions with main verbs, subject pronouns also appear in the adjacent position as opposed to subject NPs which follow postverbal adverbs or negators, as illustrated by the following sequences, cf.

(201) [4-180] eine arbeit **muß du** sehe wann iste gut
a work must you see when is good
'you have to see whether the job is alright'

(202) [4-250] de **hast du** nich gegessen
that have you not eaten
'you did not eat that'

(203) [4-251] das **esse ich** dir weg
that eat I you away
'I am eating you this away'

(204) [4-276] mit dase **gehst du** hier
with that go you here
'with this you can go here'

---

[156] This conclusion contrasts with Müller's who argues that target-like V2 is productive from the beginning.

(205) [4-294] mit   eh   **hast du**   zum   beispiele **gehst**
              with   *eh* *have you*   *to-the* *example* *go*
              du   hier
              you   *here*
              'with [that], for example, you can go here'

(206) [4-13] einmal   **komme** auch   des   chefe   von   die
              one-time *come*   *also* *the*   *boss*   *of*   *the*
              haus
              house
              'the boss of the house also came once'

(207) [4-134] vielleicht   eh   **wiederkomme** eine   male   die
              perhaps   *eh* *come-again*   *one*   *time*   *the*
              bronchite   **bronchite**   akute
              bronchitis   *bronchitis*   *acute*
              'maybe a case of acute bronchitis comes again once'

(208) [4-156] diese   film   **habe**   auch   **gemacht**   habe
              this   *film*   *have*   *also*   *made*   *have*
              auch   **gemacht**   die   in   **italien**
              also   *made*   *those*   *in* *Italy*
              'this film they also made in Italy'

(209) [4-183] dann   sinde   gekommen   die   weihnachte
              then *are*   *come*   *the*   *Christmas*
              neujahre
              New Year
              'then came Christmas, New Year'

(210) [4-311] **gefälle**   mir   nicht   **diese**
              please   *me*   *not*   *these*
              'I do not like these'

It is noteworthy that similar findings regarding a placement asymmetry between subject pronouns and subject NPs have been documented in other studies of ASLA (cf. Schwartz and Sprouse 1994) as well as in language change research (cf. the papers in Roberts and Battey 1995). In accordance with these analyses, to which I will come immediately, I want to argue that a grammar allowing for this asymmetry must be a grammar in which two alternative case-checking mechanisms are in place simultaneously, i.e. a grammar which allows subjects to be case-checked under spec-head agreement and under government. In Bruno's L2 German at this stage the former option, which is relevant to Italian-like *free inversion* applies in the case of NP-subjects.[157] Nominative case-checking under government, which is necessary for Germanic verb-subject order, occurs in constructions with subject pronouns.

Interestingly, Schwartz and Sprouse (1994) speak of similar findings in their study of an adult learner ('Cevdet') with Turkish L1 acquiring L2 German. In Cevdet's data verb-subject sequences initially occur with pronominal subjects only. According to Schwartz and Sprouse it is implausible to assume that Cevdet has implemented the government case-checking option at this point. The authors argue that if this were the case Cevdet should produce verb-subject sequences with pronominal subjects and with subject NPs. Therefore, they propose that at this stage subject pronouns are case-checked by means of the incorporation option.[158] In my view there is no reason why pronouns should not perform a kind of *pioneering function* regarding the introduction of target-like nominative case-checking under government - recall that pronominal objects also followed the order object-verb prior to object NPs.

Subsequent development of Bruno's L2 German shows that the verb-subject order is eventually implemented also with subject NPs (cf. (211) - (213)).[159]

(211) [13-76] da waren viele leute gekommen
there were many people come
'there came many people'

(212) [17-16] erste mal hat mir die sekretärin
first time has me the secretary

---

[157] What we need to take into account additionally here is the possibility of a coindexation of *pro* in preverbal position with a postverbal subject. This is a property of pro-drop languages. I will discuss the status of Bruno's L2 German in this regard in section 8.2.4.2.

[158] Schwartz and Sprouse follow Rizzi and Roberts (1989) in the assumption that case-checking can also occur through incorporation. The original proposal (cf. also Roberts 1993) intends to capture restricted French inversion. Basically, the pronominal subject is assumed to cliticise to the inflected verb in order to satisfy the Case Filter.

[159] It is noteworthy, however, that non-subject V2 sequences with subject NPs remain in the minority when compared with constructions with pronominal subjects.

gesagte (...)
said
'the first time the secretary told me (...)'

(213) [21-247] vielleicht hat nur meine schwägerin das
perhaps has only my sister-in-law the
kind gewollt
child wanted
'maybe it was only my sister-in-law who wanted the child'

8.2.3.3 Conclusion

Our analysis of nominative case-checking in Bruno's L2 German reveals that the target-like case-checking mechanism is introduced concurrently to the implementation of main verb agreement morphology. But we could also see that Bruno continued to produce Italian-like *free inversion* constructions which are deviant from target German. Once again, we acknowledge the coexistence of alternative grammatical mechanisms, a finding, which goes against the traditional assumption of *punctual* parameter (re-)setting. But, the development depicted is well in line with a dynamic understanding of language acquisition, in particular, with Hohenberger's *tripartite algorithm* (see section 7.3.2.2). Following the sub-division she proposes we can characterise Bruno's acquisition of the target case-checking mechanism in the following way:

- *preliminal state*:
  case-checking under spec-head agreement
- *liminal state*:
  case-checking under spec-head agreement and under government
- *postliminal state*:
  case-checking under government

This understanding of Bruno's development contrasts with Müller's (1996: 39):

> "To summarize the universal properties of case assignment are available to Bruno. The parameterized options are accessible as well, they are, however, determined in an item-by-item fashion. He seems to know that nominative Case assignment may depend on the lexical content of INFL. However no generalisations which extend the limits of lexical properties can be observed."

Recall that Müller favours the general assumption that restructuring in ASLA occurs in an item-by-item fashion. Once more, however, I have to contradict her arguments: the tripartite development path concerns the implementation of the relevant grammatical options. That new options are realised later with some verbs is no evidence against this claim. To the contrary: there is no evidence, for example, for the usage of the alternative options with isolated lexical items prior to the point at which these are possible, i.e. at the *liminal state*.

In sum, we can see that what Müller assumes to be an ASLA-specific version of *lexical learning* is not such. Note that she concedes that the relevant information pertains to the FCs involved in the grammatical process of case assignment (i.e. INFL). Hence it is unclear why Bruno should treat every verb as an idiosyncratic exception to the rule. Certainly, *non-subject V2* requires the target-like nominative case-checking mechanism *and* verb raising. Recall that the latter only occurs upon the correct analysis of the verb form in question. We could see above (section 8.2.2.2) that some verb forms are analysed relatively late (e.g. 'kennen', *to know*). So, if we consider the inter-play of the relevant grammatical constraints necessary for Germanic V2, the delayed appearance of these verbs in non-subject V2 contexts comes as no surprise.

And once more, evidence from research in the field of diachronic language change teaches us that such a state of affairs is not as unusual as it may seem. Several studies in the realm of language change recognise a relationship between the diachronic evolution of word order and a change in the respective nominative case-checking mechanisms. In such cases the coexistence of two nominative case-checking mechanisms has also been observed. Vance (1995), for example, discusses the status of non-subject initial sequences with non-pronominal subjects in VP final position (her "CV(X)Sn" order) in the development of Old to Middle French. The following sequences are given for further illustration (ibid.: 175 f., her transl.).

(214) et   par ceste parole   entra   en   aux   covoitise
     and   by   this word   entered   into them covetousness
                                                         (Q 103, 12)

(215) car ja   seront   repeu   li   verai chevalier de
     for now   will-be   fed   the   true   knights   of
     la   viande   del   ciel
     the food   of-the   heaven   (Q 267, 14)

(216) maintenant s'en   ala   la demoiselle   (Q 112, 22)
     now   refl-'en' went   the maiden

227

According to Vance (ibid.: 191) the CV(X)Sn order is a kind of

"... hybrid "verb second free inversion" construction, which is consistent with both a grammar in which obligatory V-to-C applies and with one in which it does not."

Vance further assumes that it is the coexistence of what she calls IP and CP inversion - which parallels with the availability of alternative case-checking mechanisms under discussion here - ultimately leads to the loss of V2:

"... the types of inverted word orders produced in IP's and those produced in CP's are fundamentally different. Specifically, CP inversion may - and, in the case of subject pronouns, must - have immediately postverbal subjects. They are of course restricted to matrix clauses, and they have an obligatory preverbal non-subject constituent. IP inversions on the other hand, generally have VP-final subjects, strictly exclude pronouns, and may occur in embedded contexts. Since they are essentially "free inversions" and not verb-second structures, they may in fact be verb-initial in MidF. It is the coexistence of these two underlyingly different inversion constructions, I claim, that sets in motion the decline of verb movement to Comp in the history of French."
(ibid.: 191)

Note that Vance claims that this is a generalised process which also applies in the history of Italian dialects or Spanish.
Other analyses, however, relativise the causality proposed by Vance. Certainly, Vance' argument is somewhat misleading. For one, coexistence represents a kind of balanced state. As seen above, coexistence may, but must not necessarily lead to *competition* among alternatives. So there must be further additional reasons why one of the options is eventually discarded. In view of our considerations regarding dynamic systems, we expect the "direction" of the development to also play a role. Recall that a system's state is always related to its previous state.
What is of crucial importance is that most of the studies agree that parametric change with regard to nominative case assignment does not unexpectedly take place (cf. Ribeiro 1995, cf. also the studies in Roberts and Battey 1995). In the course of this process some grammatical phenomena may attain a marked or residual status. Ribeiro (1995), for example, illustrates the change of Old Portuguese, which for a certain time allows both nominative case checking under government and agreement, towards Brazilian Portuguese, which only instantiates the agreement option. According to her (ibid.: 133), during a transition phase

"... the reanalysis to basic SVO structure led the child to opt for Nominative assignment under agreement, and to reanalyse XPVS evidence as marked structures involving Nominative assignment under government."

Interestingly, in the case of Bruno there is a similar development, only the other way round, i.e. from an SVO language with nominative case checking under agreement towards an SOV language with nominative case-checking under government. This option becomes productive first with subject pronouns whereas subject NPs appear in constructions which we analysed as Italian-like *free inversions*. Subsequent data proved the eventual implementation of the government option.

In concluding, evidence from language change provides additional support regarding three aspects of parametric change, which are also of relevance in ASLA, namely

(a) parametric change need not take place abruptly,

(b) grammatical restructurings may be preceded by a period in which alternative options are available simultaneously and

(c) alternative options may remain accessible as marked or residual options.

8.2.4 Non-subject topicalisation

8.2.4.1 Non-subject V2

As we could see in section 2.6 one of the crucial differences between Romance and Germanic languages pertains to the so-called *Verb-Second Constraint* (V2) which applies to Germanic languages (with the exception of Modern English). Recall that this constraint requires the finite verb to appear in sentence-second position. Furthermore, the constraint implies the topicalisation of some XP into the preverbal position. In contrast to Romance, V2 languages thus offer only one position left to the verb. Consequently, sequences with both a non-subject and a subject preceding the verb are ungrammatical in German[160] yet grammatical in Romance[161] as illustrated in (217) and (218).

(217) Italian: ieri Maria ha mangiato la insalata
              yesterday Maria has eaten the salad

---

[160] Recall that target German only allows surface V3 in structures with coordinating conjunctions (e.g. 'und', *and*) and non-coordinating particles (e.g. 'denn', *since*, 'aber', *but*).

[161] For further details on Italian syntax see Burzio (1986).

(218) German: *gestern Maria hat den Salat gegessen
yesterday Maria has the salad eaten
'yesterday Maria ate the salad'

Moreover, only non-arguments may appear before the subject in Romance. In German, by contrast, any kind of XP may be topicalised into the preverbal position. The following sequences illustrate the relevant facts:

(219) Italian: *la insalata Maria ha mangiato
the salad Maria has eaten

(220) German: den Salat hat Maria gegessen
the salad has Maria eaten

Subsequently, I will use the cover term *non-subject V2* for sequences with a topicalised non-subject obeying the V2 constraint.[162] We could see in the previous section that such sequences appear in Bruno's data as soon as the government option is implemented in his L2 German. Nevertheless the target constraint whereby topicalisation of some XP only occurs into the preverbal position is not obeyed across the board. The following sequences illustrate that Bruno also produces Italian-like XP-subject-verb sequences for which I will use the descriptive denomination *V3*:

(221) [4-174] heute isch habe gesproche mit meine
today I have spoken with my
kollegin von meine stadt
colleague of my town
'today I talked to my colleague from my home-town'

(222) [4-183] eine mal ich bin gegangen mit das freund
one time I were gone with the friend
'I went once with a friend'

(223) [7-2] und dann ich habe immer keine zeit
and then I have always no time
'and then I always have no time'

---

[162] For the time being a decision among the competing descriptive analyses of Germanic V2 (see section 2.6) will be avoided. I will touch upon this controversy in section 8.2.5 below, however, where I discuss the word order in Bruno's L2 German embedded clauses.

(224) [7-110] kuckmal viele junge leute ich habe
look-ADV *many young people I have*
schon gesprochen fü für das problem
already spoken for for the problem
von kirche
of church

'look I have talked with many young people about the problem of the church'

(225) [10-18] achso das ich habe hier gelesen
ah that I have here read
'ah, that I read here'

The sequences illustrate, additionally, that Bruno produces V3 sequences with arguments (e.g. (225)) and non-arguments (e.g. (223)) in the sentence-initial position. In figure 8.2 we can see the relative frequency of non-subject V2 sequences. The average frequency of these sequences is of 13 % for the whole recording time.

Percent

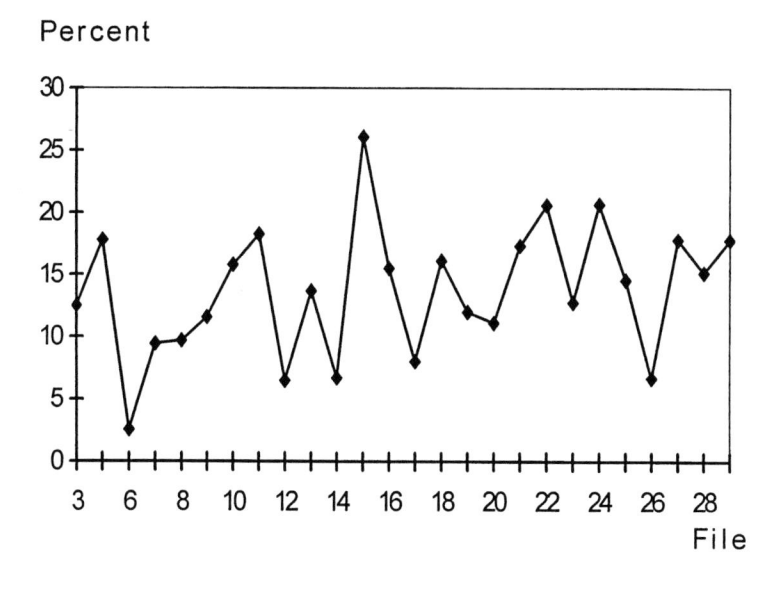

Figure 8.2 Relative frequency of non-subject initial V2 sequences

The frequency of non-subject initial V2 sequences with topicalised *arguments* increases as of file 15. Note that the number of non-arguments in

231

the preverbal position (predominant during the former period) remains somewhat constant. It is worth mentioning that in the majority of cases topicalised arguments appear in the stressed demonstrative form (e.g. 'das', *that*) as is the case in (226) - (229). Note that the usage of the stressed pronominal 'das' instead of the unstressed pronominal 'es' (*it*) is completely in accordance with the target norm which disallows the topicalisation of the latter (cf. Schwartz and Tomaselli 1991).[163]

(226) [12-83] das   hab   ich   schon   gesehen
               that   have   I   already   seen
      'I have seen that already'

(227) [15-67] das   kannst du   mir   nicht   sagen
               that   can   you   me   not   say
      'you cannot say that to me'

(228) [15-119] das   hab   ich   nicht   verstanden
               that   have   I   not   understood
      'I did not understand that'

(229) [16-74] das   kann   ich   vielleicht auch   glauben
               that   can   I   always   also   believe
      'I may possibly believe that too'

As regards the overall frequency of V3 structures in comparison with non-subject V2 sequences (see figure 8.3 below) the following observations are valid. We can see that V3 structures predominate over non-subject initial V2 sequences until file 8. From file 14, however, non-subject initial V2 sequences are clearly predominant. Nevertheless, V3 sequences are still produced with a rate which oscillates between 0 and 9 %. This is to say that by the end of the recording time non-subject V2 has not yet become obligatory.

Again, the data evidence an apparent coexistence of target-like and target-deviant structures. The overall conclusion does not tell the whole story though. A more detailed analysis reveals the following:

---

[163] The relevant contrast is illustrated in the following sequences (cf. op. cit.: 252, their transl.):
  (i)   *Es_{acc} hat   das $Pferd_{nom}$ gefressen.
        it   has   the   horse   eaten
  (ii) Das_{acc} hat   das $Pferd_{nom}$ gefressen.
        that has   the   horse   eaten

Percent

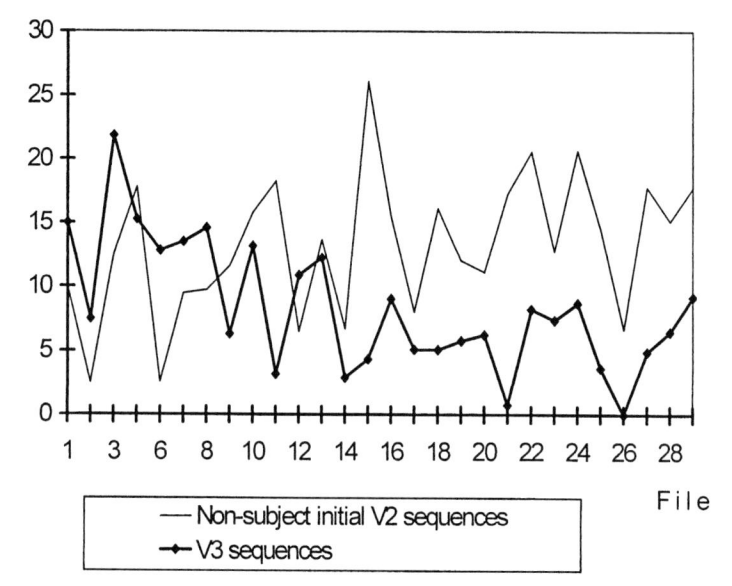

Figure 8.3 Relative frequency of non-subject initial V2 sequences and V3 sequences

- As of file 6 we can observe that the same non-arguments which appear in the sentence-initial position of V3 sequences also appear in the preverbal position of non-subject initial V2 constructions (cf. (230) - (233)).

(230) [8-82]   und **dann** ich **versteh**
              and then I   understand
              'and then I understand'

(231) [8-324] und **dann** **kommst** du mit de bus
              and then   come   you with the bus
              'and then you come with the bus'

(232) [9-84] **jetzt** **hast** du   auch mehr
              now   have   you also more
              'now you also have more'

(233) [9-101] **jetzt** ich **habe** **gelesen** in eine
              now   I   have   read   in a

233

zeitung deutsch
newspaper German
'now I have read in a German newspaper'

- Argument V3 disappears as of file 19.

- A new (target-like) option deriving "surface V3" appears as of file 14, namely the possibility of allowing sentence-initial, focused NPs, which are succeeded by a subject pronoun in preverbal position, cf.

(234) [14-17] aber   die   französisch die   haben
               but   the   French   they   have

               dreißig   prozente   die   wörter   ganz
               thirty   percent   the   words   completely

               genau   so   gleich
               exactly   like   same

               'but in French thirty percent of the words are exactly the same'

(235) [18-159] sofort   hier   die   anderen
               immediately   here   the   other

               schullehrer   die   haben angefangen
               school-teachers   they   have   begun

               zu   lachen
               to   laugh

               'the other teachers immediately began to laugh here'

In view of the preceding considerations we are led to conclude that in Bruno's L2 German a change in the status of the preverbal position affects the usage of the adjunction option deriving V3. This change is characterised by *oscillations* between target-like and target-deviant sequences. However, the data allow for the conclusion that non-subject V2 is established as of file 14 insomuch as it predominates V3. It should be thus expected that V3 gains a residual status progressively.[164] In sum, the apparent coexistence of V2 and V3 structures merits further scrutiny.

---

[164] It is noteworthy that a similar situation occurred in the case of Old High German. As pointed out by Tomaselli (1995) despite being a V2 language Old High German allowed for V3 orders, if only randomly, in main clauses with pronominal subjects.

8.2.4.2 Topic drop and pro-drop

I will finish off the discussion of non-subject topicalisation in Bruno's L2 German with a brief analysis of V1 sequences in which this process apparently fails to occur. Recall that in target German the verb appears in the sentence-initial position in yes-no questions, conditionals or imperatives (see section 2.6). Declarative (surface) V1 sequences are only possible in certain colloquial contexts.

The omission of the initial (topicalised) constituent which derives such V1 structures is termed *topic drop*. As illustrated subsequently, the element omitted can be an adverbial phrase, an object NP or even a subject pronoun[165] (the counterpart sequence without topic drop is provided in brackets), cf.

(236) Tun wir das eben nicht.   [Dann tun wir das eben nicht.]
      do we that ADV not   then do we that ADV not
      'In this case we will not do it.'

(237) Will sie nicht.   [Das will sie nicht.]
      want she not   that want she not
      'She does not want that.'

(238) Funktioniert nicht.   [Das funktioniert nicht.]
      works   not   that works   not
      'That does not work.'

The following interview passages illustrate Bruno's target-like use of topic drop.

(239) [6-199] *Interviewer:*
              hast du die von der firma oder mußt
              have you them from the office or   must
              du die selber   bezahlen?
              you them yourself pay
              'do you have them from the office or do you have to pay them yourself?'

---

[165] According to Haider (1986), colloquial German allows for the omission of nominative and accusative pronouns in the fronted position. Haider refers to Huang's (1984) analysis whereby the possibility for *pronoun drop* is related to an empty operator in the fronted position.

Bruno:

hat	mir	geholt	meine	brud-	meine
has	*me*	*taken*	*my*	*brother*	*my*

bruder	von	seine	fabrik
brother	*of*	*his*	*factory*

'my brother brought [them] from his factory'

(240) [12-102] *Interviewer:*

willst	du	ne	zigarette	haben?
want	*you*	*a*	*cigarette*	*have*

'do you want a cigarette?'

Bruno:

hab	ich
have	*I*

'I have [one]'

(241) [13-46] *Interviewer:*

machst	du	das	auch?
make	*you*	*that*	*also*

'do you do that also?'

Bruno:

hab	ich	auch	gemacht
have	*I*	*also*	*made*

'I did [that] also'

(242) [13-194] *Interviewer:*

ja	das	ist	besser	in	sizilien,	ja	mite
yes	*this*	*is*	*better*	*in*	*Sicily*	*yes*	*with*

freunde	immer	spazieren
friends	*always*	*walk*

'yes, this is better in Sicily, isn't it? To always go for a walk with friends'

Bruno:

kannst	du	auch	hier
can	*you*	*also*	*here*

'you can do [that] here also'

(243) [16-204] *Interviewer:*

der	da	hat	ein	großes	schiff -
that-one	*there*	*has*	*a*	*big*	*ship*

'the one there has a big ship'
Bruno:
hat   er   selbst   konstruiert
has   he   himself   built
'he built [it] by himself'

During files 1-20 the average rate of main clauses with the verb in initial position is of 20 % whilst non-subject V2 clauses have an average frequency of 7.50 %. The number of verb-initial sequences decreases to an average frequency of 12 % in files 21-29. The overall development is depicted in figure 8.4.

Percent

[Graph showing two lines across files 1-28, with legend:
—♦— Non-subject initial V2 sequences
——— V1 sequences]

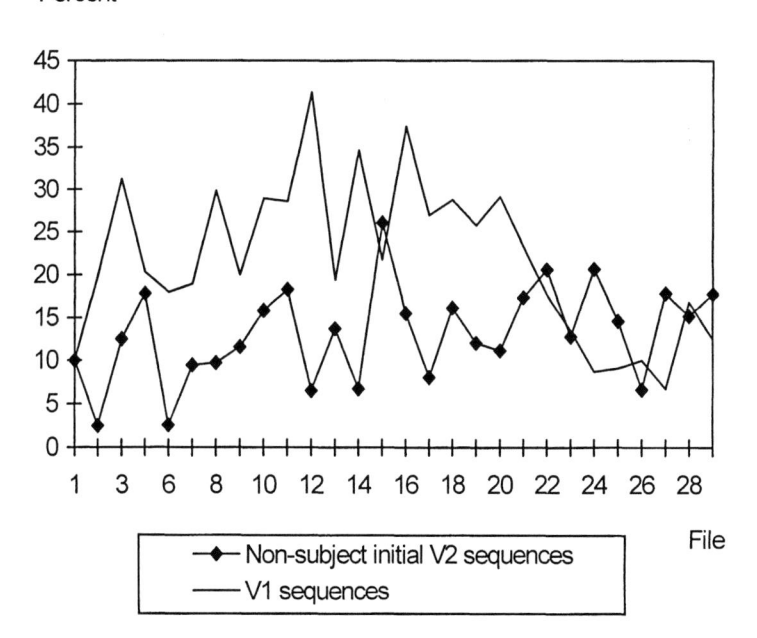

File

Figure 8.4   Relative frequency of non-subject initial sequences and verb-initial sequences

Apart from the target-like use of V1 structures Bruno also produces target-deviant ones, cf.

(244) [6-110] ja,   sind   nich   egal   probleme
               yes   are   not   the-same   problems
               'yes, the problems are not the same'

237

(245) [7-4]　　isch　sache　　wenn　isch　mache　　eine　fehler　in
　　　　　　　　I　　say　　　when　I　　　make　　　an　　error　in

　　　　　　　　meine　sprache　　　muß　korrigiere　alle　vorsicht
　　　　　　　　my　　language　　　must　correct　　　all　　care

　　　　　　　'I say that if I make an error in my language [you] must take pains to correct me'

(246) [8-133]　wenn　ich　hole　die　bus　ist schon　viertel
　　　　　　　　when　I　　take　the　bus　is already　quarter

　　　　　　　　nach　fumf
　　　　　　　　past　five

　　　　　　　'when I take the bus it is already a quarter past five'

(247) [9-79]　funktioniert　nicht　mehr　die　radio
　　　　　　　　works　　　　not　　more　the　radio

　　　　　　　'the radio does not work anymore'

We can see that these sequences differ from standard German for different reasons. In (244) and (247) the subject NP occurs in sentence-final position. So these are Italian-like *free inversion* constructions. [166]
In (245) we can see that subject drop occurs in complex structures in a way which differs from the target. In (246) the necessary expletive pronoun 'es' (*it*) is missing. In fact, the vast majority of target-deviant V1 sequences lacking a lexical subject would require such an expletive subject in order to conform to the target. This holds equally for target-deviant non-subject V2 sequences like (248) - (250).

(248) [12-93]　focus　gibt　auch　auf　deutsch
　　　　　　　　focus　is　　also　　on　　German

　　　　　　　'in German you also have the word "focus"'

(249) [13-237]　aber　für　uns　ausländer　gibet　die　regel ...
　　　　　　　　but　　for　us　foreigners　　is　　the　rule

　　　　　　　'but for us the foreigners there is the rule...'

---

[166] Nevertheless we must admit that some of these sequences would be acceptable in a colloquial situation depending on the intonation contour. Take (247), for example. As it stands this sequence reminds us of the Italian-like *free inversion* constructions discussed above. But, if "die radio" occurs as an additional remark, this sequence would be acceptable, given the interview situation. Unfortunately, the written transcripts at my disposal did not always allow for a clear-cut interpretation.

(250) [14-90] andrea de fabricio gibt nicht
"andrea de fabricio" *is not*
'there is no "Andrea de Fabricio"'

We must conclude then that Bruno does yet not obey the target-like constraints revelant for *pronoun-drop* in target German.
Note that German only allows pronoun-drop in the fronted position. The following sequences illustrate the relevant contrast (cf. Haider 1986: 56, my transl.):

(251) Gestern habe *(ich) *(es) auf den Tisch gestellt.
yesterday have I it on the table put

(252) ∅ habe es gestern auf den Tisch gestellt.
have it yesterday on the table put

(253) ∅ habe ich gestern auf den Tisch gestellt.
have I yesterday on the table put
'I put it on the table yesterday'

Later data show, however, that Bruno progressively adheres to the relevant constraint (cf. (254) - (256) and figure 8.5).

(254) [11-314] da war **es** so zwei uhr so
there was it so two clock so
'it was about two ó clock'

(255) [19-247] und ich muß immer das alles
and I have always that all
akzeptieren weile gibt keine - gibt**s**
accept because is no there-is
keine anderes mo- moglichkeit
no other possibility
'and I have to accept all this because there is no other possibility'

(256) [28-241] überall **es** gib - gibt **es** eine grenze
everywhere it is is it a limit
'there is always a limit'

239

Absolute numbers

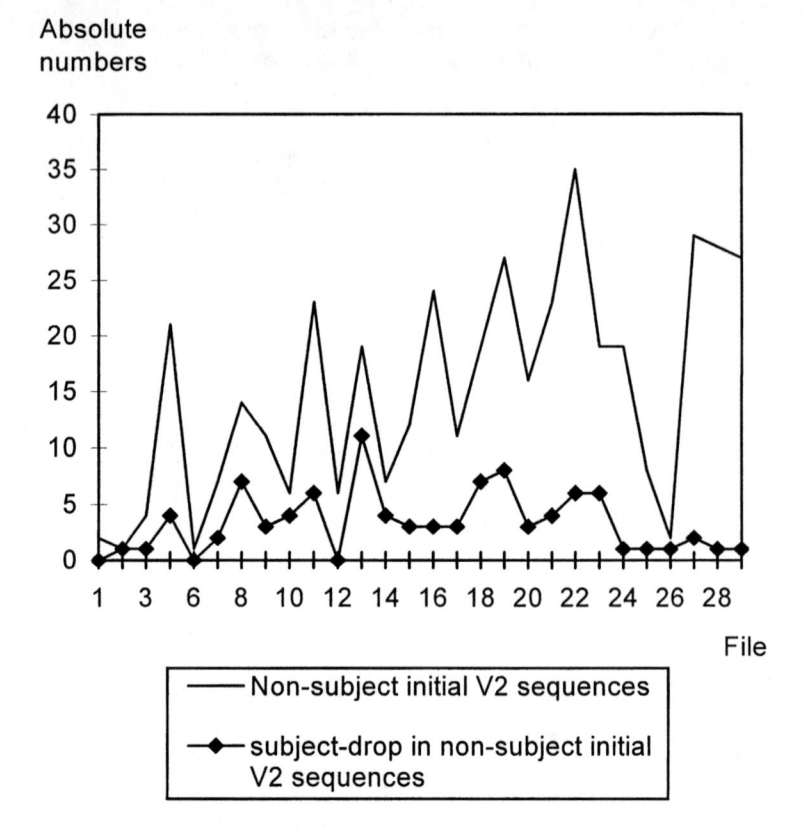

Figure 8.5   Subject-drop in non-subject initial sequences

8.2.4.3 Conclusion

The preceding examination of main clause V2 in Bruno's L2 German depicts quite a complex development. On the one hand, Bruno correctly identifies the preverbal position as a non-A position to which any kind of XP may be topicalised. The concurrent implementation of case checking under government proves that he correctly observes the correlation implicit in the V2 constraint.

But, we could also see that the acquisition of V2 does not go along with the *immediate* disappearance of target-deviant V3 sequences. Our detailed analysis of such sequences, however, revealed that the V3 option progressively becomes a residual one. All in all we are led to the conclusion that the emergence of new properties is not tied to an immediate exclusion of old ones. As in other dynamic systems *new reactions* manifest themselves in terms of *oscillations*.

It is noteworthy that this conclusion also holds true with respect to other forms of language development. Recall our discussion of inter- and intra-individual variation in child language acquisition (see chapter 7). There we discussed some of the relevant evidence which goes against the alleged instantaneous acquisition of the grammatical properties associated with V2. Recall that some of the children also produced V1 and V3 sequences in addition to target-like V2 structures.

If we turn our attention to the history of French we can also see that the change of a language disallowing V3 towards a language allowing V3 did not take place abruptly. In her analysis of the transition of Old French to Middle French, Barbara Vance points out (1995:185) that

> "[t]he competition between inversion and non-inversion becomes even more clearer when we note that the same lexical items that once required inversion now alternate between inversion and non-inversion. In some individual cases (e.g. *lors*) there is already a marked preference, in early MidF, to avoid inversion." [167]

Again, language change imposes itself as a *mirror image* to Bruno's development... Where Vance recognises a development whereby "*the initial constituent of the clause is gradually reanalyzed as being unrelated to inversion*" (ibid.: 191), Bruno's data reveal just the opposite!

Similar considerations can be made regarding the status of null subjects in Bruno's L2 German. In general terms, we can conclude that Bruno correctly analyses L2 German as a [- pro-drop]-language. But even by the end of the recording time he still makes use of null-subject sequences so that we must assume that *pro-drop* is still an option if only a residual one. Note the apparent failure of an *immediate* resetting of the pro-drop parameter is subject to a controversial debate within the framework of the so-called UG-access debate (cf. White 1989, Liceras 1988 and 1989, Hilles 1986 and 1991, Meisel 1991, Tsimpli and Roussou 1991).

---

[167] Note that Vance argues against other analyses which assume that apparent verb third clauses are the result of cliticisation of preverbal subject pronouns to the verb. According to Vance this assumption is not correct because subject pronouns are still full NP's at the syntactic level in MidF, their cliticisation being phonological only. Her revision of the texts revealed that there is no stage at which CSV is possible with pronominal subjects only. Vance speculates on a relation of the change in the evolution of rhythmic structure in French. An apparent shift of the phrasal stress to the end of the clause would be related to the rise of *free inversion*. Basically, her conclusion is that the introduction of CSV was prepared by earlier changes (syntactic and probably rhythmic ones).

The delayed implementation of the relevant constraints was contrasted with child language acquisition where the setting of the parameter was assumed to occur immediately. Recent studies, however, show that children do also produce similar errors. Hohenberger (1996), for example, remarks that her son ('Tilman') produces V2 sequences with a *pro* (cf. (257) - (258)).

(257) ränensaft   kann   *pro*   auch   trinken   (2;01,31)
      lemon juice can   also   drink
      'one can also drink lemon juice'

(258) des   mag   *pro*   nist   (2;02,03)
      this   want   not
      'I don't want this'
      (ibid: 528/9, her transl.)

Note that she also concludes that the traditional assumptions which tied the parameter setting "event" to a specific trigger fail to account for this evidence. Instead, she proposes a dynamic account which allows for a *liminal phase* in which target-like and target-deviant forms coexist until the correct option is eventually implemented. This is in line with her *tripartite model of change* (see section 7.3.2.2).

As regards topic-drop, Bruno's protracted use of this construction possibly results in an overgeneralisation of this phenomenon to situations which do not always conform to the target *pragmatic* constraints.
Note that the possibility of null subjects in a grammar obeying the V2 constraint is not as unnatural as it may seem. If we look at the history of French (cf. Lemieux and Dupuis 1995) we can see that Old French and Middle French were V2 and pro-drop languages (unlike Modern French). The coexistence of these two phenomena is illustrated in the following sequence (ibid.: 92, their transl.):

(259) Atant   regarda   *pro*   contreval   la   mer, (...)
      then   looked (3s SUBJ)   down at   the   sea...
                                                         (Bérinus, I, p. 240)
      'Then he looked down at the sea...'

Vance (1995) argues that the *dissociation* of sentence-initial non-subjects from inversion is also related to V1 orders such as (260).

(260) Fut   le   duc   de   Brunsvich   pour   l'empereur
      was   the   duke   of   Brunsvich   for   the emperor

'The duke of Brunswick was there for the emperor.'
(Saintré, 207,28)
(ibid.: 189, her transl.)

As pointed out by Vance the possibility of these orders occurring is likely among other things by a change related to the licensing of *pro* in SpecIP which is responsible for the replacement of (Germanic) V2 by *free inversion*. [168]

Again, we can see that Bruno's data reveal a development which proceeds "the other way round", i.e. towards a grammar with Germanic V2 in which V1 occurs in restricted cases only. As regards the apparent gradualness of restructuring processes in Bruno's L2 German evidence from language change proves to be quite instructive. Consider, again, Vance's assumptions (ibid.: 173) in this respect:

> "... parameter resetting takes place only after the gradual accumulation of evidence for the new grammar results in a new generation's inability to construct the old grammar out of the linguistic data it receives."

What Vance describes as a learnability problem for a new generation may also be restated in terms of grammar-internal changes. As long as the old grammar assimilates the new evidence in the input no decisive change will take place. Where this is not the case grammar-internal conflicts will force the necessary restructurings. Much like other dynamic systems' entering so-called *catastrophy folds*, we expect linguistic systems to go through restructuring processes whenever they are pushed into the vicinity of alternative *attractors* (i.e. parametric values).

---

[168] As discussed above (see section 8.2.3.3) Vance bases her assumptions on the contrast between a CP- and an IP-analysis. Her argumentation (ibid.: 191) is repeated here for convenience:
"Under my account, the types of inverted word orders produced in IP's and those produced in CP's are fundamentally different. Specifically, CP inversions may - and, in the case of subject pronouns, must - have immediately postverbal subjects. They are of course restricted to matrix clauses, and they have an obligatory preverbal non-subject constituent. IP inversions, on the other hand, generally have VP-final subjects, strictly exclude pronouns, and may occur in embedded contexts. Since they are essentially "free inversions" and not verb second structures, they may in fact be verb-initial in MidF. It is the coexistence of these two underlyingly different inversion constructions, I claim, that sets in motion the decline of verb movement to Comp in the history of French."

8.2.5 IP-headedness

8.2.5.1 Symmetric V2

One of the crucial properties which distinguishes German from other V2 languages is the verb placement asymmetry between main and embedded clauses. Whereas German generally disallows embedded V2, languages like Icelandic and Yiddish exhibit V2 in all embedded clauses (cf. Vikner 1995).[169] The following sequences illustrate this contrast (Yiddish and Icelandic examples from Vikner 1995: 66, his transl.)

(261) Yiddish:
... az	morgn	vet	dos	yingl	oyfn	veg	zen
... that	tomorow	will	the	boy	on-the	way	see
a	kats						
a	cat						

(262) Icelandic:
... að	Maríu	hefur	Helgi	aldrei	kysst
that	Maria	has	Helgi	never	kissed

(263) German:
*... daß	Maria	hat	den	Helge	niemals	geküsst
that	Maria	has	the	Helge	never	kissed

We assume that this contrast basically results from a different specification of the headedness of INFL:

- German: INFL is head-final
- Yiddish and Icelandic: INFL is head-initial

As it stands, the specification of German would imply the Symmetry Hypothesis of German sentence structure (see section 2.6). Recall that this assumption is not uncontroversial. But we will resume some of the critical aspects of the relevant hypotheses during the course of the subsequent analysis.

We have not dealt so far with the development of embedded clauses in Bruno's L2 German. The restructuring necessary for the implementation

---

[169] Yiddish and Icelandic differ from other Germanic languages such as Danish, Faroese, Norwegian and Swedish where embedded V2 is only possible in embedded clauses of certain matrix verbs (for further details see Vikner 1995).

of the target V2 asymmetry occurs only later on. In other words, for quite a long period of time word order in finite embedded clauses "reflects" main clause word order. In files 1 and 2 embedded clauses with a complementiser are not really productive with the exception of subordinated clauses introduced by the adverbial conjunction 'wenn' (*when*) (cf. (264), (267)). Clauses with a quotation reading appear in the place of indirect speech (cf. (266), (268), (269), (270)).

(264) [1-149] wenn dies   geht   kaputt   das
               if   *this* *goes* *broken* *this*
               'if it gets broken, this'

(265) [2-31]   er   sprechen etwas   das   i-ische   schon
               he *say*   *something* *that* *I*   *already*
               weiß
               know
               'he said something I already know'

(266) [2-36]   er   hate   gesagt   eeh   langsam   langsam   ische
               he *has*   *said*   *eeh* *slowly* *slowly* *I*
               gehe   reien
               go   *inside*
               'he said that I am getting slowly into the matter'

(267) [2-69]   bei   eh   wenn   isch   habe   keine   zeit   eine
               at *eh* *when*   *I*   *have* *no*   *time* *one*
               foto   allein -   eine   maschin   alleine -   eine
               photo *alone*   *a*   *maschine*   *alone*   *a*
               eine   ehm   kamera   allein   iste   gut
               a   *ehm* *camera* *alone*   *is*   *good*
               'when I have no time only one photo-camera is alright'

(268) [2-86]   er   hat   schon   gesagt   isch   [myːrshtë][170]
               he *has* *already* *said*   *I*   *want*
               das   oder   das
               this *or*   *this*
               'he has already said [that] he wants this or that'

---

[170] Bruno tries to pronounce the verb form "möchte" (*like, want*) which the interviewer has taught him.

(269) [2-149] hate   gesagt   nächste   male   fotomontage
               has   said   next   time   photo-montage
               '[she] has said next time we will do photo-montage'

(270) [2-234] meine   papier   in   schule   hat   gesagt
               my   paper   in   school   has   said
               primitiv   wiking   komme   in   sizilia
               primitive viking   come   in   Sicily
               'my school-notes said that the primitive Vikings came to Sicily'

Increased fluency and the introduction of new complementisers characterises files 3 and 4. The syntactic complementisers 'daß' (*that*) and 'ob' (*whether*) firstly appear in file 6 and 7 respectively. (271) gives an overview of the introduction of new complementisers.

(271) Overview of complementisers in Bruno's data and the time (= file) of their introduction/remarkable productivity[171]

Files 1-2	wenn (*when, if*) *wann (*when*)	das (*which*)	*warum (*why*)
Files 3-4	wo (*where*) welche (*which*) was (*what*)	wieviele (*how many*) *für (*for*)	weil (*because*) daß (*that*)
File 6	wie (*as*)		
File 7	ob (*if*)		
File 11	so – wie (*so – as*)		
Files 12 - 29	increased productivity of:	das, daß, ob	
File 16	so daß (*so that*)	bis (*until*)	
File 19	solange (*as long as*)		
File 21	der (*that, which*)	als (*when*)	wofür (*for which*)
File 22	um... zu (*in order to*)	bevor (*before*)	
File 27	die (*that, which*)		
File 28	wem (*to whom*)		

---

[171] I will comment immediately on Bruno's target-deviant use of 'warum', 'wann' and 'für'.

A few specifications are in order with respect to the overview given in (271):

- In file 1 Bruno mistakenly uses 'warum' (*why*) instead of 'weil' (*because*) (cf. (272). This is probably a transfer error as Italian instantiates the same lexical item for both wh-phrases *why* and *because*, namely 'perchè'.

    (272) [1-37] ja   hast [te:]   kucken   for   mi --   for
                  yes   *has*   *look*   *for* *me*   *for*

                  mische   in   arbeit   warum   ische   nicht
                  me   *in* *work*   *why*   *I*   *not*

                  spreche   deutschland
                  speak   *Germany*

    'yes, he looked for a job for me because I do not speak German'

- In German 'wann' (*when*) is an interrogative wh-phrase which Bruno mistakenly uses instead of 'wenn' (*when/if*) in the following utterance of file 2, cf.

    (273) [2-9] vielleicht   wann   ich   habe   keine   probleme
                 perhaps   *when* *I*   *have* *no*   *problems*

                 für   zeit   libro   (...)   vielleicht
                 for   *time*   "libro" [= Italian: *free*]   *perhaps*

                 wann   isch   habe   freizeit
                 when   *I*   *have* *free-time*

    'maybe when I have no problems in my free-time'

- Bruno mistakenly uses the preposition 'für' (*for*) in order to introduce infinitive clauses. The target-like construction would require 'um... zu' (*in order to*) (appearing as of file 22). Note that 'für' already occurs once in file 2 in the ambiguous context of an utterance which is not really comprehensible. As far as I can see the context favours the interpretation of "arbeit" (work) as a noun (i.e. 'für eine schnelle Arbeit', *for a fast work*), cf.

    (274) [2-60] (*context: Bruno and the interviewer are talking about different types of cameras*) Bruno:
                 für   arbeit   ist   gut   für   snell   arbeit
                 for   *work*   *is*   *good*   *for*   *fast*   *work*

    'for a professional and fast work [it] is good'

> *Interviewer:*
> ja   für   sport
> *yes   for   sports*
>
> 'yes, for [taking] sports'
>
> Bruno:
> aber   für   schnell   arbeite (...)
> *but   for   fast   work*
>
> 'but [especially] for a fast work [?/working fast]'

(275) [2-65] aber   hier   kein   arbeit
but   here   no   work
'but there [is] no work here'

- Bruno initially overgeneralises 'ob' (*whether*) to contexts in which target German would require the conjunction 'falls' (*if, in case*), cf.

(276) [8-188] guck   mal   ob   eine   apparade   ist   nicht
look   ADV   if   a   camera   is   not

teuer   so   wie   ich   sache   willst
expensive   so   as   I   say   will

du   kaufen   auch   du   eine
you   buy   also   you   one

'look in case a camera is not expensive, as I told you, do you also want do buy one?'

In general, the overview shows that Bruno uses complementiser introduced embedded clauses from the beginning. As mentioned previously, however, the productivity of complex structures is very low in files 1 and 2. Subsequently, however, the acquisition of the different complementisers as well as the productivity of complex structures increases rapidly. I will comment on the details as we proceed.

Figure 8.6 shows that the word order in embedded clauses is predominantly target-deviant during the first two thirds of the recording time.
In general, embedded clauses follow the order complementiser-subject-verb-object (henceforth *CV2*). But we can also see that complementiser-verb-subject sequences (henceforth *CV1*) such as the ones quoted below are equally abundant during the first half of the recording time.[172]

---

[172] Note that during this time verb-subject sequences are also quite numerous in main clauses.

Percent

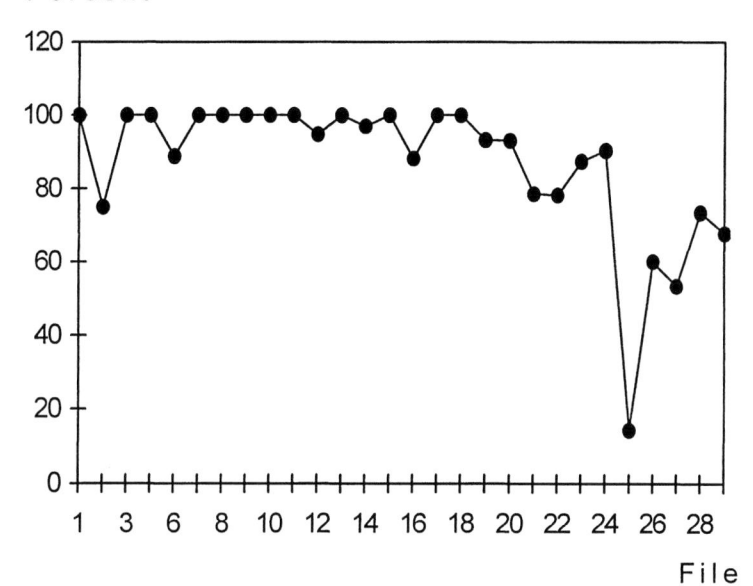

Figure 8.6   Relative frequency of embedded clauses with target-deviant verb placement

(277) [6-150] ja   wenn   **kommen**   kisten   mit   die
               yes when   come   boxes   with the

               schraube nur   eine stund in der woch(e)
               screws   only an   hour   in the week

               'yes when we get boxes with screws only an hour in the week'

(278) [7-80]   aber langsam ich habe verstande   was
               but slowly   I   have understood what

               war das   natürlich
               was   that of course

               'but slowly I understood what that was, of course'

(279) [8-141] ich habe   schon   dir   gesagt wieviel   **ist**
               I   have   already you   said   how-much   is

               die kost in italien
               the cost in Italy

               'I already told you about the costs in Italy'

(280) [8-313] vielleicht ob wenn **sagst** du die name
perhaps if when say you the name
ich mich erinn
I me remember
'maybe if you say the name I might remember'

(281) [10-21] hörst du schon so wie neugierig wenne
listen you already so as curious when
wenne **sagst** du preferida
when say you "preferida" [= Italian: *preferred*]
so wie neugierig
so as curious
'one listens with curiosity when you say "preferida"'

It is only as of the last third of the recording time that target-deviant CV1 structures decrease, exactly at the time where target-like verb final embedded clauses become productive (see figure 8.7).

Percent

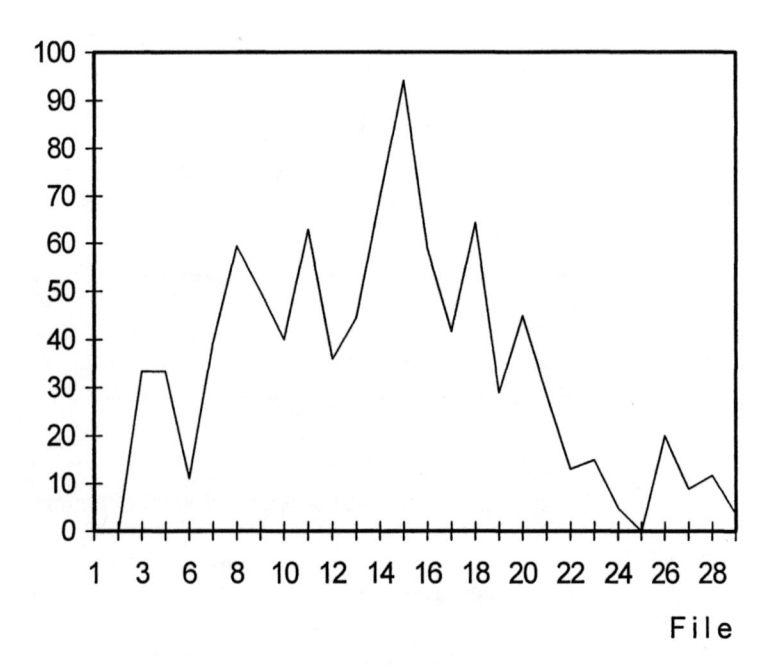

Figure 8.7   Target-deviant CV1 sequences

In descriptive terms it is noteworthy that the order complementiser-verb-subject hinges on our understanding of V2. More specifically, the question is whether embedded verb-subject sequences are CPs. The issue is especially critical if we assume that non-subject initial V2 sequences necessarily involve the CP projection (*CP analysis*) (cf. Vikner 1995, among others). Recall that the Symmetry Hypothesis of German sentence structure is based on this analysis (see section 2.6.1).
If we applied the CP-analysis in order to account for V2 sequences in Bruno's L2 German, we would have to assume CP-recursion in order to embrace embedded V2.[173]
As opposed to CV1 clauses, the order complementiser-non-subject-verb-subject (henceforth *non-subject CV2*) is fairly infrequently. The following utterances represent a comprehensive compilation of such sequences.

(282) [19-10] also   bleibt   immer   da   einfach   so
               therefore remains   always   there   simply   so

               weile   **da**   hat   angefangen zu   wohnen   und
               because   there   has   begun   to   live   and

               da   sollt   weiterwohnen
               there   should   continue-live

               'therefore he stays there simply like that because he began to live there and there he should continue to live'

(283) [23-145] weil   zum   beispiel **da** ist   nicht jeder
               because   for   example   there   is   not   everybody

               so   gut   informiert   wie   normal   soll   wie
               as   good   informed   as   normally should   as

               normal   soll
               normally should

               'since, for example, not everybody is as well-informed as he normally should be'

(284) [24-45] das   ist   eine   private frage   wenn   **das**
               this   is   a   private question if   that

               hattest   du   noch   nicht   verstande
               had   you   not   yet   understood

               'this is a personal question in case you did not understand'

---

[173] I will come shortly to Vikner's (1995) analysis upon which these considerations are based.

251

(285) [24-108] das ist aber so auch wenn **das** hatte ich
this is but so even if that had I
abgelegen
put-aside
'but it is like that even if I had put it aside'

(286) [24-135] das sag ich persönlich weile **das**
that say I personally because that
glaub ich
believe I
'I say that personally because I believe that'

(287) [24-142] das ist auch klar auch wenn **das** hab
this is also clear even if that have
ich schon erklärt
I already explained
'this is also clear even if I had explained it already'

(288) [27-48] ich ich war überlegen ob **die** konnt ich
I I was deliberate if they could I
dahin neben die mauer stellen davor
there beside the wall put in-front
'I was deliberating whether I could put them there, next to or in front of the wall'

Apart from non-subject CV2 sequences Bruno also produces complementiser introduced embedded clauses in which the verb appears in the third position (henceforth *CV3*) (cf. (289) - (293)).

(289) [11-163] ja ich komm gern weil zu hause
yes I come readily since at home
ich habe jetzte immer die selbe menu
I have now always the same menu
'yes, I will come with pleasure since we always have the same menu at home'

(290) [12-78] aber ich bin nicht ganz zufrieden
but I am not completely contented
weil mit yashica ich kann nicht
because with Yashica I can not

		fotomontage	machen	und	doppelmontage
		photo-montage	*make*	*and*	*double-montage*

              oder so
              or   so

              'but I am not completely contented because I cannot do a photo-montage or a double-montage with a Yashica'

(291) [12-104] sowieso in italien ich rauch nich mehr so
              anyway in Italy I smoke not more so

              tabak weile sonst meine freunde lachen
              tobacco because otherwise my friends laugh

              'anyway, in Italy I do not smoke tobacco because otherwise my friends would laugh'

(292) [16-117] ob eh kann ich frei sein wenne achtzehn
              if eh can I free be when eighteen

              ich werde wenn ich achtzehn werd
              I become wenn I eighteen become

              'if I shall be free when I am eighteen'

(293) [29-218] ja wenn der michel sagt daß mit hundert
              yes if the Michel says that with hundred

              liter ich würde auskommen daß mit
              liters I could get-by that with

              hundert-fünfzig liter ich würde auskommen
              hundred-and-fifty liters I would get-by

              'yes, if Michel says that I could get by with one hundred (and fifty) liters'

Apart from a few exceptions (e.g. (293)) CV3 occurs with the complementiser 'weil' (*because, since*).[174] Recall that colloquial German allows main clause word order with this complementiser. We will assume there-

---

[174] Standard German allows for an adverbial phrase to occur between the complementiser and the subject of the embedded clause in restricted cases. Note that this possibility is ungrammatical in the case of an embedded unstressed pronominal subject, cf. Vikner (1995: 103, my transl.)
   (i) *Sie hat gesagt, daß tatsächlich er dieses Buch gelesen hat.
       she has said that actually he this book read has
   (ii) Sie hat gesagt, daß tatsächlich der Junge dieses Buch gelesen hat.
       she has said that actually the boy this book read has
       'she said that it was actually the boy who read the book'

fore that Bruno has recognised this special case overgeneralising *his* main clause V3 option to embedded clauses. The overall frequency of target-deviant CV3 sequences is given in figure 8.8.

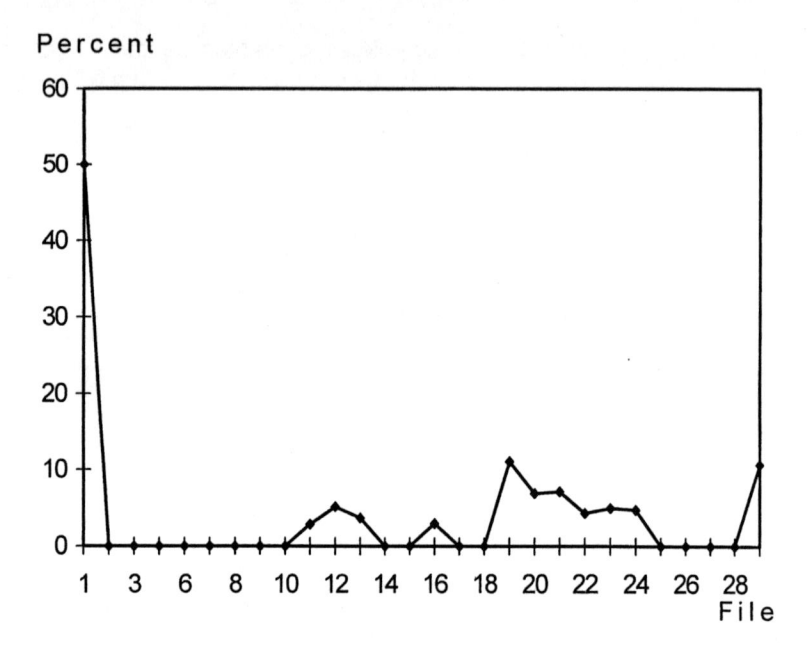

Figure 8.8   Relative frequency of target-deviant CV3 sequences

As regards the overall *symmetry* between main and embedded clauses, Bruno's L2 German grammar is analogous with the grammars of Yiddish and Icelandic (recall our introducing remarks).
Furthermore, a similar state of affairs has been acknowledged with regard to Middle French. As pointed out by Lemieux and Dupuis (1995: 99) non-subject topicalisation is productive in embedded clauses in Middle French, although they also recognise

> ".... some kind of asymmetry between root and embedded clauses since verb-second structures are used more frequently in root clauses than in embedded ones."

Interestingly, it is argued that this *asymmetry* results from "*discursive factors typically found in root contexts*" (ibid.). I take these similarities as a further indication of the fact that Bruno's L2 German does not violate universal constraints (cf. also Müller 1996). I mentioned above that there is still an ongoing discussion regarding the adequate descriptive analysis which would embrace both similarities and differences between *asymmetric* and *symmetric* V2 languages. Some authors propose a differentiation whereby only the former involves the CP analysis, the latter being derived from an IP-based analysis (cf. Lemieux and Dupuis 1995 *pace* Diesing 1990). In parametric terms the differences between languages like German and Yiddish, and for that matter Bruno's L2, would result from a different choice among the following options (cf. Lemieux and Dupuis 1995: 86):

- parameter of the landing site of the verb:
  - V-to-I: Yiddish, Icelandic, Bruno's L2
  - V-to-C: German

- parameter of the dual nature of SpecI:
  - SpecI also functions
    as an A-bar position: Yiddish, Icelandic, Bruno's L2
  - SpecI functions only
    as an A-position: German

Note that a further assumption is at stake here in order to account for non-subject topicalisation in symmetric V2 languages. According to the proposed IP analysis the subject stays in SpecVP whenever a non-subject appears in the preverbal position. Thus it has to be case-checked *in situ* under government. This is a problematic consequence of the IP-analysis as it is generally assumed that nominative case-checking involves the movement of the subject into Spec-AGR. It is certainly debatable whether this requirement need not be fulfilled in a restricted set of languages only.

Vikner (1995) intends to circumvent these problems by advancing a general V2-CP analysis also for languages like Yiddish and Icelandic. According to Vikner (1995: 67) CP-recursion is a necessary mechanism as long as the account of embedded non-subject V2 relies on the assumption that SpecIP has the same status (i.e. argument position only) cross-linguistically.[175] As Vikner remarks, subject-initial V2 is ambiguous with respect to either an IP or a CP analysis. As for language acquisition he proposes that

> '[t]he child will analyse subject-initial embedded clauses as V2 (i.e., she takes the subject to be in CPspec and the finite verb to be in C°), as this

---

[175] As pointed out by Vikner (ibid.: 81) this analysis is close to other analyses where an additional projection (call it ZP) is introduced in order to account for the relevant facts. Now whilst these analyses avoid the problem of CP-recursion they face the problem of explaining the introduction of a new projection. Eventually, it could be argued that the analyses are notational variants as noted by Vikner.

is what she does for main clauses. Main clause topicalisations give sufficient evidence that the V2 mechanism is warranted, as here V°-to-I° movement and I°-VP order will not suffice."
(op. cit.: 68)

Note, however, that the possibility of allowing CP-recursion is also open to debate. But, it seems any account which tries to cover both similarities and differences among V2 languages has to rely on additional (problematic) assumptions. As Vikner (ibid.: 83) puts it in his analysis:

"... the difference between accepting or rejecting the topicalisation to IP-spec analysis (for Yiddish and Icelandic only) is not so much a question of avoiding a disadvantage (e.g., having to claim the existence of an asymmetry that is not supported by the data), but merely a question of where to situate such a disadvantage. This can also be formulated in a different manner: Whereas rejecting the topicalisation to IP-spec analysis (for Yiddish and Icelandic only) leaves us with the difficulty of explaining why these two languages allow CP-recursion (or insertion of ZP) everywhere (given that this is not so in the other V2 languages), accepting the topicalisation to IP-spec analysis (for Yiddish and Icelandic only) merely exchanges this difficulty for another one: the difficulty of explaining why these two languages allow IP-spec to be an A-bar-position (given that this is not so in the other V2 languages)."

Similar problems are evident when considering the *Asymmetry Hypothesis* of German sentence structure. Recall that this approach claims that main clauses project to IP only as opposed to embedded clauses which project to CP (see section 2.6.2). Main and embedded clauses would thus differ with respect to the headedness value assigned to the respective IP projection. On the basis of this analysis German patterns with symmetric V2 languages with respect to main clauses but differs from these languages regarding embedded clauses due to the head-final value of the embedded IP. But further specifications would be needed in order to explain why in German embedded SpecIP can only function as an A-position. Recall that subjects appear to the right of the complementiser and that non-subjects cannot occur in this position.[176]

In concluding, none of the descriptive analyses proposed thus far provide a sufficiently conclusive account of V2 languages in a completely satisfactory way. For present purposes it suffices to say that Bruno's *symmetric* approach to German sentence structure during the first half of the recording time patterns with symmetric V2 languages.

---

[176] Note that under the *Symmetry Hypothesis* of German sentence structure this state of affairs is captured by some adjacency requirement claimed to be related to agreement features in COMP.

8.2.5.2 Restructuring of IP

It was already mentioned above that Bruno continues to produce target-deviant embedded SVO orders until the end of the recording time. As we can see in figure 8.9 target-like verb placement in embedded clauses becomes productive in the last third of the recording time.

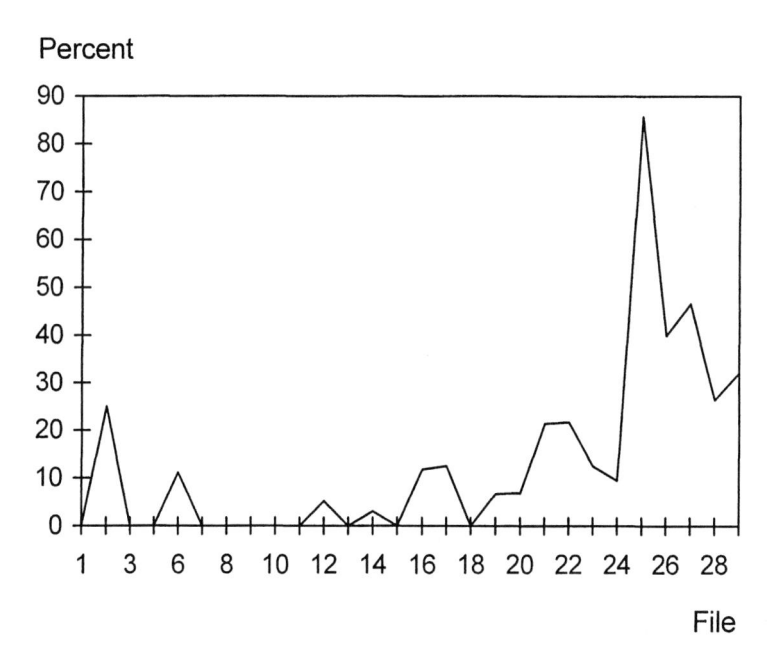

Figure 8.9   Relative frequency of embedded clauses with target-like verb placement

The following sequences illustrate the alternation of target-like and target-deviant verb placement in embedded clauses. Note that the apparent "oscillations" between alternative structural options can be observed with the same complementiser during interview passages and across files.

'wenn' (*if, when*):

(294) [19-197] manchmal   ich   werd   echt   bekloppt wenn
                sometimes *I*   *become* *really crazy*   *when*
                die beide   so   reden
                the both *so* *speak*

'sometimes I get crazy when both of them speak like that'

257

(295) [25-89] ich kaufe brot zuerst wenn ich
I buy bread firstly when I

einkaufen geh
shopping go

'when I go shopping I buy the bread first'

(296) [27-264] is auch wichtig weile wenn die luft
is also important because if the air

bleibt zu – wenn die luft zu
remains closed if the air closed

bleibt ...
remains

'it is also important because if the air remains closed...'

'der', 'das' (*relative pronouns*)

(297) [28-121] der war der einzige
the-one was the only-one

das - der gearbeitet hat
that [neuter, sing.] *that* [= masc., sing.] *worked has*

'he was the only one who worked'

(298) [28-146] ich kenn ein in Italien das
I know one in Italy that [neuter, sing.]

der braucht überhaupt nicht schlafen
that [= masc., sing.] *need at-all not sleep*

'I know somebody in Italy who needs not sleep at all'

'solange' (*as long as*):

(299) [20-181] ich kanne bei meine bruder wohnen
I can at my brother live

solange nur ein - solang - solang ich habe
as-long only a as-long as-long I have

nur eine wohnung
only an appartment

solange nur eine wohnung ich habe
as-long only a flat I have

'I can stay at my brother's place until I find a flat'

(300) [21-97] ich werde jeden samstag versuchen ein
               I   will every Saturday try   a
               zimmer solang bis ich ein finde
               room as-long as I   one find
               'every Saturday I will look for a room until I find one'

'daß' (*that*):

(301) [21-214] du weißt ganz genau kein   hat dir
               you know quite exactly no-one has you
               gesagt daß du in deutschland fahren sollst
               said that you in Germany   go   should
               'you know exactly nobody told you that you should go to Germany'

(302) [23-128] es kann eventuell auch passieren daß auch
               it can possibly also happen   that also
               die deutschland monoton werden konnt
               the Germany   monotone become could
               'it could also happen that Germany becomes monotone'

(303) [25-110] ich hoffe daß alfio hat mich verstanden
               I   hope that Alfio has me   understood
               'I hope that Alfio understood me'

(304) [29-147] ich habe gesagt daß ich krank war
               I   have said   that I   ill   was
               'I said that I was ill'

(305) [29-212] das heißt daß ich komme ganz
               that means that I   get   quite
               bestimmt   nicht mit hundert liter () aus
               definitely not   with hundred liter   by
               'that means that I definitely will not get by with one hundred liters'

As regards the rearrangement of word order in embedded clauses, it is interesting to note that, initially (i.e. files 17-22), there are sequences in which the subject and the finite verb show up sentence-finally preceded by all other elements of the clause (cf. (306) - (310)).

259

(306) [17-193] wir   können   sowieso   nur   die
                we   can   in-any-case   only   the
                dreiunddreißig   prozent   verdiene   für   ein
                thirty-three   percent   win   for   a
                gerät   das   **verkauft**   wir   haben
                machine   which   sold   we   have
                'in any case, we can only make a profit of 33 percent for a machine which we sell'

(307) [19-201] wann   **von**   **da**   **raus**   ich   komme   weiß
                when   from   there   out   I   come   know
                ich   nicht
                I   not
                'I do not know when I get out of there'

(308) [19-271] ... wie   eine   zweite   seele   das   sagt
                    as   a   second   soul   that   says
                tun   das   tun   das   tun   das   weil
                do   that   do   that   do   that   because
                der   **sohn**   isch   bin
                the   son   I   am
                '... as a second soul that tells me to do that and that because I am the son'

(309) [20-181] ... solange   **nur**   **eine**   **wohnung**   ich   habe
                    as-long   only   an   appartment   I   have
                '... until I find an appartment'

(310) [22-68]   wie   *ich*   **in sizilie**   **gehabt**   *ich*   hab
                as   I   in Sicily   had   I   have
                'as I have had in Sicily'

Certainly, the adjacency of subject and verb in these cases seems to favour an analysis whereby the subject stays in SpecVP and is case-checked under government by the verb in head-final INFL.
What remains to be accounted for is how the elements preposed to the subject get there at all, since they would have to appear between the subject and the verb in the normal case (i.e. inside the VP). In order to circumvent this problem we may consider two alternatives; namely (a) the subject is cliticised to the finite verb or (b) the elements preposed

have been scrambled out of the VP and adjoined to IP. None of these options are completely satisfactory. In view of the different possibilities Bruno tries out at this time it would appear that Bruno is similarly "undecided".
(310) is an interesting case in point as it illustrates that there are two positions for the subject. Note that this sequence occurs in file 22 - the last file in which the sequences in question appear. In dynamic terms we could conclude that during files 17-22 Bruno's L2 grammar "oscillates" among alternative analyses of subject-placement until the position right to the complementiser eventually imposes itself.

We will now consider the restructuring concerning verb placement in embedded clauses and its apparent link with the introduction of new complementisers. If we look at the overview in (271) above we can see that the introduction of different complementisers may be roughly subdivided into three phases (a) introduction and productivity of adverbial conjunctions and wh-phrases, (b) introduction of syntactic complementisers 'daß' and 'ob' (c) (morphosyntactic) specification /differentiation of d-phrases and introduction of further new (adverbial) conjunctions and 'um... zu' (*in order to*). It is certainly striking that this sub-division roughly correlates with the restructuring processes concerning both the VP and the IP. It seems it is no coincidence that the introduction of verb-final embedded clauses correlates with an increased productivity of syntactic complementisers like 'daß' (*that*) and 'ob' (*if*), the introduction of new adverbial conjunctions, the replacement of 'für' (*for*) bei 'um... zu' (*in order to*) as well as the differentiation of relative pronouns.

In this case, too, the researcher is faced with the problem of determining the causal relationship between lexical and syntactic learning. For one, as soon as they appear, new adverbial conjunctions like 'solange' (*as long*), 'bis' (*until*) and 'bevor' (*before*) occur with target-like SOV. On the other hand, there is no relevant time-lag as regards the possibility of SOV with the other complementisers. In other words, once the structural alternatives are there, Bruno uses them with all kinds of complementisers.

The following sequences are given to provide further illustration of Bruno's use of target-like CSOV with any kind of complementiser:

(311) [17-79] ich   nehme   keine   milch   nur   **wenn**   keine
              I   *take*   *no*   *milk*   *only* *when*   *no*
              da   ist
              there is

'I do not take any milk only if there is not any'

(312) [20-248] wenn sie so reagiert mein gott ich
if she so reacts my God I

kann mich nicht mehr halten
can me not anymore hold

'if she reacts that way I cannot control myself anymore'

(313) [21-108] zum beispiel **wo** - **wo** mein freund
for example where where my friend

jetzt wohnt in vohwinkel
now lives in vohwinkel

'where my friend lives now, in vohwinkel'

(314) [22-113] **bevor** er das auge rausgezeuen hat
before he the eye extracted has

'before he gouged the eye'

(315) [23-99] die deutsche men- mentalität zum beispiel
the German mentality for example

manchmal sieht die aus wie
sometime looks she [separable prefix] as

wenn zum beispiel es tut doch nicht
if for example it does anyway not

weh **wenn** zum beispiel die ausländer
hurt when for example the foreigners

alle hier bleiben
all here stay

'for example, the German mentality sometimes seems to imply that it would not matter if all the foreigners stayed here'

(316) [23-188] mir aus **wenn** ich zeit habe
me out if I time have

'I don't mind if I have time'

(317) [23-275] eine dic- eine discoteca kann gut
a discotheque a discotheque can good

werden **um** eine kontakt **zu** suchen
become in-order a contact to seek

'a discotheque can be good in order to seek contact'

(318) [25-20] **als** pisa noch grande war
when Pisa still "grande" [= Italian: big] was
'when Pisa was still important'

(319) [25-24] ich weiß nicht **ob** ich der star bin
I know not whether I the star am
'I do not know whether I am the star'

(320) [26-38] **als** ich krank war
when I ill was
'when I was ill'

(321) [27-9] ... **wenn** irgend - irgend ein neuigkeit rauskommt
when any any a new comes-out
'when any news comes out'

(322) [27-23] unsere produktion das heißt die gerät
our production that means the machines
die ich selbst in meine firm -
that I myself in my company
in meine arbeitsplatz produziere
in my place-of-work produce
'our production, that is, the machines that I produce at work'

(323) [27-110] die giovanni die hab ich nicht mehr
the Giovanni the-one have I not more
geseh von letztes mal **als** wir bei
seen of last time when we at
ihne vorbei gefahren sind
them past driven were
'I have not seen Giovanni anymore since we visited them'

(324) [27-202] irgend – ist für dich egal **was**
any is for you equal what
vorkommen wird
happen will
'anything - it does not make any difference to you what will happen'

263

(325) [28-51] und   **wo**   de   weg   zu   ende ist da
                and   *where*   *the* *path* *to* *end* *is* *there*
               ist de   bar
               is *the* *bar*
               'and at the end of the path there is the bar'

(326) [28-187] du   weißt   **wie** die   gemacht sind
               you *know* *how*   *they* *made*   *are*
               'you know how they are made'

(327) [28-208] zu   **wem**   der   die   produkte   verkauft das
               to *whom*   *he* *the* *products* *sells*   *that*
               ist ganz   einfach zu   sagen
               is *quite* *simple* *to* *say*
               'it is quite simple to tell to whom he sells the products'

(328) [29-205] aber   bei   kochen ich   brauch   mehr   warten
               but *at* *cook* *I*   *need*   *more* *wait*
               bis   das   wasser   heiß   wird
               until   *the* *water* *hot*   *becomes*
               'but when I cook I have to wait longer until the water gets hot'

8.2.5.3 Conclusion

The development of Bruno's L2 German with regard to word order in embedded clauses is analogous with the other restructurings we discussed in previous sections: Bruno produces target-deviant CSVO sequences until, at a certain point in time, he produces target-like sequences. But the realisation of the target grammatical properties does not lead to the immediate exclusion of target-deviant structures. Again, we observe the coexistence of both options. As already stated, recording finished at this time. So any consideration about the eventual implementation of the target-like order remains speculative.

As pointed out above, the issue of whether a phase in which alternative options are available simultaneously is transitory can only be determined *a posteriori*. Coexistence may not result in competition but rather stabilise or *fossilise*. But in view of the overall picture of Bruno's development it seems plausible to assume that the target-like option will eventually impose itself as much as it did in other grammatical areas. Thus the analysis proposed here contrasts with Müller's (to appear: 20) in which lexical learning in an item-by-item fashion is also claimed to determine word order variation in embedded clauses:

"As in the case of participles, Bruno learns the target-like position of finite verbs in embedded clauses in an item-by-item fashion, i.e. separately for each complementizer. Each complementizer passes through the three developmental phases independently."

According to Müller, two general observations support the lexical learning based approach, namely (a) acquisition is a gradual learning process and not an instantaneous one and (b) the correct order and target-deviant orders coexist with the same complementisers and the same finite verbs. In my opinion, the acquisition of target-like verb placement in embedded clauses being time-consuming is no definitive argument which could help decide whether learning in ASLA is "only lexical", i.e. item-based. For one, the introduction of complex structures also occurs "late" in child LA. Furthermore, the global picture of restructuring proves to follow a well-determined order which parallels with the different levels in the structure tree (cf. also Schwartz 1991). As pointed out by Tracy (1994/5: 154), *"we have to keep the temporal unfolding distinct from claims of internal logic."* The introduction of CSOV is not a gradual item-dependent process in the context of the overall development: at a certain point in time CSOV becomes possible and not before. It is unclear why lexical learning should obey such temporal delimitations. In sum, the structural development should be given more prominence.

If we have a look at other forms of language acquisition or language change, we can discern, once more, similarities with Bruno's development. Santorini (1995), for example, notes that apart from INFL-final subordinate clauses, early Yiddish also exhibited subordinate clauses that were derived from an INFL-initial structure (her *INFL-medial*) prior to the eventual implementation of the INFL-initial structure. [177] This is illustrated in the following sequences (ibid.: 60/61, her transl.):

(329) ven   der   vatr   nur   doyts   leyan   **kan**
      if   the   father   only   German   read   can
                                                                         (Anshel 11, ca. 1534)
      'provided only that the father can read German'

---

[177] Santorini further considers the possibility that the loss of INFL-final is related to the loss of hybrid COMP. This she assumes is due to the ambiguity in the data: "It might therefore be argued that although the first Infl-medial clauses in Yiddish may have been produced by a grammar with hybrid Comp, they would provide children with no positive evidence for it and that at least some children would therefore analyze Infl in Infl-medial clauses as the highest [+ I] category." (ibid.: 68)

(330) vi   es   **iszt** mir   zu   klt   (Purim-shpil 424, 1697)
      how   it   is   me   so   cold
      'how I feel so cold'

Again, it is striking that restructuring in diachronic language change represents a kind of mirror image to Bruno's development, even when taking into account in his case the last 'step' is missing. From a phase with INFL-final structures only, early Yiddish develops into a language with INFL-medial structures only and it does so by going through a phase in which both options are possible.

Recall, additionally, our discussion of intra-individual variation in child language acquisition (see chapter 7). There we concluded that one of the children ('Benny') also made use of both a head-initial and a head-final IP (for both main and embedded clauses). In the light of our discussion of Bruno's data, the similarity between his and Benny's CV1, CV2 and CVE patterns is certainly striking. Consider in this respect the following utterances (Gawlitzek-Maiwald et al. 1992: 78/79, their transl.):

(331) wenn   hab   ich   geburtstag habt   dann   han
      when   have   I   birthday   had   then   have

      ich   nein   nein   ich   ganz   au   mal   burtstag   habt
      I   no   no   I   very   too   once   birthday   had

      dann   krieg ich   das   au   mal   pispi
      then   get   I   this   too   once   frisbee
                                                       Benny 09 (3;01.04)
      'when I have my birthday then I'll get a frisbee, too'

(332) will   die   meerjungfrau haben   daß   du   has
      want   the   mermaid   have   so-that   you   have

      net   die   meerjungfrau
      not   the   mermaid   Benny 08 (3;00.19)
      'I want to have the mermaid [figure] so that you don't have the mermaid'

(333) weil   dann   kannst   du   mich   nicht   heben
      because   then   can   you   me   not   lift
                                                      Benny 10 (3;01.13)
      'because then you can't lift me'

Recall that Gawlitzek-Maiwald et al. (ibid.) also raise the critical question of how target-deviant structures eventually disappear. As already mentioned they essentially propose that the child is *forced* to decide on the headedness of IP[178] and that he eventually does so by a differentiation among sentence types.[179]

This proposal contrasts with Müller's (to appear) analysis of the child 'Ivar', who initially produces only CSVO orders. From a certain point in time, however, target-like CSOV orders appear in the data. According to Müller target-like verb placement in embedded clauses is introduced for every complementiser separately. She assumes that this is a consequence of the initial miscategorisation of complementisers.[180]

In this case also Müller argues that the necessary restructuring occurs by means of item-by-item learning. According to her the learner has to resort to this strategy because a grammar in which V2 is generalised to embedded clauses is a superset grammar. In other words, the child, in having to unlearn certain properties of his superset grammar, is faced with a situation which goes against the subset principle. So the child is left with lexical learning as the only means of narrowing down a superset grammar.

The reasons why I do not agree with Müller's lexical learning approach have already been mentioned. Suffice it to say that this approach ignores that the learnability problem with which the learner is confronted is still a structural one. Consequently, we have to look at the grammar-internal reasons for why the eventual implementation of the target-like grammatical option takes the form it does. Variation, be it intra-individual or inter-individual is not an exclusive property of lexical learning. On the basis of a dynamic approach to language and its acquisition variation is a natural consequence of the self-organisation of complex systems.

---

[178] According to Gawlitzek-Maiwald et al. the eventual fixation of the headedness parameter is only part of the problem as failing verb movement in structures like "was ich kann machen" needs to be explained also.

[179] Note that this analysis differs somewhat from d'Avis and Gretsch's (1994) study, which focuses on the way Benny introduces this structural variation. Benny is characterised as a "bottom-up learner, who abstracts a type on the basis of several tokens" (ibid.: 82) with a semantic orientation. According to the authors the semantic orientation is evident in that Benny uses precursor structures and overt complementisers at the same time with varying verb placement. *Structural narrowing* (ibid.: 80) is claimed to apply in a *token-by-token strategy* (ibid.: 80), developing type(s) only late.

[180] As pointed out by Müller (ibid.: 31), Ivar's bilingualism (German/French) is unlikely to be the reason for his problems with German sentence structure. Ivar produces CXVS structures which could not have been derived from the French grammar. Furthermore, there are some utterances in which the verb appears in the second and in the clause-final position, a pattern which was not acknowledged in his French data.

9 Final remarks or "opening the windows"

9.1 Linguistic theory and ASLA: The dynamics of their relationship

One of the main topics of the present investigation is the assessment of the implications of UG theory for the theory of ASLA. In the field of ASLA research much controversy has arisen around the question of whether adult learners have access to UG at all. We could see that the Modularity Hypothesis plays a crucial part in this controversy. For some researchers the differentiation between modular and central cognitive systems parallels with different forms of language learning. Roughly speaking, the generalisations made in the framework of the Fundamental Difference Hypothesis relate child language learning with modular, i.e. task-specific cognitive systems and adult second language learning with central, i.e. non-task-specific cognitive systems.

For various reasons hypotheses based on this line of reasoning cannot provide a satisfactory account of ASLA. In view of the vague ideas characteristic of such hypotheses one often wonders whether a conclusive account is intended at all...

If we were to agree with the assumption that our language faculty is based on *specific* cognitive capacities it is barely conceivable how language acquisition in adulthood could rely exclusively on non-language-specific mechanisms. Moreover, the apparent *general* problem solving mechanisms which proponents of the Fundamental Difference Hypothesis claim to underly ASLA are not so general. As we could see in chapter 1 they are descriptive generalisations which refer to *linguistic* elements and sequences. But the centralist approach to ASLA completely ignores the *linguistic* creativity which is manifest in the development of L2 grammars. Nor does is account for the ample evidence that learner grammars are UG constrained.

It is not without irony that the cognitivist approach which was originally designed so as to embrace adult and child language acquisition ended up as a kind of "last resort explanation" for some ASLA researchers. The cognitivist approach was discarded as an explanatory account of child language acquisition. But supporters of the centralist approach to ASLA fell back on cognitivist assumptions as they concluded that the Principles and Parameters model does not apply in ASLA.

The assumption that parametric learning is not given in ASLA originates in a misguided interpretation of the instantaneous model of language acquisition. This lies at the heart of the evaluation of adult second language development against the allegedly "ideal" development in child language acquisition. Deviances from this standard are taken as evidence against the applicability of a learning model where the possibility of variation, the coexistence of alternative options or fossilisation is not conceived. From such a point of view something has to be "wrong" with ASLA. The line of argumentation could be summarised as follows: either ASLA is "fundamentally" different from L1A such that there is no access to UG or it is different to the extent that it lacks either adequate learning mechanisms or the necessary "source" for the acquisition of a language-specific grammar, *viz.* the Functional Module.

The idealisation implicit in the instantaneous model of language acquisition also influences researchers who support the UG Hypothesis in the field of ASLA. UG-based hypotheses of adult second language learning, too, have sought to embed ASLA into the "scaffolding" of generally valid ASLA trajectories. The revelatory potential of deviances from such idealisations is not conceived. In sum, since variation has been considered as irrelevant "noise" for researchers working in the realm of UG theory, researchers in the field of ASLA were left with two possibilities. Either they turned their attention to the analysis of the findings which revealed uniformity across learners or they went beyond the bounds of UG theory falling back into behaviouristic or cognitivistic theories in trying to account for variability. In any case, the possibility of embracing both aspects of ASLA seemed to be an impossible task.

We could see in chapter 5 that the Developmental Problem of child language acquisition raises a number of interesting questions related to the development of learner grammars which the instantaneous model of language acquisition ignores. In essence the debate centres around the issue of determining the differences between early and end state grammars and the implications following thereof for an account of language development. We noticed that similar empirical data are subject to quite different hypotheses regarding language development in childhood. Our conclusion hinted at the possibility that the dichotomies determining the debate (e.g. continuity vs. discontinuity, lexical vs. syntactic learning) are the result of a learning model which adheres to a linear conception of development. This shortcoming also affects our understanding of language development in adulthood. We could see in chapter 6 that the weaknesses of a linear conception becomes most evident here: hypothetically ASLA would be like L1A but devoid of any maturation effects. In other words, ASLA would be a *continuous* process in which the relevant primary linguistic data would trigger the necessary parametric options immediately. But language development in adulthood also "takes time" and there is also evidence for discontinuities: parameter (re-)setting does not take place overnight, the mother tongue plays a part, triggering elements of the L2 appear in learner languages without the necessary restructurings... It is clear that such findings do not fit into a linear model of language development. But nobody in the field of ASLA questioned the weaknesses of the learning model as such.

In the light of these considerations the relevance of recent research in the field of child language acquisition is of double importance: not only do we reckon that variation is not an exclusive property of ASLA. But we also acknowledge that learning concepts based on the "ideal" acquisition trajectory cannot be maintained anymore. Recent studies on bilingual acquisition and diachronic language change also point to the necessity to reconsider the Principles and Parameters model in dynamic terms.

As noted in chapter 7 research in other scientific fields shows that a linear or reductionistic conception cannot account for the development of complex systems. The more we become aware of the role of non-linearity the more we acknowledge the relevance of self-organising principles. The realisation that language *qua* functionally complex system is also subject to processes of self-organisation allows us to investigate further the role of the system-internal processes and how they interact with the environment. It is important to note therefore that one of the driving forces for language change is the type of *tension* that arises between the non-reducibility and the inter-relation between linguistic levels. We could see in chapters 7 and 8 that processes of differentiation and integration play a crucial role at different levels of linguistic analysis. They apply in the organisation of multilingual knowledge and they are relevant in the internal organisation of a language-specific grammar. Apparent *conflicts* resulting from linguistic *contact* situations gain a new significance under a dynamic approach: they pave the way for necessary changes. In our discussion of Bruno's data we could see that the relevant restructurings of his L2 grammar were always preceded by periods of instability or incongruency.

On the basis of a dynamic approach we realise that the similarities and the differences between child and adult language development and diachronic language change are in conformity with the self-similar or *fractal* nature which is characteristic of dynamic systems. In other words, each type of language development has its peculiarities but they also have something in common. UG delimits the range of variation but it does not prescribe the actual developmental path.

We can deduce from the preceding considerations that the Principles and Parameters theory can only profit from the research in different linguistic fields, among them ASLA.

In summarising, much of what has been proposed in the present analysis goes against long-standing "prejudices" which seem to be typical for research dealing with bilingual or adult second language acquisition. The assumption that the attainment of the competence of a language other than the mother tongue is something *out of the ordinary* still enjoys considerable support. The short-sightedness implicit in such prejudices becomes evident once we become aware of the multiple dimensions implicit in the dynamics of our language faculty.
If we look at the last two decades of research in the field of ASLA we could conclude, using dynamic theory's terminology, that the relationship between linguistic theory and ASLA is marked by "oscillations". But oscillations are, as we learn from chaos theory, indispensable for further progress.

9.2 Lexical and syntactic development: What triggers what?

In this analysis we explored the relationship between the lexical and the syntactic development in ASLA. Whilst functionalist theories assume that referential or informative aspects prevail in the course of language development, most syntacticians dismissed the role of non-syntactic aspects as irrelevant to grammatical development. However, the modular grammar as conceived in the Principles and Parameters theory relies on the *interaction* of its sub-parts as much as it does on their respective autonomy. Recall that the Projection Principle, the Principle of Structure Preservation or the Theta Criterium fulfill a "guarantee" function at the interfaces between different linguistic levels. In other words, non-linearity is implicit to such a modular conception of grammar. Consequently, it is unclear why we should stick to a linear concept of language learning, which, as we discussed in this study, faces quite a number of problems.

The Functional Parametrisation Hypothesis ties cross-linguistic variation to a specific sort of lexical elements, namely, functional categories. The crucial implication following thereof being that grammar development depends upon the correct acquisition of these elements and their language-specific properties. If we assume that universal principles are available from the beginning of language acquisition, then the acquisition of a language-specific grammar turns out to be the specification of "lexical idiosyncracies", i.e. the language-specific properties of FCs. It is commonly assumed that these specifications are acquired by means of lexical triggers.
The discussion of these assumptions in the light of the empirical studies on child and adult language acquisition proves that the usage of *lexical learning* as a cover term for different forms of learning is rather mis-

leading. As we could see in chapters 3 and 6 the confusion is especially evident in ASLA research where lexical learning is also used as a characterisation of *non-parametric* learning which would be specific to ASLA. Recall that opponents of the UG Hypothesis of ASLA argue that adult learners use the relevant functional items which should function as triggers without the corresponding restructuring. These findings leave them to conclude that ASLA consists basically of a relexification of the L1 grammar.

In response to these claims some authors have sought to determine alternative, i.e. ASLA-specific, triggers in order to prove that lexical learning in parametric terms applies in ASLA too. Other authors have assumed that the causal relationship between the acquisition of certain lexical items and the setting of the respective parameters is also given in ASLA only if the adults' temporal realisation of the lexically triggered restructurings differs from the children's. In the context of our analysis of the L2 German of an adult learner ('Bruno') we also discussed a third proposal which claims that the L2-specific syntactic properties are acquired in an item-by-item fashion. Following this assumption parametric properties are learned as idiosyncratic properties of every single lexical instantiation of the relevant functional category.

Our discussion of the weaknesses of these hypotheses led us to conclude that the ongoing discussion suffers from the conceptual and empirical shortcomings of too restricted a concept of lexical triggering and, accordingly, of lexical learning.
The assumption of certain linguistic elements acting as generally valid triggers ignores the intricacy of the learnability task, i.e. the structural analysis of these linguistic elements on the multiple levels where they are embedded. We could see in chapter 7 that some learners engage in the determination of the target-like phonological and referential properties of the relevant lexical items before going on to determine the appropriate grammatical properties of the respective functional category. Some other learners proceed the other way round. We have to realise therefore that different forms of *bootstrapping* apply in the course of language acquisition and that even the notion of a *learner type* is a generalisation which fails to account for the intricate system-internal dynamics which is unique to any individual developmental path. Actually, this potential for inter- and intra-individual variation is only a natural consequence of the modularly organised human language faculty.
If we extend these considerations to ASLA we can conclude that adults profit from the modular organisation of grammar in a similar way apart from the "difference" that the L1 also plays a part in the dynamics of L2 development.

We deduce from this that the notion of trigger needs to be revised in the following terms. Firstly, we have to look at the system-internal organisation which is responsible for the *reactions* of system to the new "external" data. How do the new constituents *take part* in the system's organisation? In self-organising systems minor changes may have major effects but only when the system is far from the equilibrium, as we could see in chapter 7. Therefore the emphasis has to be put on the system-internal dynamics responsible for its *sensitivity* to the new information from "outside". Under this line of reasoning the alleged triggering element is like the figurative straw that breaks the camel's back (cf. also Hohenberger 1996).

In a way this is putting on its head the traditional notion of trigger where the trigger was conceived as *the* element which undertakes the change. Our insight into the ongoing discussion in the field of diachronic language change provided additional support for our scepticism against any proposal which seeks to single out the very elements responsible for the respective diachronic changes.

Therefore I preferred to speak of the *pioneering function* of certain elements which first realised new grammatical properties. Such pioneering elements are important since their *information* gets amplified by means of iteration and self-reference. From other dynamic systems we know that their bifurcations involve the amplification of minor fluctuations. In Bruno's L2 German we could observe that pronominalised forms assume such a pioneering function in the introduction of new parametric options. By means of feedback processes the new structural option is amplified, eventually driving the system into the vicinity of a "catastrophy fold" beyond which we find the implementation of the L2 *attractor*. The necessity of such amplification processes lies in the "conservative" nature of complex systems which is responsible for the apparent hysteresis effects in bifurcation regions.

This understanding of triggering effects resolves the apparent paradox implicit to the traditional linear concept of lexical trigger: the triggering effect of the relevant lexical items presupposes the recognition of their syntactic properties - but the implementation of these is assumed to be the result of the triggered parameter setting. Under a dynamic conception of development the apparent circularity is constitutive.

That changes depend on the respective state of the system is especially evident in ASLA where the very same lexical items which were incorrectly analysed at the beginning appear later in their correct structural context. We discussed several such cases in our analysis in chapter 8. An illustrative example is the use of complementisers which occurs quite early for some learners in ASLA at a point where they do not yet master the target-like word order in embedded clauses. This certainly disproves the argument that complementisers are the triggers for the V2 asymmetry characteristic of German sentence structure. The appearance of complementisers may be related to the projection of a CP level which is, however, not yet specified as to the target-like properties. As we could see this occurs at a later point, alongside a further differentiation of complementisers which we observed in Bruno's L2 German.

The preceding considerations illustrate how we have to view the relationship between lexical and syntactic learning.
If, as traditionally believed, a certain size of the lexicon represents a precondition for the development of syntax the opposite holds as well. This was pointed out by Radford (1990) who acknowledged lexical spurts upon the implementation of FCs in the grammatical system of the child. Our analysis of Bruno's data also revealed that the stabilisation of certain grammatical phenomena was succeeded by an increased diversity of the related lexical items. Syntax "triggering" an increase of the lexicon? This is not so surprising in view of the fact that in a complex system every part depends on each other. At a particular time, the increase of the lexicon may trigger new syntactic properties, another time the implementation of certain syntactic properties may enhance the increase of the lexicon.

9.3 The "shifting web": Hysteresis effects and bifurcations in ASLA

One of the central questions in ASLA research pertains to the role of the mother tongue knowledge in the acquisition of a second language in adulthood. We could see that there are two main views on this issue which we may roughly summarise as the view which emphasises structure-building processes in ASLA as opposed to the view which conceives L2 development as a succession of restructurings of the L1 determined L2 grammar.
This apparent contradiction can be solved under a dynamic approach to language acquisition according to which processes of integration *and* of differentiation are characteristic of self-organising systems. We could see in chapter 7 that the notions of coexistence and competition are crucial for our understanding of the evolution of grammars. Coexisting or competing grammars are evident in mono-lingual, in bilingual acquisition as much as in ASLA or language change. For the overall development of dynamic systems the resulting fluctuations are of crucial relevance as mentioned previously.
In ASLA the interwovenness of structure-building *and* of restructuring processes is explained by the fact that L2 development is tied to the linguistic knowledge already attained (i.e. the L1 or other foreign languages

the adult learner knows already and UG) by means of self-reference. Recall that autocatalytic processes are well-documented phenomenon in biology. To the same extent the L1 may serve as a "bootstrap" for the L2. Implicit in this consideration is the assumption that bootstrapping occurs across languages as much as it does across linguistic modules as if "opening the windows" onto autonomous linguistic components.
Consequently, the alleged ASLA-specific *permeablity* of L2 learner grammars highlighted in early inter-language studies fits into a dynamic theory of language acquisition.

That both structure-building and restructuring are necessary for a successful acquisition of the L2 can be deduced from "fossilised" L2 learner grammars which consist of a VP only. In such cases we find no evidence for functional categories which would be essential for L2 grammar-building. We can assume that the necessary complexity of the L2 lexicon which would have required the implementation of the functional category systems was never established for various internal and external reasons. As outlined in section 7.3.3 dynamic systems can resist change by means of feedback remaining within the bounds of structural stability which will make it impossible for any "intruder" to affect its internal organisation.
The apparent optionality of verb raising in Bruno's early L2 grammar, on the other hand, signals the progressive implementation of the IP grammar and therefore the activity of structure-building processes.
As much as in child language acquisition, the bifurcation between lexical and functional categories is decisive for ASLA to be successful.

Our data of the adult learner Bruno does not provide evidence for a VP stage as such since he is already at a stage where functional categories play a role in his L2 grammar. The apparent L1-determined specifications reveal the relevance of self-reference along the lines outlined above: the L1 attractors subdue the functional categories of the incipient L2 grammar. It seems the system "knows", due to UG, that the architecture of languages is universally constrained. By means of feedback processes, however, the L2 attractors begin to exert their influence. The system begins to fluctuate between alternative grammatical options, as if the system would not give up the former attractors. This reminds us of the hysteresis effects documented in the development of other dynamic systems. In Bruno's L2 German we could observe several such situations. To many researchers such a situation does not fit in their conception of how a UG based development should look alike.
From a dynamic point of view, however, this kind of instability is of special interest since it is at the point where the system is far from the equilibrium that its internal organisation is prone to dramatic changes.

We could see that UG plays a central role here: learner grammars are constrained by UG; universal principles lie at the heart of the necessary correlations across linguistic levels; the interaction of the different sub-theories of UG is the basis for the succession of restructuring processes, and so on. Additionally, UG ultimately is responsible for the self-similarity which characterises different forms of language development. The apparent mirror image of Bruno's development to evolutions in the history of English or French is a good example. The range of variation is universally delimited - there is order in the apparent chaos!

We can conclude that the unstable phases are critical for the future of the system. Against the backdrop of the ongoing debate in the field of ASLA the observed oscillations are of critical importance: they evidence the availability of alternative grammatical options and therefore the accessibility to the Functional Module in adulthood. As much as other dynamic systems in states far from the equilibrium the L2 learner grammar opens a "window onto the whole". Note that the accessibility to "the whole" is given in apparently stable grammars in the form of marked or residual options evident in ASLA or language change. This is consistent with the assumption of the fractal nature of language (cf. also Hohenberger 1996).
The role of functional categories in the processes described is crucial: not only are they essential to grammar they are also the "crystallised memory" of language and the bifurcations it underwent. They are therefore the locus of the *bifurcation sensitivity* of the system.

For multiple external and internal reasons it could be that L2 learner grammars "resist" necessary changes remaining in a stable state which is deviant from the L2 attractor. In such cases the result is a fossilised or hybrid grammar. We could speculate on whether such a situation will hold forever or if a future change in one of the multiple variables involved could spur the system into further development. In fact there is a familiar situation which illustrates the relevant phenomenon. Consider an adult learner whose contact with the L2 input is interrupted, for whatever reasons, at a certain point whilst he was acquiring the L2. This learner is then exposed once more to L2 input, experiencing a progression of his previous knowledge. In such an event we can say that the apparent stability of his former knowledge is disrupted upon the renewed exposure to L2 input.

As mentioned previously there are many external but also internal factors which may affect the system's sensitivity to changes. In this analysis we concentrated on the system-internal conflicts. In our investigation of Bruno's L2 German development we could see how his learner grammar is pushed again and again into unstable states at which crucial bifurcations take place. In accord with the Functional Parametrisation Hypotheses these bifurcations affect the implementation and specification of functional categories. Much like in fractal trees the decision points are evident on ever finer scale indicating the "independisation" of the L2 as much as its progressive internal organisation. At all different levels of linguistic analysis we can therefore observe the relevance of autonomy and interaction. The question raised in section 4.3.2 of how we should conceive multilingual competence has to be answered in the following terms: multilingual knowledge unfolds the multiple aspects of the intricate interplay of autonomy and interaction which is constitutive of our human language faculty.

9.4 ASLA: A window onto the whole

If the assumption of the fractal nature of language is correct, then our understanding of the human language faculty will profit from each contribution coming from different fields of linguistic research. Following these considerations we assume that acquisition processes are not identical but self-similar as much as everyone acquired his mother tongue in a unique fashion. With all its peculiarities ASLA offers a wide field for analysing aspects of all different sorts which are relevant for a better comprehension of how we know, acquire and use language. Insofar as the dynamics of chaos and order uncover a *looking glass world* our analysis of adult learners acquiring a second language uncovers the chaotic and the ordered dimensions of the processes underlying our language faculty. The present analysis is but a small contribution. There is still much work to be done - so we should be encouraged to take up the challenge of looking through the multiple windows into the dynamic landscape of language.

Let us close therefore with the following statements of Briggs and Peat (1990: 154):

> "Each autopoietic structure has a unique history, but its history is tied to the history of the larger environment and other autopoietic structures: an interwovenness of time's arrows. Autopoietic structures have definite boundaries, such as a semipermeable membrane, but the boundaries are open and connect the system with almost inimaginable complexity to the world around it."

10 Bibliography

Adjemian, Christian (1976) "On the nature of interlanguage systems." *Language Learning* 26: 297-320

Atkinson, Martin (1992) *Children's syntax: An introduction to Principles and Parameters Theory.* (Oxford: Blackwell)

Baker, Mark C. (1988) *Incorporation: A theory of grammatical function changing.* (Chicago: The University of Chicago Press)

Bates, Elizabeth and Brian MacWhinney (1982) "Functionalist approaches to grammar." In: Eric Wanner and Lila R. Gleitman (eds.) *Language acquisition: The state of the art.* (Cambridge: Cambridge University Press) pp. 173-218

Battye, Adrian and Ian Roberts (eds.) (1995) *Clause structure and language change.* (Oxford: Oxford University Press)

Belletti, Adriana (1990) *Generalised verb movement.* (Torino: Rosenberg & Sellier)

Birdsong, David (1991) "On the notion of "critical period" in UG/L2 theory: A response to Flynn and Manuel." In: Lynn Eubank (ed.) *Point counterpoint: Universal grammar in the second language.* (Amsterdam: John Benjamins) pp. 147-166

Birdsong, David (1992) "Ultimate attainment in second language acquisition." *Language* 68: 706-755

Bley-Vroman, Robert (1989) "What is the logical problem of foreign language learning?" In: Susan M. Gass and Jacquelyn Schachter (eds.) *Linguistic perspectives on second language acquisition.* (Cambridge: Cambridge University Press) pp. 41-68

Borer, Hagit and Kenneth Wexler (1987) "The maturation of syntax." In: Thomas Roeper and Edwin Williams (eds.) *Parameter setting.* (Dordrecht: D. Reidel) pp. 123-172

Briggs, John and F. David Peat (1990) *Turbulent mirror: An illustrated guide to chaos theory and the science of wholeness.* (New York: Harper & Row)

Brown, Roger A. (1973) "The first sentences of child and chimpanzee." In: Charles A. Ferguson and Dan I. Slobin (eds.) *Studies of child language development.* (New York: Holt, Rinehart and Winston) pp. 295-332

Burzio, Luigi (1986) *Italian Syntax: A Government-Binding approach.* (Dordrecht: D. Reidel)

Chomsky, Noam (1970) "Remarks on nominalisation." In: Noam Chomsky, *Studies on semantics in generative grammar.* (The Hague: Mouton)

Chomsky, Noam (1980) *Rules and Representations.* (Oxford: Basil Blackwell)

Chomsky, Noam (1981) *Lectures on government and binding: The Pisa Lectures.* (Dordrecht: Foris)

Chomsky, Noam (1982) *Some concepts and consequences of the theory of government and binding.* (Cambridge, Mass.: The MIT Press)

Chomsky, Noam (1986) *Knowledge of language: Its nature, origine and use.* (New York: Praeger)

Chomsky, Noam (1988) *Language and problems of knowledge: The Managua Lectures.* (Cambridge, Mass.: The MIT Press)

Chomsky, Noam (1989) "Some notes on the economy of derivation and representation." *MIT Working Papers on Linguistics* 10: 43-74

Chomsky, Noam (1992) "A minimalist program for linguistic theory." *MIT Occasional Papers in Linguistics* 1

Clahsen, Harald (1982) *Spracherwerb in der Kindheit: Eine Untersuchung der Entwicklung der Syntax bei Kleinkindern.* (Tübingen: Gunter Narr)

Clahsen, Harald (1984) "The acquisition of German word order: A test case for cognitive approaches to L2 development." In: Roger W. Andersen (ed.) *Second languages: A cross-linguistic perspective.* (Rowley, Mass.: Newbury House) pp. 219-242

Clahsen, Harald (1988a) *Normale und gestörte Kindersprache: Linguistische Untersuchungen zum Erwerb von Syntax und Morphologie.* (Amsterdam: John Benjamins)

Clahsen, Harald (1988b) "Parameterized grammatical theory and language acquisition: A study of the acquisition of verb placement and inflection by children and adults." In: Suzanne Flynn and Wayne O'Neil (eds.) *Linguistic theory in second language acquisition.* (Dordrecht: Kluwer) pp. 47-75

Clahsen, Harald (1988c) "Kritische Phasen der Grammatikentwicklung: Eine Untersuchung zum Negationserwerb bei Kindern und Erwachsenen." *Zeitschrift für Sprachwissenschaft* 7: 3-31

Clahsen, Harald (1990a) "Constraints on parameter setting: A grammatical analysis of some acquisition stages in German child language." *Language Acquisition* 1: 361-391

Clahsen, Harald (1990b) "The comparative study of first and second language development." *Studies in Second Language Acquisition* 12: 135-153

Clahsen, Harald (1992) "Learnability theory and the problem of development in language acquisition." In: Jürgen Weissenborn, Helen Goodluck and Thomas Roeper (eds.) *Theoretical issues in language acquisition.* (Hillsdale: Lawrence Erlbaum Associates)

Clahsen, Harald and Pieter Muysken (1986) "The availability of universal grammar to the adult and child learners - a study of the acquisition of German word order." *Second Language Research* 2: 93-119

Clahsen, Harald and Pieter Muysken (1989) "The UG paradox in L2 acquisition." *Second Language Research* 5: 1-29

Clahsen, Harald, Anne Vainikka and Martha Young-Scholten (1990) "Lernbarkeitstheorie und lexikalisches Lernen: Eine kurze Darstellung des LEXLERN-Projekts." *Linguistische Berichte*: 466-477

Clahsen, Harald, Jürgen M. Meisel and Manfred Pienemann (1983) *Deutsch als Zweitsprache: Der Erwerb ausländischer Arbeitnehmer.* (Tübingen: Gunter Narr)

Clahsen, Harald, Sonja Eissenbeiss and Anne Vainikka (1994) "The seeds of structure: A syntactic analysis of the acquisition of case marking." In: Teun Hoekstra and Bonnie D. Schwartz (eds.) *Language acquisition in generative grammar: Papers in honor of Kenneth Wexler from the 1991 GLOW workshops.* (Amsterdam: John Benjamins) pp. 85-118

Cook, Vivian (1991) "The poverty-of-stimulus argument and multicompetence." *Second Language Research* 7: 103-117

Cook, Vivian (1992) "Evidence for multicompetence." *Language Learning* 42: 557-591

Coppietiers, René (1987) "Competence differences between native and near-native speakers." *Language* 63: 544-573

Cramer, Friedrich (1993) *Chaos and order: The complex structure of living systems.* (Weinheim: VCH)

D'Avis, Franz-Josef and Petra Gretsch (1994) "Variations on "Variation": On the acquisition of complementizers in German." In: Rosemarie Tracy and Elsa Lattey (eds.) *How tolerant is Universal Grammar?* (Tübingen: Niemeyer) pp. 59-110

Demonte, Violeta (1991) *Detrás de la palabra: Estudios de la gramática del español.* (Madrid: Alianza)

Di Sciullo, Anna Maria and Edwin Williams (1987) *On the definition of word.* (Cambridge, Mass.: The MIT Press)

Diesing, Molly (1990) "Verb Second in Yiddish and the nature of the subject position." *Natural Language and Linguistic Theory* 8: 41-79

Dittmar, Norbert (1982) "'Ich fertig arbeite, nich mehr spreche Deutsch': Semantische Eigenschaften pidginisierter Lernervarietäten des Deutschen." *Zeitschrift für Literaturwissenschaft und Linguistik* 45: 9-34

Du Plessis, Jean, Doreen Solin, Lisa Travis and Lydia White (1987) "UG or not UG, that is the question: A reply to Clahsen and Muysken." *Second Language Research* 3: 56-75

Ebeling, Werner (1991) *Chaos - Ordnung - Information: Selbstorganisation in Natur und Technik.* (Frankfurt M.: Harri Deutsch)

Eubank, Lynn (1992) "Verb movement, agreement and tense in L2 acquisition." In: Jürgen M. Meisel (ed.) *The acquisition of verb placement: Functional Categories and V2 phenomena in language acquisition.* (Dordrecht: Kluwer) pp. 225-244

Eubank, Lynn (1994) "Optionality and the initial state in L2 development." In: Teun Hoekstra and Bonnie D. Schwartz (eds.) *Language acquisition in generative grammar: Papers in honor of Kenneth Wexler from the 1991 GLOW workshops.* (Amsterdam: John Benjamins) pp. 369-388

Eubank, Lynn (1996) "Negation in early German-English interlanguage: more valueless features in the L2 initial state." *Second Language Research* 12: 73-106

Eubank, Lynn and Bonnie D. Schwartz (1996) "What is the 'L2 Initial State'?" *Second Language Research* 12: 1-6

Fanselow, Gisbert and Sascha W. Felix (1990a) *Sprachtheorie: Eine Einführung in die Generative Grammatik. Band 1: Grundlagen und Zielsetzungen.* (Tübingen: Francke)

Fanselow, Gisbert and Sascha W. Felix (1990b) *Sprachtheorie: Eine Einführung in die Generative Grammatik. Band 2: Die Rektions- und Bindungstheorie.* (Tübingen: Francke)

Felix, Sascha (1984) "Das Heranreifen der Universalgrammatik im Spracherwerb." *Linguistische Berichte* 94: 1-26

Felix, Sascha (1985) "More evidence on competing cognitive systems." *Second Language Research* 1: 47-72

Felix, Sascha (1987) *Cognition and language growth.* (Dordrecht: Foris)

Felix, Sascha (1991) "The accessibility of universal grammar in second language acquisition." In: Lynn Eubank (ed.) *Point counterpoint: Universal grammar in the second language.* (Amsterdam: John Benjamins) pp. 89-104

Felix, Sascha and Henning Wode (eds.) (1983) Preface to: *Language development at the crossroads: Papers from the Interdisciplinary Conference on Language Acquisition at Passau.* (Tübingen: Gunter Narr) pp. 5-7

Felix, Sascha and Wilfried Weigl (1991) "Universal grammar in the classroom: The effects of formal instruction on second language acquisition." *Second Language Research* 7: 162-181

Flynn, Suzanne (1988) "Nature of development in L2 acquisition and implications for theories of language acquisition in general." In: Suzanne Flynn and Wayne O'Neil (eds.) *Linguistic theory in second language acquisition.* (Dordrecht: Kluwer) pp. 76-89

Flynn, Suzanne and Sharon Manuel (1991) "Age-dependent effects in language acquisition: An evaluation of "critical period" hypothesis." In: Lynn Eubank (ed.) *Point counterpoint: Universal grammar in the second language.* (Amsterdam: John Benjamins) pp. 117-146

Fodor, Jerry A. (1983) *The modularity of mind: An essay on faculty psychology.* (Cambridge, Mass.: The MIT Press)

Fritzenschaft, Agnes, Ira Gawlitzek-Maiwald, Rosemarie Tracy and Susanne Winkler (1990) "Wege zur komplexen Syntax." *Zeitschrift für Sprachwissenschaft* 9: 52-134

Garfield, Jay L. (1987a) "Introduction: Carving the mind at its joints." In: Jay L. Garfield (ed.) (1987) *Modularity in knowledge representation and natural-language understanding.* (Cambridge, Mass.: The MIT Press) pp. 1-13

Garfield, Jay L. (ed.) (1987b) *Modularity in knowledge representation and natural-language understanding.* (Cambridge, Mass.: The MIT Press)

Gawlitzek, Ira and Rosemarie Tracy (1994) "Bilingual bootstrapping." To appear in: Aldridge, Michelle (ed.) *Proceedings of the child language seminar 1994.* Bangor

Gawlitzek-Maiwald, Ira, Rosemarie Tracy and Agnes Fritzenschaft (1992) "Language acquisition and competing linguistic representations: The child as arbiter." In: Jürgen M. Meisel (ed.) *The acquisition of verb placement: Functional categories and V2 phenomena in language acquisition.* (Dordrecht: Kluwer) pp. 139-179

Givón, Talmy (1979) *On understanding grammar.* (New York: Academic Press)

Givón, Talmy (1985) "Function, structure, and language acquisition." In: Slobin, Isaac D. (ed.) *The crosslinguistic study of language acquisition. Volume 2: Theoretical Issues.* (Hillsdale, Lawrence Erlbaum) pp. 1005-1028

Gleitman, Lila R. and Eric Wanner (1982) "Language acquisition: the state of the state of the art." In: Eric Wanner and Lila R. Gleitman (eds.) *Language acquisition: The state of the art.* (Cambridge: Cambridge University Press) pp.3-48

Goodluck, Helen (1986) "Language acquisition and linguistic theory." In: Paul Fletcher and Michael Garman (eds.) *Language acquisition.* (Cambridge: Cambridge University Press)

Goodluck, Helen and Dawn Behne (1990) "Development in control and extraction." In: Jürgen Weissenborn, Helen Goodluck and Thomas Roeper (eds.) (1992) *Theoretical issues in language acquisition.* (Hillsdale: Lawrence Erlbaum) pp. 173-190

Grewendorf, Günther (1990) "Verb-Bewegung und Negation im Deutschen." *GAGL* 30: 57-125

Grewendorf, Günther (1991) "Parametrisierung der Syntax. Zur "kognitiven Revolution" in der Linguistik." *Arbeitspapiere Frankfurt* 1

Grewendorf, Günther, Fritz Hamm and Wolfgang Sternefeld (1987) *Sprachliches Wissen: Eine Einführung in moderne Theorien der grammatischen Beschreibung.* (Frankfurt a.M.: Suhrkamp)

Grimshaw, Jane (1990) *Argument structure.* (Cambridge Mass.: The MIT Press)

Guilfoyle, Eithne and Máire Noonan (1988) "Functional categories and language acquisition." (Unpublished manuscript, McGill University)

Haider, Hubert (1986) "V-Second in German." In: Hubert Haider and Martin Prinzhorn (eds.) *Verb Second phenomena in Germanic languages.* (Dordrecht: Foris) pp. 49-76

Haken, Hermann (1988) *Information and Self-organisation: a macroscopic approach to complex systems.* (Berlin: Springer)

Haken, Hermann (1990) "Synergetics as a tool for the conceptualization and mathematization of cognition and behaviour – how far can we go?" In: Hermann Haken and M. Stadler (eds.) *Synergetics of cognition: Proceedings of the International Symposium at Schloß Elmau, 1989.* (Berlin: Springer)

HPD (= Heidelberger Forschungsprojekt "Pidgin-Deutsch") (1977) "Die ungesteuerte Erlernung des Deutschen durch spanische und italienische Arbeiter: Eine soziolinguistische Untersuchung." *Osnabrücker Beiträge zur Sprachtheorie* 2

Hilles, Sharon (1986) "Interlanguage and the pro-drop parameter." *Second Language Research* 2: 33-52

Hilles, Sharon (1991) "Access to Universal Grammar in second language acquisition." In: Lynn Eubank (ed.) *Point counterpoint: Universal Grammar in the second language.* (Amsterdam: John Benjamins) pp. 305-338

Hohenberger, Annette (1992) *Funktionale Kategorien und Spracherwerb.* (Master Thesis, J.-W.-Goethe Universität Frankfurt/M.)

Hohenberger, Annette (1996) *Functional categories and language acquisition: Self-organisation of a dynamic system.* (Ph Dissertation, J.-W.-Goethe Universität Frankfurt/M., to appear in Tübingen: Niemeyer)

Huang, C.-T. James (1984) "On the distribution and reference of empty pronouns." *Linguistic Inquiry* 15: 531-574

Hyams, Nina (1986) *Language acquisition and the theory of parameters.* (Dordrecht: D. Reidel)

Hyams, Nina (1994) "VP, null arguments and COMP projections." In: Teun Hoekstra and Bonnie D. Schwartz (eds.) *Language acquisition in generative grammar: Papers in honor of Kenneth Wexler from the 1991 GLOW workshops.* (Amsterdam: John Benjamins) pp. 21-56

Hyltenstamm, Kenneth and Loraine K. Obler (eds.) (1989) *Bilingualism across the lifespan: Aspects of acquisition, maturity, and loss.* (Cambridge: Cambridge University Press)

Ioup, Georgette, Elizabeth Boustagui, Manal El Tig and Martha Moselle (1994) "Reexamining the Critical Period Hypothesis: A case study of successful adult SLA in a naturalistic environment." *Studies in Second Language Acquisition* 16: 73-98

Jackendoff, Ray (1972) *Semantic interpretation in generative grammar.* (Cambridge, Mass.: The MIT Press)

Jackendoff, Ray (1983) *Semantics and cognition.* (Cambridge, Mass.: The MIT Press)

Jackendoff, Ray (1990) *Semantic structures.* (Cambridge, Mass.: The MIT Press)

Jaeggli, Osvaldo and Ken Safir (1989) "The null subject parameter and parametric theory." In: Osvaldo Jaeggli and Kenneth J. Safir (eds.) *The null subject parameter.* (Dordrecht: Kluwer) pp. 1-44

Johnson, Jacqueline and Elissa L. Newport (1991) "Critical period effects on universal properties of language: The status of subjacency in the acquisition of a second language." *Cognition* 39: 215-258

Karpf, Annemarie (1990) *Selbstorganisationsprozesse in der sprachlichen Ontogenese: Erst- und Fremdsprache(n).* (Tübingen: Gunter Narr)

Karpf, Annemarie (1993) "Chaos and order in morphology (neuron watching included)." In: L. Tonelli and W. U. Dressler (eds.) *Natural morphology - perspectives for the nineties.* (Padova: Unipress) pp. 7-20

Kiparsky, Paul (1995) "Indo-European Origins of Germanic Syntax." In: Adrian Battye and Ian Roberts (eds.) *Clause structure and language change.* (Oxford: Oxford University Press) pp. 140-170

Klein, Wolfgang (1986) *Second language acquisition.* (Cambridge: Cambridge University Press)

Koopman, Hilda and Dominique Sportiche (1991) "The position of subjects." *Lingua* 8: 211-258

Köpcke, Klaus-Michael (1987) "Der Erwerb morphologischer Ausdrucksmittel durch L2-Lerner am Beispiel der Personalflexion." *Zeitschrift für Sprachwissenschaft* 6: 186-205

Kratzer, Angelika (1984) "On deriving syntactic differences between English and German." (Unpublished manuscript, TU Berlin)

Lebeaux, David (1988) *Language acquisition and the form of grammar.* (Ph Dissertation, University of Massachusetts, Amherst)

Lemieux, Monique and Fernande Dupuis (1995) "The locus of verb movement in non-asymmetric Verb-Second languages: The case of Middle-French." In: Adrian Battye and Ian Roberts (eds.) *Clause structure and language change.* (Oxford: Oxford University Press) pp. 80-109

Lenneberg, Eric (1967) *Biological foundations of language.* (New York: Wiley)

Leuninger, Helen (1989) *Neurolinguistik: Probleme, Paradigmen, Perspektiven.* (Opladen: Westdeutscher Verlag)

Liceras, Juana M. (1988) "Syntax and stylistics: more on the pro-drop parameter." In: James Pankhurst, Mike Sharwood-Smith and Paul Van Buren (eds.) *Learnability and second languages: A book of readings.* (Dordrecht: Foris) pp. 71-93

Liceras, Juana M. (1989) "On some properties of the "pro-drop" parameter: Looking for missing subjects in non-native Spanish." In: Susan M. Gass and Jacquelyn Schachter (eds.) *Linguistic perspectives on second language acquisition.* (Cambridge: Cambridge University Press) pp. 109-133

Lightfoot, David (1991) *How to set parameters: Arguments from language change.* (Cambrige, Mass.: The MIT Press)

Marantz, Alec (1984) *On the nature of grammatical relations.* (Cambridge, Mass.: The MIT Press)

Marslen-Wilson, William and Lorraine Komisarjevsky Tyler (1987) "Against modularity." In: Jay L. Garfield (ed.) (1987) *Modularity in knowledge representation and natural-language understanding.* (Cambridge, Mass.: The MIT Press) pp. 37-62

McMahon, April M. S. (1994) *Understanding language change.* (Cambridge: Cambridge University Press)

McShane, John (1991) *Cognitive development: An information processing approach.* (Oxford: Blackwell)

Meisel, Jürgen M. (1990) "Grammatical development in the simultaneous acquisition of two first languages." In: Jürgen M. Meisel (ed.) *Two first languages: Early grammatical development in bilingual children.* (Dordrecht: Foris)

Meisel, Jürgen M. (1991) "Principles of Universal Grammar and strategies of language learning: Some similarities and differences between first and second language acquisition." In: Lynn Eubank (ed.) *Point counterpoint: Universal Grammar in the second language.* (Amsterdam: John Benjamins) pp. 231-276

Meisel, Jürgen M. (ed.) (1992) *Bilingual first language acquisition: French and German grammatical development.* (Amsterdam: John Benjamins)

Müller, Natascha (1993) *Komplexe Sätze: Der Erwerb von COMP und Wortstellungsmustern bei bilingualen Kindern (Französisch / Deutsch).* (Tübingen: Gunter Narr)

Müller, Natascha (1996) "UG access without parameter fixing: A longitudinal study of (L1 Italian) German as a second language." (Ms. Universität Hamburg) Appears in: Maria Beck (ed.) (1998) *Morphology and its interfaces in second language knowledge.* (Amsterdam: John Benjamins) pp. 115-164

Müller, Natascha (to appear) "Subordinate clauses in second and first language acquisition: a case against parameters." *Studies in Second Language Acquisition*

Neisser, U. (1967) *Cognitive Psychology.* (New York: Appleton-Century-Crofts)

Newport, Elissa L. (1990) "Maturational constraints on language learning." *Cognitive Science* 14: 11-28

Ouhalla, Jamal (1991) *Functional categories and parametric variation.* (London: Routledge)

Ouhalla, Jamal (1992) "Functional categories, agrammatism and language acquisition." *Sprachwissenschaft in Frankfurt* 9

Parodi, Teresa (1990) "Funktionale Kategorien im bilingualen Erstspracherwerb und im Zweitspracherwerb." In: Monika Rothweiler (ed.) *Spracherwerb und Grammatik: Linguistische Untersuchungen zum Erwerb von Syntax und Morphologie.* (Opladen: Westdeutscher Verlag; Linguistische Berichte, Special Issue 3) pp. 152-165

Piaget, Jean (1972) "Problems of equilibration." In: C. F. Nodine, J. M. Gallagher and R. H. Humphreys (eds.) *Piaget and Inhelder on equilibration.* (Philadelphia)

Piaget, Jean (1981) "The psychogenesis of knowledge and its epistemological significance." In: Massimo Piatelli-Palmarini (ed.) *Language and learning: The debate between Jean Piaget and Noam Chomsky.* (London: Routledge & Kegan Paul) pp. 23-34

Pienemann, Manfred (1989) "Is language teachable? Psycholinguistic experiments and hypotheses." *Applied Linguistics* 10: 52-79

Pinker, Steven (1984) *Language learnability and language development.* (Cambridge, Mass.: Harvard University Press)

Pintzuk, Susan (1991) *Phrase structures in competition: Variation and change in Old English word order.* (Ph Dissertation, University of Pennsylvania)

Platzack, Christer (1983) "Germanic word order and the COMP/INFL parameter." *Working Papers in Scandinavian Syntax* 2: 1-45

Platzack, Christer and Anders Holmberg (1989) "The role of AGR and finiteness." *Working Papers on Scandinavian Syntax* 43: 51-76

Poeppel, David and Kenneth Wexler (1993) "The Full Competence Hypothesis and clause structure in early German." *Language* 69: 1-33

Pollock, Jean-Yves (1989) "Verb movement, universal grammar and the structure of IP." *Linguistic Inquiry* 20: 365-422

Prigonine, Ilya and Isabelle Stengers (1984) *Order out of chaos: Man's new dialogue with nature.* (Boulder: Shambhala)

Radford, Andrew (1990) *Syntactic theory and the acquisition of English syntax: The nature of early child grammars of English.* (Oxford: Blackwell)

Randall, Monika (1992) "The catapult hypothesis: An approach to unlearning." In: Weissenborn, Jürgen, Helen Goodluck and Thomas Roeper (eds.) *Theoretical issues in language acquisition.* (Hillsdale: Lawrence Erlbaum) pp. 93-138

Ribeiro, Ilza (1995) "Evidence for a Verb-Second in Old Portuguese." In: Adrian Battye and Ian Roberts (eds.) *Clause structure and language change.* (Oxford: Oxford University Press) pp. 110-139

Rieck, Bert-Olaf (1989) *Natürlicher Zweitspracherwerb bei Arbeitsimmigranten: Eine Langzeituntersuchung.* (Frankfurt a.M.: Peter Lang)

Rizzi, Luigi (1982) *Issues in Italian Syntax.* (Dordrecht: Foris)

Rizzi, Luigi (1990) "Speculations on Verb Second." In: Joan Mascaró and Marina Néspor (eds.) *Grammar in progress: GLOW essays for Henk van Riemsdijk.* (Dordrecht: Foris) pp. 375-386

Rizzi, Luigi and Ian Roberts (1989) "Complex inversion in French." *Probus* 1: 1-30 (re-published in: Adriana Belletti and Luigi Rizzi (eds.) (1996) *Parameters and functional heads: Essays in comparative syntax.* (Oxford: Oxford University Press) pp. 91-116

Roberts, Ian (1993) *Verbs and diachronic syntax: A comparative history of English and French.* (Dordrecht: Kluwer)

Roeper, Thomas (1992) "From the Initial State to V2: Acquisition Principles in action." In: Jürgen M. Meisel (ed.) *The acquisition of verb placement: Functional categories and V2 phenomena in language acquisition.* (Dordrecht: Kluwer) pp. 333-370

Roeper, Thomas and Jill de Villiers (1992) "Ordered decisions in the acquisition of wh-questions." In: Jürgen Weissenborn, Helen Goodluck and Thomas Roeper (eds.) (1992) *Theoretical issues in language acquisition.* (Hillsdale: Lawrence Erlbaum) pp. 191-236

Rothweiler, Monika (1993) *Der Erwerb von Nebensätzen im Deutschen: Eine Pilotstudie.* (Tübingen: Niemeyer)

Santorini, Beatrice (1995) "Two types of Verb Second in the history of Yiddish." In: Adrian Battye and Ian Roberts (eds.) *Clause structure and language change.* (Oxford: Oxford University Press) pp. 53-79

Schachter, Jacquelyn (1989) "Testing a proposed universal." In: Susan M. Gass and Jacquelyn Schachter (eds.) *Linguistic perspectives on second language acquisition.* (Cambridge: Cambridge University Press) pp. 73-88

Schwartz, Bonnie D. (1986) "The epistemological status of second language acquisition." *Second Language Research* 2: 120-159

Schwartz, Bonnie D. (1991) "Conceptual and empirical evidence: A response to Meisel." In: Lynn Eubank (ed.) *Point counterpoint: Universal grammar in the second language.* (Amsterdam: John Benjamins) pp.277-304

Schwartz, Bonnie D. and Alessandra Tomaselli (1991) "Some implications from an analysis of German word order." In: Abraham, Werner, Wim Kosmeyer and Eric Reuland (eds.) *Issues in Germanic syntax.* (Berlin: de Gruyter) pp. 251-276

Schwartz, Bonnie D. and Lynn Eubank (1996) "What is the 'L2 initial state'? *Second Language Research* 12: 1-6

Schwartz, Bonnie D. and Rex Sprouse (1994) "Word order and nominative case in non-native language acquisition: A longitudinal study of (L1 Turkish) German interlanguage." In: Teun Hoekstra and Bonnie D. Schwartz (eds.) *Language acquisition studies in generative grammar: Papers in honor of Kenneth Wexler from the 1991 GLOW workshops.* (Amsterdam: John Benjamins) pp. 317-368

Selinker, Larry (1972) "Interlanguage." *International Review of Applied Linguistics* 10: 209-231

Sharwood-Smith, Michael (1988) "On the role of linguistic theory in explanations of second language developmental grammars." In: Suzanne Flynn and Wayne O'Neil (eds.) *Linguistic theory in second language acquisition.* (Dordrecht: Kluwer) pp. 173-198

Slobin, Dan I. (1973) "Cognitive prerequisites for the development of grammar." In: Charles A. Ferguson and Dan I. Slobin (eds.) *Studies of child language development.* (New York: Holt, Rinehart and Winston) pp.175-276

Slobin, Dan I. and Thomas G. Bever (1982) "Children use canonical sentence schemas: A crosslinguistic study of word order and inflections." *Cognition* 12: 229-265

Smith, Neil and Ianthi-Maria Tsimpli (1995) *The mind of a savant: Language learning and modularity.* (Oxford: Blackwell)

Sorace, Antonella (1993) "Incomplete vs. divergent representations of unaccusativity in non-native grammars of Italian." *Second Language Research* 9: 22-47

Sportiche, Dominique (1988) "A theory of floating quantifiers and its corollaries for constituent structure." *Linguistic Inquiry* 19: 425-449

Stowell, Timothy (1981) *Origins of phrase structure.* (Ph Dissertation, Massachusetts Institute of Technology)

Tomaselli, Alessandra (1995) "Cases of Verb Third in Old High German." In: Adrian Battye and Ian Roberts (eds.) *Clause structure and language change.* (Oxford: Oxford University Press) pp. 345-369

Tomaselli, Alessandra and Bonnie D. Schwartz (1990) "Analysing the acquisition stages of negation in L2 German: support for UG in adult SLA." *Second Language Research* 6: 1-38

Tracy, Rosemarie (1991) *Sprachliche Strukturentwicklung: Linguistische und kognitionspsychologische Aspekte einer Theorie des Erstspracherwerbs.* (Tübingen: Gunter Narr)

Tracy, Rosemarie (1994/5) *Child languages in contact: Bilingual language acquisition (English/German) in early childhood.* (Unpubl. Habilitationschrift, University of Tübingen)

Tsimpli, Ianthi-Maria (1992) *Functional categories and maturation: The prefunctional stage of language acquisition.* (Ph Dissertation, University College London)

Tsimpli, Ianthi-Maria and Anna Roussou (1991) "Parameter resetting in L2." *UCL Working Papers in Linguistics* 3: 171-183

Vainikka, Anne and Martha Young-Scholten (1994) "Direct access to X-bar theory: Evidence from Korean and Turkish adults learning German." In: Teun Hoekstra and Bonnie D. Schwartz (eds.) *Language acquisition in generative grammar: Papers in honor of Kenneth Wexler from the 1991 GLOW workshops.* (Amsterdam: John Benjamins) pp. 265-316

Vainikka, Anne and Martha Young-Scholten (1995) "Tree Growth and morphosyntactic triggers in adult SLA." Paper presented at the GASLA conference, New York.

Vainkka, Anne and Martha Young-Scholten (1996a) "Gradual development of L2 phrase structure." *Second Language Research* 12: 7-39

Vainikka, Anne and Martha Young-Scholten (1996b) "The early stages in adult L2 syntax: additional evidence from Romance speakers." *Second Language Research* 12: 140-176

Vance, Barbara (1995) "On the decline of verb movement to Comp in Old and Middle French." In: Adrian Battye and Ian Roberts (eds.) *Clause structure and language change.* (Oxford: Oxford University Press) pp. 173-199

Verrips, Maaike (1990) "Models of development." In: Monika Rothweiler (ed.) *Spracherwerb und Grammatik: Linguistische Untersuchungen zum Erwerb von Syntax und Morphologie.* (Opladen: Westdeutscher Verlag; *Linguistische Berichte, Special Issue* 3) pp. 11-21

Vikner, Sten (1995) *Verb movement and expletive subjects in the Germanic languages.* (Oxford: Oxford University Press)

Von Stechow, Arnim and Wolfgang Sternefeld (1988) *Bausteine syntaktischen Wissens.* (Opladen: Westdeutscher Verlag)

Weissenborn, Jürgen (1990) "Functional categories and verb movement: The acquisition of German syntax reconsidered." In: Monika Rothweiler (ed.) *Spracherwerb und Grammatik: Linguistische Untersuchungen zum Erwerb von Syntax und Morphologie.* (Opladen: Westdeutscher Verlag; *Linguistische Berichte, Special Issue* 3) pp. 190-224

Weissenborn, Jürgen, Helen Goodluck and Thomas Roeper (1992) "Introduction: Old and new problems in the study of language acquisition." In: Jürgen Weissenborn, Helen Goodluck and Thomas Roeper (eds.) (1992) *Theoretical issues in language acquisition.* (Hillsdale: Lawrence Erlbaum) pp. 1-24

Wexler, Kenneth and Rita Manzini (1987) "Parameters and learnability in binding theory." In: Thomas Roeper and Edwin Williams (eds.) *Parameter setting.* (Dordrecht: Reidel) pp. 41-76

White, Lydia (1982) *Grammatical Theory and Language acquisition.* (Dordrecht: Foris)

White, Lydia (1988) "Island effects in second language acquisition." In: Suzanne Flynn and Wayne O'Neil (eds.) *Linguistic theory in second language acquisition.* (Dordrecht: Kluwer) pp. 144-172

White, Lydia (1989) *Universal grammar and second language acquisition.* (Amsterdam: John Benjamins)

White, Lydia and Fred Genesee (1996) "How native is near-native? The issue of ultimate attainment in adult second language acquisition." *Second Language Research* 12: 233-265

Wode, Henning (1981) *Learning a second language: I. An Integrated View of Language Acquisition.* (Tübingen: Gunter Narr)

Wode, Henning (1988) "Language transfer: A cognitive, functional and developmental view." In: Eric Kellerman and Michael Sharwood-Smith (eds.) *Crosslinguistic influence in second language acquistion.* (New York: Pergamon Institute of English) pp. 173-185

Young-Scholten, Martha (1993) "The L2 acquisition of informal speech in German." In: Bernhard Kettemann and Wilfried Wieden (eds.) *Current issues in European second language acquisition research.* (Tübingen: Narr) pp. 11-124

Zobl, Helmut (1990) "Evidence for parameter-sensitive acquisition: a contribution to the domain-specific versus central processes debate." *Second Language Research* 6: 39-59

Zobl, Helmut and Juana M. Liceras (1994) "Functional Categories and acquisition orders." *Language learning* 44: 159-180

Zubizarreta, Maria Luisa (1987) *Levels of representation in the lexicon and in the syntax.* (Dordrecht: Foris)